THE FACES OF TERRORISM

Books in the **SCIENCE ESSENTIALS** series bring cutting-edge science to a general audience. The series provides the foundation for a better understanding of the scientific and technical advances changing our world. In each volume, a prominent scientist— chosen by an advisory board of National Academy of Sciences members—conveys in clear prose the fundamental knowledge underlying a rapidly evolving field of scientific endeavor.

The Faces of **Terrorism**

SOCIAL AND

PSYCHOLOGICAL DIMENSIONS

Neil J. Smelser

PRINCETON UNIVERSITY PRESS

PRINCETON AND OXFORD

Copyright © 2007 by Princeton University Press
Published by Princeton University Press, 41 William Street,
Princeton, New Jersey 08540

In the United Kingdom: Princeton University Press,
3 Market Place, Woodstock, Oxfordshire OX20 1SY

Library of Congress Cataloging-in-Publication Data

Smelser, Neil J.
The faces of terrorism : social and psychological dimensions / Neil J. Smelser
    p.   cm.   (Science essentials)
Includes bibliographical references and index.
ISBN-13: 978-0-691-13308-9 (hardcover : alk. paper)
1. Terrorism. 2. Terrorism—Social aspects. 3. Terrorism—Psychological aspects. I. Title
HV6431.S63 2007
303.6′25—dc22   2007004837

British Library Cataloging-in-Publication Data is available

This book has been composed in Minion
Printed on acid-free paper. ∞
press.princeton.edu

Printed in the United States of America

10 9 8 7 6 5 4 3 2 1

Contents

PART I

INTRODUCTION

CHAPTER 1

The Paradoxes of Terrorism

TERRORISM as a contemporary phenomenon teems with paradoxes. For at least three decades, many who have studied it have regarded it as the "conflict for our time" (Clutterbuck, 1977, p. 13). Yet the same author who advertised it in those words also regarded it as "rooted in history" (ibid., p. 22), to be found in military, political, and religious annals since classical times. Despite this duality of vision, it is true that terrorism has irregularly emerged as the world's most salient and worrisome form of combat during the past several decades, and to many it promises to remain so indefinitely into the twenty-first century.

It is also paradoxical that, despite being so conspicuous on the current scene, terrorism has never been defined properly by either scholars or political officials. Nor, with the exception of some political scientists and policy analysts, have behavioral and social scientists studied this critical phenomenon very much or very well. This situation is all the more curious because only a little observation or reflection is needed to conclude that the human sides—the psychological, social, political, economic, and cultural—are universally present dimensions in terrorism and the responses to it.

A third paradox is that observers frequently describe post–cold war or post-9/11 terrorism as something new—the end of war as we knew it, a facet of globalization, an aspect of postmodernity—yet close inspection of the actual goals, ideologies, strategies, and tactics reveals how few of these ingredients are novel. In light of this circumstance, in this book I treat terrorism not as a special thing or creature but as a kind of human behavior that has some distinctive characteristics but that also lends itself to explanation by mobilizing existing theoretical and empirical knowledge in the behavioral and social sciences.

In a single volume added to the increasing cascade of books, articles, and media discussion, I cannot hope to resolve these paradoxes fully, though one of my aims is to cast light on understanding them. I will do so in part by self-consciously shunning cosmic and dramatic depictions—some of which, I argue, are reactions to our ignorance and anxiety about terrorism. Instead, I treat contemporary terrorism as a peculiar combination of ingredients culminating in a specific form of violent behavior.

Although behavioral and social scientists have fallen short in studying and understanding terrorism, some knowledge has accumulated. In addition, we know much about phenomena that are parts of the terrorism package. This knowledge can be brought to bear on understanding it. Among the relevant areas of knowledge are the structural bases—economic, political, social, and cultural—of deprivation, dispossession, and protest; the nature and role of ideologies that accompany extremist behavior; the dynamics of recruitment to social movements, behavior in them, and political reactions to them; the dynamics of small groups and networks; public reactions to uncertain threats and actual disasters; deterrence; and the politics of fear. I will mobilize selected knowledge on these and other topics in the book.

A few words on my credentials—whether they are strengths or liabilities—are in order. I am a sociologist by profession, but prior to my retirement in 2001, I, like almost all my colleagues, was not a student of terrorism. Within sociology I have studied collective behavior, social movements, cultural traumas, organizational responses to uncertainty, and comparative social structure and social change. For better or for worse, my work has almost always been interdisciplinary, and at different times I have had one foot in history, economics, anthropology, and political science. I also mention research that has reached into psychology. As part of this effort, I have undertaken full psychoanalytical training, including some practice. For the study of terrorism I regard interdisciplinarity as a strength, because the topic itself knows no disciplinary boundaries and spreads into all of them.

My direct introduction to terrorism occurred almost immediately after my retirement on September 1, 2001. Shortly after the September 11 attacks in New York City and Washington, D.C., the presidents of the National Academies wrote a letter to President George W. Bush pledging the support and cooperation of scientists in dealing with the national crisis created by those events. The first tangible manifestation of this support was the creation of the Committee on Science and Technology for Countering Terrorism, which, within less than a year, issued a major report on scientific understanding and applications to defending the nation against most types of potential terrorist attack (Committee on Science and Technology for Countering Terrorism, 2002). I was one of two social scientists on that committee, and I drafted the chapter on terrorism and human populations. In addition, I chaired two National Research Council committees, one dealing with the social and psychological dimensions of terrorism generally (Smelser and Mitchell, 2002a) and one on the possibilities and limitations of deterrence theory in dealing with contemporary international terrorism (Smelser and Mitchell, 2002b). Subsequently I have been involved in a diversity of the National Academies' activities relating to research and policies on terrorism. Engaged in these experiences, I was more or less forced to become a scholar of the subject. The experiences with the National Academies, moreover, provided the background for my decision to write a general book on the subject.

This book is mainly academic in emphasis in that it synthesizes behavioral and social science research and seeks general understandings and explanations. To deflect any message of grandiosity that may be inferred from this statement of purpose, I hasten to add that no effort is made to cover all relevant social science materials; rather, I use materials selectively according to my own judgments of relevance and priority. Nor do I pretend that I am simply, automatically, and impersonally applying objective knowledge with no intrusion on my part. Some interpretations are my own, consistent, it is hoped, with our general knowledge of psychological and social processes. Nor, finally, can I avoid topics that are controversial. Terrorism in all its international and domestic ramifications is by now thoroughly politicized, and even statements intended to be objective about it excite partisan reactions. To take only one example, to "objectify" the ideological bases of terrorism and counterterrorism and to attempt to understand them as natural phenomena is to adopt a political distance from these ideologies that is offensive to those who believe in them. And as the shrillness of the American presidential campaign of 2004 amply demonstrated, almost no facet of our nation's policies toward terrorism escapes partisan tint. All one scholar can do is to strive (but never succeed fully) to overcome partisan implications by bringing the best knowledge available to bear on any issue.

I have supplemented my general analysis in two particular ways. First, in working through all the issues involved in the subject of terrorism, I came to locate a number of snarls in our thinking about it and practical predicaments in our dealing with it. I call these entrapments. Many of them arise because terrorism has foisted them on democratic societies. They are points of confusion and controversy—many touching the fundamentals of our political system—that result in repeated and seemingly irresolvable debates and conflicts. Furthermore, the entrapments do not yield solutions, because discourse seldom moves outside or rises above their own internal dynamics. Examples of entrapments are conflicts over defining terrorism, diagnosing the role of the media, and understanding the tension between security and civil liberties in responding to terrorism. I identify a number of points of entrapment as the work proceeds.

Second, I have taken the occasion to add an autobiographical dimension in the form of boxed material in many of the chapters. These entries are illustrative personal experiences and observations arising from my work on terrorism, including work with other social scientists. They are designed to provide vivid and concrete illustrations of general issues and topics discussed in the text.

I have arranged the chapters in a mainly analytical way. One could argue that issues of definition should come first. However, this item is so nettlesome and so demanding of conceptual throat clearing that I decided to begin straightaway with substance, and discuss definitions in the appendix. Chapter 2 takes up the causes and conditions of terrorism, focusing on its insurgent and international forms but not on state terrorism—historically an equally important and certainly a more lethal form than the first two but the product of a quite different set of determining conditions. This chapter is a complex one, corresponding to the complexity involved in sorting out the multiple causes, their significance at different levels, and their permutations and combinations. Chapter 3 singles out the ideologies that inspire terrorism. Concentrating on them helps elicit their crucial importance in unraveling and explaining terrorist behavior. In chapter 4 I turn to a combination of topics: the motivation of individual terrorists, their recruitment, the significance of the groups they form, their decline, their audiences, and the roles of the media in terrorism. These topics are often treated separately in the literature. For reasons that will become clear, however, I will argue that all of them—and ideology, too, for that matter—are inseparable parts of the driving motivational complex for terrorists and the commission of terrorist acts.

Chapter 5 turns to the study of target societies and deals with the social psychology of anticipating. experiencing, and coping with the threat of rare but potentially catastrophic events; the social and psychological aspects of educating, preparing, and warning the population about terrorism; and the diversity of responses to terrorist threats and attacks. In chapter 6 I deal with the complexities involved in living with the possibility of terrorist attacks, including defending democratic societies against them. Chapter 7 takes up even more general historical issues involved in dealing with international terrorism and is concerned directly with the contemporary world situation, especially the United States' place in it, as well as domestic and foreign public policies. Chapters 6 and 7 are more reflective and evaluative than the others and include many judgments of my own that seem plausible in light of what we know, but they are in no sense disciplined "applications" of sure knowledge.

I envision that the book will have three audiences—other scholars, public officials concerned with terrorism and responsible for confronting it, and interested general readers. Communicating with the first and third of these audiences is relatively nonproblematical, but I am fully aware of the limitations of academic material for policy makers and policy executors. There are inherent reasons why knowledge produced by academics does not interest—and may even irritate—those in policy arenas. At the most general level, academics and policy makers (and most military officers and journalists) have different and noncomparable priorities. The former are typically interested in general explanations arrived at by objective examination of available evidence (Wieviorka, 1995, p. 605). Many of the explanatory factors they identify, moreover, lie beyond the possibility of political or public intervention. The latter are interested in applied, timely decisions and implementations intended to have desired effects. In consequence, people on both sides of the academy–policy divide often cannot hear one another, and become impatient as a result.

Terrorism policy reflects this disconnect in an extreme way. By its very nature, terrorism demands focus and urgency, because it is uncertain and because it carries threats of death and destruction. Most policy makers cannot afford to appreciate the nicety, conditionality, and qualifications of academic analysis (Ezekiel and Post, 1991, pp. 118–19). This tension is superimposed on a traditional residue of mutual stereotyping and distrust between "academic" people of thought and "policy" people of action (Merari, 1991, p. 88). Despite these general limitations, some parts of this book may be directly relevant to policy. For example, my analysis produces a critique of the reliance on "gadgets, game theory, and goodness"—that is, the combination of technological solutions, instrumentalism, and moralism—that appears to have dominated our nation's response to terrorism since September 11, 2001. In addition, the discussions of counterproductive effects of overreacting to terrorist threats, underpreparing and overpreparing populations for danger, and the vulnerabilities of first-responding agencies are surely relevant to planning and policy. Many other points on the political, economic, social, and cultural aspects of terrorism and terrorist groups should be relevant for longer-term policy. One must acknowledge, however, that in democracies facing danger and among politicians sensitive to the media and public opinion and ultimately accountable in the electoral process, short-term reactions and accommodations typically trump longer-term polices and general reflection.

PART II

CAUSES AND DYNAMICS

CHAPTER 2

Conditions and Causes of Terrorism

IN THE LAST DECADE of the nineteenth century, Émile Durkheim, one of the founders of sociology, launched his campaign to establish the field as a science (Durkheim, 1958 [1893]). He was a positivist, insisting on the independent significance of social facts (institutions, rates of behavior, collective sentiments). Among the scientific tenets he propounded was the principle that an observed social fact (for example, a group suicide rate) has a single cause that produces that effect (in the case of suicide, the cause was found in the force of social cohesion) (Durkheim, 1951 [1895]). He held to this principle of single cause → single effect tenaciously: "*A given effect always has a single corresponding cause*" (Durkheim, 1958 [1893], p. 128, italics in original). In his actual interpretation of statistical and historical events, however, his analyses usually revealed a more subtle and complicated view of social processes than a literal application of his favored principle would have yielded (Smelser, 1976).

Writing a decade later, Max Weber, an equally eminent founder, voiced a more qualified version of sociology as a science. With respect to the issue of causation in particular, he envisioned the confluence of multiple causes to produce a given historical phenomenon, and, by implication, a single cause in combination with others to produce multiple effects (and by further extension, the interaction and feedback among multiple causes) (Weber, 1949). In explaining the rise of rational bourgeois capitalism, for example—one of his enduring preoccupations—Weber acknowledged the causal role of technology, legal conditions, a stable monetary system, and a facilitative administrative apparatus of the state (Weber, 1950). Much of his comparative work was dedicated to teasing out the significance of these respective conditions and to establishing the causal role of different religious traditions on economic growth and rationalization.

When confronting a historical phenomenon such as terrorism, it seems advisable to side with Weber on the issue of causation (for further defense of this position, see Crelinson, 1987, pp. 5–6). For one thing, I establish in the appendix that it is impossible to consider terrorism as a single effect at all; rather, the phenomenon as it has been identified seems to beg for disaggregation along several dimensions. Furthermore, it is possible to identify several different kinds of causes, ranging from very general (remote) to highly specific (immediate) causes (see Tocqueville, 1955 [1856], on the causes of the French Revolution). Some causes, such as predisposing economic, political, and cultural conditions, may facilitate the growth of organized movements that engage in terrorism, but those conditions do not guarantee the appearance of violence. Indeed, such conditions may persist for decades without producing such a consequence. For violence to develop, the facilitative conditions must combine with other factors, such as a special ideology enunciated by charismatic leaders, the development of effective recruiting machinery, and substantial support for protest on the part of relevant publics. Moreover, some factors in the causal nexus are neither predisposing nor impelling but are primarily inhibitive measures, such as co-opting terrorist-prone movements into institutionalized political channels or protecting targets against attacks. In a word, everything points to the advisability of identifying and arranging multiple causal factors acting in combination with one another and to assess the specific value that is added by each factor to the explanation.

It is important to recognize the principle of multiple and multilevel causation of a phenomenon such as terrorism, because many forces pull us toward thinking about it in simplified if not single-cause terms. We hear in political and public discourse and in the media—and from scholars, who normally love complexity—that terrorism is "caused" by psychopaths, fanatics, religious fundamentalism, Islam, American support for Israel, oil, economic penetration, globalization, inadvisable foreign policies, "failed states," or states that harbor or are permissive of terrorism. The tendency to oversimplify lies in the fact that terrorism itself is simultaneously dangerous, uncertain, terrifying, and cognitively destabilizing. A certain unjustified but substantial psychological comfort is gained by simplification, because simplification suggests that the threat is more readily comprehensible and therefore controllable or preventable by working on *the* single cause. In reality, terrorism is an unusually complex phenomenon and demands sorting out its conditions and causes.

The purpose of this chapter is to array the range of conditions and causes of terrorism—so far as we can understand them through behavioral and social science knowledge—and to demonstrate how they funnel by different processes toward the special violent outcomes that constitute terrorism. Consistent with reasoning advanced in the appendix, my focus is on "agitational terrorism" or "terrorism from below," and I do not consider "enforcement terrorism" or "state terrorism" (Wardlaw, 1989, pp. 10–11), because the causal patterns for each differ so much from one another.

A promising way of confronting this formidable task is to conceive of the causal processes leading to acts of terrorism behavior as a series of transitions from extremely general processes involved in the genesis of terrorism to its specific manifestations. This means that we do not leapfrog from general conditions to specific outcomes. Rather, we think in terms of analytically identifiable situations—call them phases, if you will, though linear temporality is not asserted—each of which sets the stage for the transition to the next identifiable situation. Different complexes of conditions and causes play their respective roles at each transition, as the whole process marches forward as a continuous combination and recombination of causal factors.

The major identifiable transitions are:

- What are the conditions, both national and international, that affect the differential propensity for alienation and dissatisfaction to develop?
- What are the conditions under which political alienation and dissatisfaction crystallize into politically conscious collectivities and audiences supportive of them?
- What are the conditions under which such collectivities—or, more typically, subgroups of them—become prone to violence?

- What conditions the movement of violence in the direction of one of its subtypes, terrorism?
- Under what conditions does the impulse to terrorism result in terrorist actions?

Our knowledge about these transitions is incomplete, sometimes woefully so, but disaggregating the process into the transitions suggested is a fruitful way of addressing its otherwise bewildering complexity.

In contemplating and undertaking this task, we run headlong into the general dilemma of historical specificity versus general patterns, a dilemma that arises when striving for explanations of historical phenomena. No final solution to this dilemma has ever been put forth. One of the best scholars of terrorism, Martha Crenshaw, in her respect for the uniqueness of historical contexts of terrorism, declared simply that "the causes and consequences of terrorism are comprehensible only in terms of political conflicts in specific historical periods" (Crenshaw, 1995a, p. 24). At the same time, also adopting the logic of the "narrowing funnel" of causes, she moved in the direction of seeking generalizations about "which elements in what situations encourage oppositions or states to turn to terrorist tactics" (ibid., p. 5) while at the same time denying the possibility of a completely general theory or "deterministic explanations" (ibid., p. 4). In my estimation, the only sensible strategy is to walk such a middle line, though as a lifetime practicing social scientist, my inclination has been and will be to lean toward pushing the search for regularities. At the same time, decades of research have taught me that to press theoretical certitude beyond the limits of our conceptual and empirical knowledge is also a pitfall.

The Structural Origins of Discontent

Early in my career I wrote an ambitious treatise that tried to establish a common framework for explaining a wide variety of collective actions—panics, crazes, violent outbursts, reform movements, revolutionary movements, and religious sects (Smelser, 1962). One of the main classes of variables I identified at that time was what I called "structural strain"—the presence of deprivation; the presence of fault lines such as racial and ethnic divisions; and ambiguities, anomalies, and discontinuities occasioned by irregular social change. I interpreted these conditions as the bases of individual and group dissatisfaction that underlay all the kinds of collective responses that interested me. The language of strain has been superseded by other terms, but the underlying logic remains in the literature on social movements (see Buechler, 2004).

Even at that time, I came to some conclusions that still apply to understanding the significance of strains:

- After examining a range of literature on the origins of social movements, I concluded that the variety of strains was almost endless—dislocation through migration, unemployment and poverty, anomic conditions, downward mobility, cultural (especially religious, ethnic, and racial) divisions, colonial domination, disenfranchisement, political persecution, and many others.
- As a corollary to this multiplicity, it followed that no single type of strain could be identified as the single cause for one type of collective response or another (thus defying Durkheim's canon); as a consequence, looking for strong correlations between types of strain and types of collective action was of limited value. Some kind of strain (and resultant dissatisfaction) seemed to be a necessary cause for such action, but it had to combine with a variety of other conditions to be activated as a causal variable.
- Strains could not be identified solely as objective conditions, such as absolute level of poverty, but always had to be assessed in relation to some kind of expectation on the part of the population that was experiencing it. This is, of course, the principle of relative deprivation, which seems to be a universal feature of dissatisfaction. This principle often leads to the apparently ironic result that when a group is actually advancing, it feels itself worse off. For example, Tocqueville (1955 [1856]) described heightened dissatisfaction among the middle classes and peasants in eighteenth-century France, even though their well-being, from a material point of view, was improving. This improvement made other, remaining foci of exclusion more visible and aggravating.

These three principles should govern our search for the broadest determining conditions that lead to those group dissatisfactions that sometimes generate impulses to collective action and, in their respective forms, may turn toward expressions of violence, including terrorism.

Dispossession: A Key Predisposing Condition

By dispossession I refer to perceptions on the part of a group that it is systematically excluded, discriminated against, or disadvantaged with respect to some meaningful aspect of social, economic, and political life to which it feels entitled. There is no society in the world that does not have many groups that feel illegitimately dispossessed. Despite its widespread if not universal existence, this phenomenon of dispossession must be invoked as a necessary condition for dissatisfaction and collective mobilization. As a general principle, those contented with their lot do not protest, unless they feel imperiled—in which case they fear dispossession.

Historical illustrations. I begin by illustrating dispossession, as well as its relative deprivation aspect, with three empirical examples:

- Most of the "nation-building" efforts on the part of the Western nations have involved a systematic effort to homogenize the language and political cultures of their peoples through educating their children in schools, using the media to create national symbols, myths, and memories, and other means (Anderson, 1991; Gellner, 1983). More recently, the sustained efforts of the last Shah in the mid-twentieth century to develop Iran into a Western-style country simultaneously aimed to suppress clerical influences, ethnic differences, and nomadic uprisings (Green, 1995, 557–58). We should also remind ourselves that much of contemporary Muslim fundamentalism rose to salience in the wake of disillusionment with other secular nation-building efforts (many including religious repression) in a number of other Arab countries (Kamrava, 2005). This process of cultural homogenization, at the very least, offended the sensibilities of particular groups, and in many cases occasioned political persecution of them. These efforts to homogenize have never been completely successful.

Turbulence and violence occur especially in the early stages of state formation (Chopra, 2001, pp. 15–16). Europe today bears dozens of historical residues of its relative incompleteness in the presence of regional communities: the Bretons, the Basques, the Tyroleans, the Welsh, and the Scots, to say nothing of the religious-ethnic-linguistic subnational groups in Central and Southeastern Europe. Typically these people feel dominated and dispossessed in various ways, and this constitutes a basis for latent and sometimes openly expressed antagonism toward the parent state and other groups.

· Slavery could be said to be a source of absolute deprivation for black Americans in almost every respect. In the decades that followed emancipation, many black leaders hailed its end and foresaw full incorporation of the race as American citizens. After decades of disappointment, however, occasioned by the reimposition of harsh Jim Crow arrangements in the South and continuing discrimination elsewhere, a deep disillusionment set in. This disillusionment was "relative" because it was experienced in the context of earlier high hopes. For a variety of reasons it did not generate revolutionary protest, but it did occasion remarkable efforts to revitalize black American culture, the most notable of which was the Harlem Renaissance. Some of this effort even incorporated the experience of slavery into a new positive identity (Eyerman, 2004).

· The civil rights movement of the 1950s and early 1960s, under the leadership of Martin Luther King, Jr., was by all realistic standards a resounding success, leading to the formal desegregation of eating establishments, public transportation, and other facilities and stimulating the government to introduce many reforms. It was also a movement that raised expectations not only among black citizens but among other groups as well (youth, women, other ethnic groups). Yet the imperfect realization of these successes in practice and the persistence of other deprivations (primarily economic) led to a renewed dissatisfaction and a radicalization of at least a minority of black activists. In this case, the movement spawned a submovement of violence (through mechanisms to be identified later) that has been treated as terrorism in the literature, especially as manifested in the activities of the Black Panthers.

These examples provide an idea of the processes and mechanisms by which relative deprivation and dissatisfaction are generated and which in many cases have spawned domestic social movements, a few of which have resorted to violence.

Illustrations from the international scene. It is also instructive to identify some long-term international processes that have heightened the disjunction between the nation-state (and nationalism) and ethnic-regional-religious particularism around the world, and, as a corollary, a predisposition to the emergence and multiplication of dispossessed groups. The following are relevant:

- The colonial era, in which the world's major colonial powers—Spain, Portugal, the Netherlands, Great Britain, France, and Germany—divided up the colonized world into territories in ways that took little or no account of the tribal, religious, and other characteristics of those territories except sometimes to exploit them for political purposes. Clutterbuck chided the British for having "no rivals in history" in "creating intractable communal problems":

   > They attempted to form a unified sub-continent in India, instead of allowing it to take its course in shaking out into a Balkanized patchwork of independent states. . . . It was under British rule that Chinese and Indian labour migrated into Malaya, with the result that, when they inherited independence, the Malays made up only forty-nine per cent of the population of that country. It was largely under British administration that Greeks poured into Cyprus and outnumbered the indigenous Turks. The massive Jewish migration into Palestine, which passed the point of no return in the 1930s, took place under the British mandate. And, of course, it was the migration of English and Scottish Protestants into a Catholic Ireland which created a problem which no government has been able to solve since Queen Elizabeth I sent in the English Army. (1977, p. 61)

   The diagnosis is correct, but it should be added that the British did not have a monopoly among the colonial powers in generating the political bases for antagonistic communalist sentiments.

- The postcolonial heritage, in which many of the newly independent colonies adopted the model of the nation-state—the mode of political organization represented by their former colonizers and the political mode preferred by the diplomatic communities and the United Nations for membership in the world system of nations (Gurr and Harff, 1994). "The result was one dominant ideal (in theory but not practice): the belief in the coherence of nation-states and the desire to maintain their territorial integrity. From these norms grew the grievances of territorial separatists and national independence movements" (Flint, 2003, p. 54).

- The *formal* adoption of the traditional characteristics of nation-states by the new states (political self-sufficiency, insistence on monopoly of violence, the focus on a national identity, and recognition as a nation by other nations) but their *actual* lack of effectiveness in many cases in developing the nation-state form, which was realized in the West only after a long and irregular historical process. In some cases the result was "failed states" (Zartman, 1995). In a survey of 275 communal groups that existed in the 1980s and 1990s, Gurr (2000) concluded that "[deadly] rounds of ethnopolitical conflict are likely to occur or reoccur in new, impoverished states with ineffective governments and sharp communal polarities" (p. xv). In other cases, "the insistence on the right to conduct internal affairs without outside interference gave unscrupulous dictators like Macias and Amin freedom to commit atrocities against their subjects in the name of 'nation-building'" (Gurr and Harff, 1994, p. 12). In fact, much of the "ethnic cleansing" of modern times has been perpetuated by political leaders from one particularistic group securing state power and attempting to crush violently or eradicate other groups (Naimark, 2001; for the importance of this factor in postcolonial Africa, see Otubanjo, 1994).

- The dramatic "third wave" of democratization (Huntington, 1991), which began in 1974 and affected dozens of nations throughout the world. This development, combined with the spread of education, generated a great deal of relative deprivation, that is, heightened expectations for recognition, rights, and interests on the part of political groups—expectations that the idea of democracy typically fosters—as well as a more widespread sense of injustice. In the words of Friedland,

> The evolution and growing acceptance of democratic philoso-
> phies has fostered the view that discriminatory social structures and political systems are neither immutable nor legitimate. The view of authority as a prescribed right is no longer accepted. It was replaced with the attitude that authority has to be earned, constantly justified, and, by the same token, challenged. (1992, p. 83; see also Narang, 2001)

The general shift was toward the dismantling of authoritarian regimes and the development of democratic institutions, but the results of this movement have been mixed in terms of the actual realization of stable democracies. The transition to democracy implies a formal commitment to deal with contending opposition voices (including particularistic groups), thus giving them—legitimately—more political salience, but the transition did not guarantee effectiveness in dealing with conflicts among such groups or between them and the state.

- The even more dramatic dismantling of the communist and socialist countries in 1989–90, which not only permitted the emergence of multiple ethnic, religious, and local forces that had been held under by repression for decades but also resulted in the formation of a number of new states. Moreover, almost none of these states "solved" issues of internal diversity, because in almost all cases residual minorities remained (for example, the Russian population in Latvia).

- An accelerating process of international migration. Although international migrants make up only 2 percent of the world's population, their absolute numbers accelerated from approximately 75 million in 1965 to perhaps 129 million at the end of the 1990s (Castles, 2001, p. 9826). The occasions for migration have been both economic and political. The process inevitably has resulted in some kind of multiculturalism both for the receiving countries and for the migrant populations who are caught in the struggle between inherited particularistic loyalties and the "pressures of the varied ideologies of cultural and legal inclusion which characterize their new homes" (Appadurai, 2001, p. 6289).

I have dwelt on these international political conditions because the anomalous position of national subpopulations has been at the root of many if not most of the identity-based conflicts in the world and because so many terrorist activities of the past half-century have been by or on behalf of such groups. In addition, all the preconditions for generating them have moved in the same direction, toward increasing the disconnect (or contradiction) between nation-based identity and subnational identity based on region, race, ethnicity, religion, and language.

There is another reason for concentrating on this range of political conditions. The cultural beliefs that bind most of these groups together are *primordial* in character, stressing membership on the basis of blood, ancestry, language, and custom (see Geertz, 1973). These are compelling bases; they give membership an absolute, sometimes sacred aura, and they are salient in defining the individual identities of their members. When such groups experience some kind of dispossession or disadvantage, this tends to be experienced in totalistic terms, as an assault on a people. This complex of particularistic identity and conflict encourages the solidification of absolute, principled beliefs in these kinds of groups, and these kinds of beliefs are the raw material for legitimizing extreme measures of defense and conflict on their part.

Economic Deprivation

One factor that reappears in discussions of the causes of terrorism is the economic one. In its simplest form it is asserted that conditions of "[lack of] food, poverty, and hunger" and the accompanying "misery" (Arnold, 1988, pp. 135–36, 142–44) breed desperation and extreme responses. The operative causal model relates real economic deprivation (the independent variable) to frustration and aggression (dependent variable). It is a model that has appeal among the political left, which traditionally favors explanations of protest based on economic suffering and class oppression. More conservative explanations focus more on moral or psychological factors, which more or less explicitly place responsibility on individuals and minimize impulses to ameliorate the putative conditions of misery.

Economic factors evidently have to be taken seriously in considering the conditions inducing terrorism, but the simple model outlined is inadequate, for two reasons. First, participation in terrorist movements reveals a diversity of economic backgrounds. In some salient terrorist movements, notably the left-inspired Weather Underground in the United States and the Red Army Faction in West Germany in the 1960s and 1970s, the composition of these fringe political movements was primarily middle-class, relatively comfortable young people protesting on behalf of the poor and oppressed, but not from these classes. In others, those recruited to terrorist tactics do come from conditions of extreme poverty—for example, economically displaced, unemployed, and disposed Palestinian Arabs—but often these participants are foot soldiers. Their leaders come from more comfortable economic backgrounds that have often included direct contact, through education and participation, with Western societies (Smith, 2002). Hewitt (2003) reported different economic backgrounds for the Ku Klux Klan (mostly working class, with a handful of small business owners, self-employed and white-collar workers), the Weatherman (privileged backgrounds), and black militants (working class, some lumpenproletariat), concluding that "no single [occupational] factor can explain their resort to terrorism" (p. 73).

Second, the history of economic deprivation and poverty in the world reveals that these conditions have existed forever and everywhere, and if militant protest is thought to be a product of this, it "begs the question why . . . militancy is not pandemic throughout the Third World" (Toth, 2005). In most cases the poverty-stricken do not protest but bear their suffering passively and silently. This overwhelming fact suggests that, when poverty plays a role, it is as a result of its being elevated to political consciousness in combination with a number of other conditions. Absolute economic deprivation in itself is a poor predictor (for an empirical evaluation, see Krueger and Maleckovà, 2002).

What are some of these other conditions? One is *structural economic dislocation*, which may not directly induce poverty but may increase the vulnerability of the affected groups to market forces. I refer to traditional peasant subsistence farmers who are drawn into producing food for the market, laborers in traditional economies who are drawn into wage labor, technologically displaced craftsmen, workers in the former socialist countries who enjoyed a relative degree of economic security but who find themselves at the mercy of uncertain markets under the new, quasi-capitalist conditions, and even new middle-class occupational groups whose position in the economic and status order is ambiguous. This variable of structural dislocation is an economic one, to be sure, but it is not a process that necessarily produces poverty. In fact, it may accompany a general improvement in economic conditions. Its primary effect is to produce economic uncertainty and the sense of being at the mercy of economic forces that are beyond one's control; this is not economic deprivation as such, although it often carries a threat of economic dispossession.

Structural dislocation is often closely related to relative economic deprivation. This term implies that economic conditions come to be experienced as satisfying or frustrating not according to absolute levels of poverty or welfare but *in relation to perceptions of other groups' fortunes or in relation to cultural expectations.* A particularly telling example of this phenomenon emerged in Peru in the 1960s and 1970s, which witnessed efforts and government economic reforms (increased expectations), the failure of these reforms to relieve the economic suffering of the peasants (dashing of expectations), and, in the 1970s especially, a radicalization of the government itself, and permission if not encouragement of radical protest (a sense of opportunity). Such were the conditions that made the scene ripe for the appearance of the noted Peruvian terrorist movement, the Shining Path (Palmer, 1995).

If we apply the logic of relative deprivation broadly, it is possible to claim that almost every group can experience deprivation because there are inevitably other groups in relation to which it can feel disadvantaged. In practice, however, relative deprivation is more likely to be felt in relation to groups that are historical or new competitors (for example, women versus men in the labor force, or recent Central American Hispanic immigrants versus Cuban immigrants in Florida).

International economic penetration of all kinds, but the recent spread of global capitalism over the world is particularly likely to generate multiple kinds of relative economic deprivation. First, in less developed countries it creates new classes of low-paid wage labor whose economic position may be low in absolute terms but high in relation to traditionally very poor groups in those countries. The seeking of low-cost labor abroad clearly generates feelings of apprehension among higher-paid workers in wealthier countries, who feel themselves threatened with displacement. Often, too, the economic returns of international penetration are differentially distributed in the host countries (the history of oil production in the Middle East is the readiest example), occasioning reality-based perceptions of a worsening distribution of wealth. International economic fluctuations and crises also involve rapid changes in economic fortunes; the radical increases in energy costs in the 1970s affected most Third World countries' economies strongly and negatively (Toth, 2005, p. 118).

Cultural disruptions. For decades, cultural anthropologists have documented the consequences of cultural domination, a regular accompaniment of colonialism. It took the form of different efforts to "civilize" the dominated peoples, whether as a matter of direct colonial policies (as in the case of French cultural colonialism) or more indirectly, through the efforts of missionaries. Such efforts were self-consciously directed toward acculturation. Their typical effects were to create conditions of cultural confusion and a double ambivalence in the dominated population: simultaneous attraction and repulsion to the cultural values of the oppressors and a similar attraction and repulsion to the traditional way of life. The international migration of groups into host societies creates similar effects, often described as "culture shock," by setting up the four-way struggle among attraction to and rejection of the host society and attraction to and rejection of the society of origin. Thus, the possibilities of dissatisfaction under conditions of cultural domination and immigration are multiple.

The era of classical colonialism has passed, but the process of the international diffusion of competing cultural worldviews, values, and expectations has not. In fact, under conditions described under the heading of cultural globalization, the process has become magnified. The cultural diffusion of globalization supplies above all new cultural standards that give realistic situations their depriving bite. We may identify three principal forms of cultural diffusion.

Economic culture: Materialism. The presence of wealthy foreigners and wealthy natives who have profited from the economic presence of those foreigners introduces two new groups who constitute an immediate source of envy. In addition, the growing presence of mainly American films and television conveys images of economic plenty into households and public places of less advantaged nations. This spread of material values, labeled variously according to the process involved ("globalization"), the nation that most personifies the material values ("Americanization"), or vivid commercial symbols ("McDonaldization"), constitutes an extremely powerful source of both relative deprivation and cultural conflict. The potency is illustrated by a story spread in the 1980s. This had to do with an end-of-the-world scenario in the Hollywood film *The Day After*, which portrayed life in Topeka, Kansas, after the explosion of a nuclear weapon. The film drew great interest in other countries, including the Soviet Union, where it was shown. The story was that the only portions of the film that were censored by Soviet authorities were the scenes of supermarket shelves teeming with food and other material goods, as though the sight of these was more threatening than the postnuclear horror. The avid materialism in long-deprived Eastern European countries before and immediately after the end of the communist-socialist era reveals the same potency of material values.

The impact of materialist values in deprived countries is thus the focus of deep ambivalence, of simultaneous envy and desire, on the one hand, and disgust and rejection of the presumed corrupting force of material desires on the other. In this regard, attitudes in these countries echo the deep Western ambivalence over the power of materialism to corrupt, proclaimed mainly by religious leaders and political protesters (see Wuthnow, 1995).

Secularization. Colonial powers and missionaries wished to Christianize native populations and did so to some degree. In more recent times, the religious impact of Western penetration has included continued missionary efforts (mainly by Roman Catholic, Mormon, and fundamentalist Protestant churches), but these efforts have been overwhelmed by the forces of secularization that have eclipsed traditional religions in the West. This influence has been of greatest consequence in the Muslim world, where fundamentalists and others decry the threats to Islam and regard secularized leaders of their countries with almost as much venom as they do the foreign nonbelievers who have brought secularism to their lands (Williams, 2002).

Democracy and human rights. Earlier I mentioned the third wave of democratization in the last third of the twentieth century, the effect of which has been to bring new standards and higher expectations of political participation to countries long deprived of it. This democratic pressure is complemented by the contemporary worldwide concern with human rights, long a feature of Western political culture, made salient by the United Nations declaration of 1945 and pressed strongly if intermittently and somewhat inconsistently by the United States (Falk, 2003). The international human rights movement, widely regarded as admirable in its aims, is also, in effect, an extension of the missionary impulse in the sense that it is an effort to import if not impose putatively universal but mainly Western-invented values in parts of the world where these values are often not appreciated. In any event, they constitute a major source of cultural domination, cultural clash, and the resulting cultural confusion experienced in the contemporary world.

The scholarly and ideological literature regarding the international spread of Western-associated values such as materialism, democracy, secularization, and human rights has polarized around two extreme positions. The first, voiced both by radical critics and by avid proponents such as neoliberal capitalists, is that the spread of these values is leading, inevitably if irregularly, toward a cultural homogenization of the world (usually via an American-dominated version of global capitalism and cultural hegemony). The essence of this position has been voiced by Fukuyama: "modernity, as represented by the United States and other developed democracies, will remain the dominant force in world politics, and the institutions embodying the West's underlying principles of freedom and equality will continue to spread around the world" (2002, p. 28). The second, voiced by traditionalists, localists, and antiglobalists, stresses opposition to globalization and the reassertion of local social and cultural diversities (Beyer, 2001). The foci of resistance are regional and include groups that are ethnic, racial, indigenous, ethnonationalist, religious, linguistic, and cultural (Robertson, 2001). The dichotomization of the debate is unfortunate, because it obscures the evident truth that although the homogenizing forces are both powerful and universal, their effects are always muted by the modifying and resisting influences on the part of peoples in the settings in which they are received (Hannerz, 1990). Above all, however, the result of these mixed effects is almost universally to create a double ambivalence toward both Western and indigenous cultural values and beliefs, as well as confusions and instabilities of identity.

Such are the main sources and mechanisms of deprivation, dislocation, and dispossession in the contemporary world. They more or less ensure that high levels of dissatisfaction and ambivalence are the order of the day in this world—and the menu of the future as well. We now turn to some of the processes by which these reservoirs of dissatisfaction come to be expressed in protest movements and their derivatives.

The Crystallization of Dissatisfaction: Ideology, Motivation, Group Mobilization, Leadership, and Audience Support

Later in the book I develop separate accounts of several social-psychological aspects of terrorism: ideologies that shape, drive, and legitimize terrorist behavior through the specification of grievances, the identification of enemies, the statement of goals and objectives, and the formulation of ultimate ideals; the individual psychology of terrorists; the role of the group, group processes, and the group's leadership in extremist movements; and the role of audiences in determining the direction and the success or failure of terrorist activities. The task at the moment is to place this class of variables in the overall structure of conditions that combine to produce extremist movements. It is appropriate to focus on extremism, because as a general rule "support for terrorism is linked with the existence of extremist movements" (Hewitt, 2003, p. 19).

The general contribution of this set of variables is that they shape, give meaning to, and channel the diffuse kinds of structurally based dissatisfactions reviewed above, thus moving them closer—in the "value-added" process—to producing definite and tangible collective responses to those dissatisfactions and to generating protest against and attacks on definite targets. These social-psychological processes arise from the seedbed of dissatisfactions, but they are not caused by them in any automatic way. A partially independent set of dynamics comes into play as they unfold.

I group the elements of ideology, motivation, group processes, leadership, and audience together because they mesh as aspects of the process of mobilization, and because each is a partial component of the others. When ideology, for example, is internalized by those with grievances, it becomes *part of* individual motivation. It is often remarked in the literature that a sense of injustice and victimization is an important part of the motivational complex of those who become involved in protest movements. It must be noted, however, that this sense gains its motivational strength and potency only when *framed in a meaning system* that we refer to as an ideology. Individual drives or conflicts (for example, narcissistic rage, need for social support) play a role in protest groups as well, but do not operate as autonomous drivers of action. Rather, they are activated when they become embedded in a belief system and are reinforced by group processes involved in recruitment, indoctrination, and enforcement of group norms. Leaders arise and succeed not as an independent force but only insofar as they articulate their message effectively with the ideologically and motivationally defined individual and group psychology. Finally, audience support is one of the determining conditions for the development of protest. Seeking and securing of support or other reactions from audience communities and the media becomes part of the social psychology of the protesting groups.

When these social-psychological processes congeal into a viable extremist movement, they constitute a conduit between the real and perceived structural conditions and derived dissatisfactions, on the one hand, and collective action, including violence, on the other. Whether this action occurs at all, and if it does, what form it takes, are largely a function of the opportunity structure (which includes both facilitative and inhibitive forces) confronting the movement (see Kriesi, 2004). We now turn to this class of determinants.

What Turns Collective Protest Action in a Violent Direction?

Structural Opportunities: Political Structures, Avenues, and Processes

A principle that has emerged in the study of social movements is that their structural features, strategies, and tactics are largely determined by the political contexts in which they develop. This principle is encapsulated in the aphorism "protest follows politics." Decades ago (Smelser, 1962), I discussed this principle under the headings of "structural conduciveness" (that is, which avenues of collective action are available to concerned groups, and which are not) and "social control" (that is, the reactions of political authorities to protest movements once they become active). The principle that protest follows politics has survived in the literature and now is usually discussed under the rubric of "opportunity structure" (see Tarrow, 1996; McAdam, Tarrow, and Tilly, 2001).

Political opportunity connotes several possibilities: (1) to organize into collectivities, (2) to express grievances, and (3) to have access to the political structure so that these grievances can be heard. At one end of the spectrum of opportunities are cases of extreme totalitarianism and state terror, manifested in different ways in Hitler's Germany and Stalin's Soviet Union and exercised by the Argentine government and military against the urban guerrilla movement in the 1970s (Gillespie, 1995). Effective totalitarianism denies all three aspects of political opportunity through extreme repression, making any kind of political protest, including those that use terrorism as a method, "impossible to organize" (Laqueur, 1999, p. 6). Although many of the structural conditions for dissatisfaction and protest—especially political disenfranchisement—are experienced by the subject populations in these situations, they are ruthlessly denied opportunities for association and political expression. Similar difficulties in mounting protest are found in cases of heavy-handed and effective repression by one ethnic group of others, as in Saddam Hussein's Iraq, in the Serbian and Albanian repression in Kosovo, in Sudan, and in Ethiopia. These cases are the most likely settings for state terrorism in the form of "ethnic cleansing" to occur, which is designed in part to stamp out political opposition in lethal ways (Falkenrath, Newman, and Thayer, 1998, pp. 201–2).

When, however, the repressiveness of totalitarian regimes is incomplete, inept, or sapped by political corruption, the balance shifts and disaffected groups, while still officially excluded from formal participation, can better mount underground, guerrilla, revolutionary, and terrorist activities. The case of the decay of the repressive tsarist regimes in nineteenth-century Russia is an apt example of totalitarian ineptness. The rise of anticolonial and nationalistic protest in the colonies of European countries in the decades following World War II resulted not only from the resolve of protesting anticolonial groups but also from the diminished power of the colonial powers to sustain the colonies after the war, the rise of domestic opposition to colonialism in the populations of the colonial powers, the increasing cost of maintaining order in faraway lands, and the momentum for national self-determination emphasized in the United Nations charter.

The general historical map of extremist protest, then, is determined by a combination of general factors: structural conditions that generate some form of dispossession, along with "(a) oppressive foreign rule and conquest or (b) oppressive domestic rule without any expectation of institutionalized, legalized avenues of change" (Gross, 1969, p. 464). We may refine the latter factors, however, by saying that extreme and effective oppression discourages or even renders mobilization of violence impossible, whereas some weakness or vulnerability on the part of oppressive or unresponsive rulers permits insurrection on the part of the disaffected and alienated. It has to be added that the "weakness or vulnerability" is a matter of perception on the part of potential insurgents, a perception often generated by their own ideology. For example, the ideologies among the Weather Underground in the United States, the Red Army Faction in West Germany, and the Red Brigades in Italy— all informed by a neo-Marxist worldview—depicted contemporary capitalism and its pseudo-democratic political system as corrupt, vulnerable, and capable of being destroyed if assaulted (Alexander and Pluchinsky, 1992, pp. 20–27), even though these expectations proved to be false in all three cases. In all events, the combination of conducive factors involves the experience of dispossession and oppression, the unavailability of political channels of influence, and a perception of oppressors' vulnerability.

The importance of the defining ideology in establishing these conditions must be underscored, because from a historical point of view political violence, including terrorism, has not been absent in those liberal democracies that are built on democratic principles of free elections, political parties, and elaborated administrative procedures for airing grievances and expressing political voice. For example:

- The violence associated with the Basque nationalist movement actually increased after the end of the totalitarian regime of Generalissimo Franco and as democratic reforms were introduced under the new republican regime. The movement was split among the moderates who wished to seek legitimacy through electoral means and those who, for ideological reasons, believed that "nothing had changed" for the Basques and that violence remained the only possibility to gain their nationalist goals (Shabad and Ramo, 1995, pp. 420–22).
- Whole volumes have been written on the frequent historical occurrence of terrorism in the United States and in Western European democracies (Rubin, 1990; Lodge, 1981; Alexander and Myers, 1982).
- Even Holland, which is probably the most extreme example of toleration, co-optation, and negotiation with protest movements, has, in the context of a general picture of success against terrorism, experienced a few instances of domestic terrorist activity (Schmid, 1993b), including the assassination of Theo van Gogh in 2004.

The truth is that, while we may point to the general fact that democratic institutions and access to legitimate channels for political expression discourage violence by providing alternatives, so long as even small militant groups develop perceptions and hold beliefs that assert repressiveness or neglect by political authorities or "the system," then the possibility of political violence is always present (Gilbert, 1994). Furthermore, as discussed in chapter 3, historical memories and ideologies are readily available on both the right (for example, fundamentalist ideologies) and the left (for example, varieties of Marxist thought), and these offer a reservoir of raw materials for such beliefs.

This principle of structural opportunity has its analogue at the international level. In the history of the modern nation-state, the typical form of international violence has been some variety of war, often called "conventional war," in which the armies of two powers engage in violent conflict in an effort to defeat one another's armies and bring the political leaders of the enemy to heel by destroying them or forcing them to lay down their arms. One corollary of the willingness to enter a war is what one might call "imagined parity," or the belief on the part of each side that it is possible to win the war, or if not to win, to force the enemy into some kind of political settlement. So long as these conditions held, it was reasonable to expect that military wars would dominate the international scene.

World War II can be described as the last great conventional war, but even that war ended on a note—America's dropping of atomic devices on Japan—that foretold the future. Japan surrendered almost immediately after those events, and the age of atomic, later nuclear, war was born. From that war emerged a new if temporary constellation of two huge superpowers, which, after the Soviet Union developed nuclear weapons and systems of delivery, reached a kind of parity in the capacity of both the United States and the Soviet Union to wreak terrible destruction on the other. The hallmarks of the forty years of the cold war were the standoff between the nuclear superpowers with respect to nuclear attack on one another, many small wars and uprisings in which the superpowers sometimes meddled to protect or enhance their own interests, and two larger wars, in Korea and Vietnam, that were direct expressions of the larger struggle between world capitalism, represented by America and its allies, and world communism, represented by Soviet bloc countries and sometimes communist China. The less developed countries were marginalized in this larger conflict, but in some cases (Nasser's Egypt and Qadaffi's Libya, for example), these countries made efforts to play the superpowers off against one another.

The collapse of the Soviet bloc and international communism in 1989–90 brought a rapid end to the uneasy equilibrium of the cold war, and the United States emerged as the sole effective nuclear superpower, even though some other nations possessed nuclear weapons. Without entering the dispute among political scientists as to how hegemonic the United States is at the beginning of the twenty-first century, it is clear it is massively dominant on the world scene technologically, economically, politically, and above all militarily. The CIA's own diagnosis of the world scene in 2002 runs as follows:

> Experts agree that the United States, with its decisive edge in both information and weapons technology, will remain the dominant military power during the next 15 years. Further bolstering the strong position of the United States are its unparalleled economic power, its university system, and is investment in research and development—half of the total spent annually in the advanced industrial world. Many potential adversaries, as reflected in doctrinal writings and statements, see US military concepts, together with technology, as giving the United States the ability to expand its lead in conventional war fighting capabilities. (Central Intelligence Agency, 2002, p. 24)

It remains that the United States' domination is muted, variably from situation to situation, by influence from other countries, especially those in its alliances built up after World War II, by some, if halting, influence from the United Nations, and by its economic dependence on those nations that supply it with imports needed to fuel its vast economy. This line of analysis is elaborated in chapter 7.

The inevitable conclusion from this diagnosis of international dominance is that in many respects, the option of challenging the United States militarily is not now open to any nation in the world, and, again in the CIA's words, none of them "want to engage the US military on its own terms" (ibid., p. 24). Cooper (2003) put it dramatically if unrealistically: "were all the rest of the world to mount a combined attack on the United States they would be defeated" (p. 45). From the standpoint of the present analysis, this situation constitutes a blocking of structural opportunities for those who fear and are antagonistic to the United States. Weaker countries cannot challenge the United States

politically, economically, or militarily. They confront a situation that
has radically narrowed their political options. Those who remain
committed to fight must turn to other avenues, often referred to as low-
intensity, asymmetric warfare (Jones and Smith, 2004). This fundamental structural fact of the world power situation goes far toward explaining the acceleration of much of the world's clandestine terrorism
in an international direction. It also verifies the principle contained in
the aphorism, "terrorism [is] the coercion of the strong by the weak,"
and by the weak we mean those who regard themselves as oppressed
by the United States and its foreign involvements, who see little recourse
in the proceedings of international law, diplomacy, alliances, economic
sanctions, or wars, and who as a result turn to more radical options.

The Sense of Opportunities in the Shorter Term

The foregoing diagnosis of structural opportunities is a valid
principle for understanding the general distribution of political violence, but that factor in itself is historically nonspecific and does not
tell us very much about the timing and occasions for group violence,
including terrorism. That logic is found in the flow of historical events,
and that flow can be expected to have unique contours in different
societies that have experienced episodes of political violence.

The historical literature on terrorism reveals one principle about the
timing of the crystallization of violence-based groups: when a disaffected group is either emboldened by a dramatic episode of success or
discouraged or made desperate by a reversal of fortunes, then the
group—or, better, one or more of its subgroups—is likely to revert to
violent means.

In one respect this is not a scientifically attractive principle, because
it seems to predict the same outcome from opposite causes, thus creating an explanatory indeterminacy. This difficulty recedes, however,
when we take into account the structure of the ideologies that accompany extremist movements. As I argue in chapter 3, such ideologies
contain ingredients that invite and encourage actual and potential believers to experience a wide range of emotions—anxiety, hopelessness,
despair, rage, hope, and elation—and these emotional possibilities provide the template for interpreting different experiences that affect the

movement. Within such an ideological context, a setback constitutes evidence for believers that they are beleaguered and in danger of defeat, and moreover evidence that more radical means must be sought. A success, on the other hand, feeds the emotions of hope and elation and encourages bolder and more aggressive action. Although by some logics the conclusions drawn from these kinds of evidence are not consistent, within the context of the guiding ideologies of extremist groups they have their own internal and compelling logic.

The historical record yields ample evidence of the invigorating effects of both unsuccessful and successful moments for extremist movements. I turn first to some illustrations of the effect of discouragement.

- Crenshaw (1990) cited a number of historical examples of terrorism arising in the wake of perceived failures of moderate tactics, as in the case of the failure of nonviolent movements that preceded nineteenth-century Russian terrorism and the burst of terrorism that followed the failure of Parnell's "constitutionalism" in Ireland, also in the nineteenth century.
- The crystallization of the Red Brigades into a terrorist organization in the 1970s was occasioned in part by the reconciliation between the Italian Communist Party (PCI) and the Christian Democrats, which generated the sense on the part of radicals that the left was selling out and that their futures could not lie with the communists (Schraub, 1990, pp. 142–45). The kidnapping and killing of Aldo Moro by the Red Brigades in 1978 was clearly symbolic of this, as he had been the principal architect of the "historic compromise" between the two parties; so was the grisly dumping of his body at a spot in Rome exactly halfway between the headquarters of the Christian Democratic and Communist parties (Jamieson, 1989).
- Similarly, among the causes occasioning the rise of the Baader-Meinhof (Red Army Faction) terrorist group in West Germany in the 1970s was the formation of the Grand Coalition between the Social Democrats (SPD) and the Christian Democrats, which was viewed by the radical student movement as evidence that the left

was compromising and that the SDP could not be counted on (Pridham, 1981, p. 17).

- Gush Eunim was a right-wing messianic group that arose in Israel after the Six Days' War of 1967 and agitated for Israeli settlements on the West Bank. It experienced a deep sense of setback with the signing of the Camp David accords in 1978, which involved the return of Sinai to Egypt and a plan for the autonomy of the West Bank and Gaza. This radicalized the group, and after the killing of six Yeshiva students by Arabs on May 3, 1980, it turned to underground violence (Sprinzak, 1988, p. 207).

- When it became apparent in 1993 that the movement to reform apartheid initiated by South African state president F. W. de Klerk was in effect irrevocable, episodes of terrorism on the part of extreme right-wing groups broke out in South Africa (Welsh, 1995, p. 253).

- The emergence of terrorism on the part of radical Sikh groups in Punjab in the 1980s followed a series of failures of moderate leaders to get grievances of the Sikh population addressed (Arora, 1999). In fact, this was a mixed case of promise followed by failure. The promised accord between the Indian government and the Sikhs, ventured by Prime Minister Rajiv Gandhi in 1985, was meant to accommodate the Sikhs after a period of harsh treatment by the Indira Gandhi government. The projected accord was received well by most moderate Sikhs, but the split between moderate and extremist Sikhs over the accord, plus its breakdown when the Rajiv Gandhi government reneged on some of its promises, gave heart and encouragement to the extremist terrorist element (Wallace, 1995).

A kindred invigorating effect occurs when internal divisions over strategies give rise to splits within protest parties, with subgroups forming along the dimension of peaceful protest or reform strategies versus disruptive or violent strategies. The reason this effect is kindred is that one subgroup, usually the more radical, typically issues accusations that the movement is failing because of ineffective moderate strategies. Following are some illustrations of such internal splits:

- The Provisional Irish Republican Army (the faction responsible for most terrorist activities from the Catholic side of the Ulster divide) was officially formed in 1970, but it origins lie in a long-standing split beginning with the radical accusation of betrayal by those who supported the Anglo-Irish treaty of 1921, which divided Ireland into two parts instead of creating a single, Catholic Ireland (Wilkinson, 1983, p. 116).

- Students for a Democratic Society, a major organizational force behind the student movement in the 1960s in the United States, grew rapidly in membership between 1964 and 1968 but split into warring factions at its 1969 convention, after which its membership plummeted. In this context of division and disappointment, the Weatherman faction seized control of the organization. Out of this development grew the revolutionary terrorist organization, the Weather Underground (Hewitt, 2003, p. 53).

- The Black Panther Party was founded in 1966 in the context of the general radicalization of the black movement and the success of the Nation of Islam and later the Black Muslim movements. Factional disputes between Huey Newton and Eldridge Cleaver led to a split in the Black Panthers and the appearance of the Black Liberation Army, the militant wing of the Cleaver faction, which advocated a more violent course of action against police and other authorities (ibid., p. 55).

- The history of the Palestinian struggle has been characterized by political fragmentation and factionalization, with the repeated appearance of more radical terrorist factions (for example, the Popular Front for the Liberation of Palestine [PFLP], Black September, and Abu Nidal group) appearing both as radical anti-Israeli terrorist groups and as factions protesting against more moderate tendencies within the Palestine Liberation Organization (Gearty, 1991).

In their quantitative study of more than 400 terrorist groups in the twentieth century Weinberg and Pedahzur found that more than 100 fell into the category of "party creates terrorist group" and "party faction breaks away and creates terrorist group" (2003, p. 29), suggesting that the internal divisions within political groups over their political effectiveness and political fortunes are among the most important precipitants of terrorist activity.

On the breeding of terrorism by dramatic success, we must first note the historical fact that in terms of achieving long-term political goals, terrorism as a political strategy has a very meager record of outright successes. Hoffman (1998, p. 63) identified only a handful of political successes on the part of terrorist campaigns: the terrorist campaign in Israel of 1944–48, leading to the establishment of the state of Israel, the campaign of the Ethniki Organosis Kyprion Agonston (EOKA) on behalf of the Greek Cypriots, and the Front de Liberation Nationale (FLN), leading to Algerian independence (see also Crenshaw, 1995b). Even in these cases it is doubtful whether terrorist activity was the decisive causal factor, because in each case the parties toward whom the terrorists directed their campaign had their own political reasons for wanting to quit the scene.

Despite this limited political record, terrorists have obtained quite spectacular success in the short run, and this has widened support for the groups among relevant audiences and encouraged others to emulate their strategies and tactics (identified as the "bandwagon or echo effect" by Addison, 2002, p. 29). I consider four examples, all relating to international terrorism:

- It is widely agreed that the genesis of the modern era of international terrorism arose from the dynamics of the Palestinian-Israeli struggle (ibid., chap. 3; see also Wilkinson, 1987, p. xiii). The long period of border raids and sabotage within Israel on the part of Palestinians leading up to 1967 had not won over world opinion against Israel. The dramatic Six Days' War was a disastrous development for the cause, leaving the armies of several Arab states defeated and in disarray, the Palestinians isolated and even opposed by King Hussein of Jordan, and the Israelis in possession of the Sinai, the West Bank, the Gaza Strip, and the Golan Heights. Out of this defeat and disillusionment arose a new strategy: the export of terrorist activities abroad to gain concessions from and otherwise influence European countries and the United States. This phase began with the hijacking of the El Al airliner in 1968

(Gearty, 1991, p. 8), executed by the PFLP and the Black September group, radical organizations among the congeries of groups that constituted the Palestinian Liberation Organization.

Thus far the story is one of terrorism bred by disappointment and failure. But in the turn toward international terrorism, a number of spectacular successes were scored, at least from the standpoint of drawing the attention of the world to the Palestinian plight. Among these, the most dramatic was the massacre of Israel athletes at the Munich Olympic games in September 1970. In addition, the attacks on the U.S. Embassy in Beirut and the U.S. Marines at Beirut International Airport in Lebanon in 1983 contributed to the decision of the Reagan administration to withdraw U.S. forces from Lebanon, and Hezbollah (the Lebanon-based terrorist organization) claimed credit for ending the Israeli occupation of Lebanon. The kidnapping of the OPEC representatives in Vienna in 1975, engineered by the terrorist entrepreneur "Carlos," was another dramatic terrorist coup. These early successes, scored while the various target countries were either unprepared for terrorism or were only beginning to develop their strategies to contend with it, were the defining episodes for the proliferation of hostage taking, airline hijacking, and murder that characterized modern international terrorism in its first two decades.

- Also as a general rule, the spectacular media success of a given terrorist event or series of events—even if not an unequivocal political success—emerges historically as a model for future spread. The successes of the Irgun movement in Israel became a "template for subsequent anticolonial uprisings elsewhere" (Hoffman, 1998, p. 56). The successes of the FLN in Algeria inspired the Palestine Liberation Organization, and the latter inspired the renewal of Armenian terrorism, Quebec nationalist strategies, Argentine urban guerrillas, the Free South Moluccan Organization in Indonesia, the turn toward violence by left-wing radical movements in Western Europe (notably West Germany, France, and Italy) in the 1970s, and the trend toward international terrorism generally in the 1970s and 1980s (Crenshaw, 1995a, Hoffman, 1998).

- The students' capture of the American embassy in Tehran in 1979, shortly after the accession of the Ayatollah Khomeni, and the subsequent catastrophic failure of an American raid to free the hostages just before the 1980 American presidential election emboldened not only the terrorist movement in general but that wing of it that subsequently came to be dominant, Islamic fundamentalism, and demonstrated to many that the American giant was vulnerable. The success of the insurgency (including its terrorism) against the Soviet presence in Afghanistan in the 1980s (supported by the American government) also had the effect of demonstrating that the mighty could be defeated and elevated the religiously inspired Al-Qaeda movement, including its leader, Osama bin Laden, to a new level of visibility and support as it subsequently turned its attention to a terrorist campaign against the United States.

- Finally, there seems little doubt that the dazzling success of the attack on the World Trade Center and the Pentagon on September 11, 2001, while horrifying the vast majority of Arabs and Muslims, had the effect of buoying and consolidating the support of anti-American sentiment throughout the Muslim fundamentalist world (and perhaps more widely) and provided a kind of positive demonstration effect that terrorism was the weapon to be employed against America and the West generally.

More systematic evidence for "contagion" was presented in an early study by Midlarsky, Crenshaw, and Yoshida (1980). In a careful quantitative study of 503 terrorists incidents in Latin America between 1968 and 1974, the authors uncovered a pattern whereby incidents tended to spread from countries with high status to others. They also discerned a kind of "reverse hierarchical" borrowing of ideology, rhetoric, and methods of terrorist activities from Third World countries by groups engaged in the wave of terrorism in Western Europe in the 1970s.

The emboldening-discouraging logic applies to the specific selection of targets as well. In general, the selection of targets is determined by a variety of factors, including the ideology of the terrorist groups, the symbolic relation of the target to that ideology, its functional significance (for example, is it a part of the political apparatus of the target society), and whether the intent of the attack is to eliminate a threat, disorient the enemy, gain an endorsement from an audience, or force concessions (Drake, 1998). However, once a target is successfully attacked, this constitutes proof at some level that it is vulnerable, and invites repetition. Once the attacked societies begin to shore up defense against this particular target, however, this constitutes discouragement at some level and invites turning to another target. This logic helps explain the wave effect of targets, manifested, for example, in the sequencing of targets from political and military and military facilities (1970–72) to assaulting diplomatic targets (1973–75) to emphasizing business targets (1975–87) (Alexander, 1990). Another example is the introduction of metal detectors in airports in the 1980s, which appeared to reduce terrorist incidents at airports but triggered a search for new evasive technologies on the part of terrorists, and an apparent turn to kidnapping as an alternate form (Enders, Sandler, and Cauley, 1988). The diversion of massive resources to protecting commercial airlines since September 2001, however effective or ineffective that has been, no doubt increases the probability of attacks on other types of targets. Finally, the turn from detectable weapons to liquid explosives uncovered in the foiled plot of Islamic extremists in England in the summer of 2006 is the most recent instance of the principle of substitution.

The Availability of Resources as Opportunity

The Mass Media as Resource

Many writers stress that terrorist acts are a form of communication (Schmid and de Graaf, 1982)—propaganda by deed, and even a form of theater (Combs, 2003). Such characterizations are both instructive and incomplete. They do underscore the fact that terrorism without publicity is bound to be limited in its capacity to instill terror, because publicity is the main mechanism for spreading terror-inducing information. The evolution of the mass media over the past several decades, especially the development of television and the electronic media, has guaranteed that any dramatic act of terror occurring anywhere in the world will be widely available to the public within minutes after its occurrence. The fact that virtually every medium and its viewers regard terrorism as newsworthy makes this effect inevitable. In addition, the presence of potentially critical media, widely regarded as a necessary feature of a democratic society, also guarantees that counterterrorist activities on the part of a government will also be the object of close public knowledge and scrutiny, and that this shapes their repertoire of responses to terrorism. The role of the mass media is complex, and we will have occasion to revisit it in chapter 4, but at this point it can be stressed that the mass media cannot be left out of account in assessing the resources available to contemporary terrorism and that they contribute to its potency.

Financial Resources

No terrorist organization—or any other kind of organization, for that matter—can carry out its mission without financial resources. Over the course of history, most terrorist organizations have had small numbers of adherents and have been subterranean and secretive, with no regular sources of payment for individual members. Because of the reliance of such groups on personal commitment to idealistic goals, they may have an antimaterial bias (like Weber's charismatic groups; Weber, 1968, vol. III, p. 1115), even though the realistic needs of survival dictate require some material support. These rudimentary terrorist groups have survived in a variety of ways but mainly hand-to-mouth, including irregular gifts from supporters, theft, extortion, and kidnapping and ransom payments (Adams, 1987, p. 393).

As these organizations become larger, better organized, and more enduring, more sophisticated and systematic forms of support appear—again, varying according to opportunities and the ingenuity of leaders. The Irish Republican Army, for example, began like most rudimentary terrorist organizations but gradually developed more diverse and sizable flows of funds, including income from taxi businesses, illegal drinking clubs, tax frauds, and donations of unknown and disputed amounts from sympathetic Irish-American individuals and organizations. The Palestine Liberation Movement has lived on support from wealthy Palestinians and sympathetic Arab governments, but beyond this it has developed its own developed financial empire by investing its funds worldwide (ibid.). Al-Qaeda, under the leadership of Osama bin Laden, relied in part on his wealth and on funds donated by sympathetic Saudis and others (Greenberg, Wechsler, and Wolosky, 2002), but it also developed a completely independent financial and investment branch as an integral part of its organizations. Its typical mode of operation in the 1990s was to supply allied cluster organizations in different countries and regions with seed money to begin their own jihad, but the local groups were then thrown on their own to raise money or receive support from Muslim charity organizations (Sageman, 2004, p. 38). The financial strategies of those two Middle East-based, international terrorist organizations brought the business side of terrorism to new levels. In addition, international terrorist groups have increasingly relied on the efficiency, confidentiality, and capacity for instant electronic transfer of funds to lubricate for their activities.

State-supported terrorist activities fall into another category. During the cold war era both the Soviet Union and the United States supported and supplied resources (usually in the form of arms sales and military advisers) to terrorist groups (Gareau, 2005). State-sponsored and state-supported terrorism rose to salience in the 1980s, when the regimes of Colonel Qadaffi of Libya and others were directly engaged in financing and executing terrorist activities. With the end of the cold war and the decline of state-sponsored terrorism, along with the efforts of governments to interdict terrorist finances and close down "charitable" and other institutions in the 1990s, terrorist organizations have increased their reliance on drug trafficking as a way of financing, trading drugs for weapons, laundering drug money, and corrupting government officials. This is a worldwide trend, most evident in Afghanistan, Colombia, and Peru, but fundamentalist Islamic organizations, including Al-Qaeda and its associated groups, have become increasingly involved in the drug trade to finance their activities (Federal Research Division, Library of Congress, 2002). Other recently developed sources of income include trafficking in precious metals, gems, contraband, and stolen goods, and armament sales and shipment (Mathewson and Steinberg, 2003; Winder, 2002). Some of the changing patterns of finance have developed in response to the United Nations' actions after September 11, 2001, and efforts on the part of member states to freeze assets (see Biersteker, 2004). These efforts were only partially enforced and touched only a portion of assets available (Greenberg, Wechsler, and Wolosky, 2002), but they did result in the shifting of resources by Al-

Qaeda and other groups to precious metals and gems and the transfer of many of these groups' funds not through banks but via hawalas, longstanding informal exchange channels in Arab and Asian countries (Schoenberg, 2003; Farah, 2004).

Terrorist activity is inexpensive when compared with the costs involved in sending armies into war. The National Commission on the Terrorist Attacks Upon the United States estimated that the September 11 attacks were carried out at a cost of $400,000 to $500,000 (2004, p. xcviii). If the infrastructural costs of Al-Qaeda, responsible for organizing and directing the attack, are taken into account, the total sum would be considerably higher. In the last analysis, however, the double fact remains: while relatively inexpensive, terrorism involves essential costs for paying the expenses of operatives, finding safe homes, transporting terrorists from place to place, producing documents, and securing and distributing weapons. If such activities cannot be maintained, then financial resources available to terrorist organizations become one of the conditions limiting the scope and effectiveness of terrorist organizations' operations.

Weapons and Weapons Technology as Resources

Much of the history of war is the history of the advance of the technological means of executing it, and the advantages obtained by these advances. Examples are gunpowder and guns, the armored tank, the airplane, radar systems, atomic and nuclear weapons, and computerized target locators and guidance systems. The potential availability of many of these weapons to terrorists and other groups is evident (for a catalogue of agents and their destructive consequences, see Falkenrath, Newman, and Thayer, 1998). In practice, however, the modern history of terrorism has been one of reliance on guns and bombs. Certain lines of escalation toward the spectacular are observable: before 1965, most terrorism was associated with rural insurgencies; by 1975, aircraft hijackings, kidnappings and newsworthy assassinations dominated; by 1985, international terrorism included massive bombing attacks, spectacular hostage taking, and embassy takeovers (Goss, 1986, p. 39). The attacks on the World Trade Center in 1993 and 2001 brought terrorism to the American mainland in a dramatic way. But these developments brought little evolution in weaponry. Some evidence indicates Al-Qaeda's interest in acquiring nuclear weapons (Daly, Parachini, and Rosenau, 2005). There are only two known instances of terrorist attacks using chemical substances—the release of sarin nerve gas in the Tokyo subway system in March of 1995 by the Buddhist cult, Aum Shinrikyo, and the fleeting anthrax episode in Washington, D.C. shortly after the September 11 attacks. The historical record does show many efforts to use chemicals and biological agents in mass poisonings and assassinations and assassination attempts, as well as in hundred of hoaxes (ibid., pp. 30–31).

It is of interest to ask, but almost impossible to answer, why terrorist organizations have remained so conservative, in spite of the fact that much of the relevant technology is known and readily available, radioactive substances can be secured, and that Al-Qaeda and related organizations have shown an interest in nuclear, chemical, and biological resources and weaponry. Several hints at an answer are (1) the costs and difficulties of obtaining some of the weapons; (2) the risks involved to the users themselves; (3) the possibly counterproductive political effects of seemingly gratuitous slaughter of large numbers of innocents (Post, 2004); (4) the difficulties faced by small, highly decentralized, mobile cell organizations in transporting and delivering more complex technology and; (5) a learning principle: many terrorist organizations learn their techniques from other terrorist organizations (for example, through the visits of members of West Germany's Red Army Faction to Palestinian organizations), and this makes for a continuity of weapons and techniques of delivering them. To note this disconnect between theory and practice, however, does not give much cause for comfort. There is little reason to believe that terrorist organizations in the future will not seek more destructive nuclear, chemical, and biological technologies as they become more sophisticated and better supported financially and as highly destructive weapons and techniques become better known and more widely available.

The Vulnerability of Targets as Opportunities

A primary assumption guiding the analysis in this chapter is that terrorism is a relational phenomenon—for example, expressing the interaction between disaffection and opportunities to express it and the relationship between both of those to an ideology that identifies and explains them. In addition, I have endorsed the idea that state terrorism expresses a relationship between a relatively strong government and relatively weak victims, and that agitational terrorism expresses a relationship between weaker and stronger parties.

Nowhere does this relational principle express itself more clearly than in the assessment of the points of weakness of (otherwise stronger) target societies. Terrorism is a relationship between the strength, strategies and tactics of terrorist organizations, on the one hand, and points of vulnerability in their targets on the other. This relationship reveals itself in a number of ways in contemporary democratic societies.

It is often asserted in the literature that terrorism is a product of the globalization of the contemporary world (Burbach, 2002; Bresser-Pereira, 2002). One of the problems of such an assertion is that globalization is such a multifaceted phenomenon that it does not offer very precise explanations. Accordingly, the specific meanings assigned to this assertion are often not available. The fact that terrorist organizations are "stateless" and operate without regard to national boundaries and have ready access to internationally transmitted information (Maniscalco and Christen, 2001) is sometimes cited as an indicator of the "global" nature of terrorism. So is the parallel between multinational corporations and international terrorist organizations such as Al-Qaeda. Such references are not without value, but they do not directly address the issue of the special potency of contemporary terrorism. To address that issue I note four sources of vulnerability of target societies:

Technology and Vulnerability

As a general rule, technology can be described as significant in three ways: first, it is an engine that drives economic efficiency, new lines of activity, and progress; second, it generates new forms of vulnerability to and opportunities for accidents (see Perrow, 1984), disruption, and attack; and third, it may provide the means for preventing or controlling those effects. I consider the third in chapter 6 on the preparation for and defense against terrorism. At the moment I mention the vulnerability aspects:

- The phenomenon of piracy on the high seas—not terrorism, but a cousin of it—could not have become a historical reality were it not for the invention, design, and construction of ocean shipping and its derivative, vastly increased international trade (see Keohane, 2002).
- Computer crimes such as theft, hacking, and fouling express a relationship between the cleverness of the perpetrator and the actual availability of computer technology, which provides the target for the crimes. Without the technology there would be no object of criminal activity and no category of crime.
- The September 11 attacks on the World Trade Center and the Pentagon could not have happened without the availability of aircraft filled with flammable fuel. The event expressed a relationship between the terrorists' ingenuity and their access to an appropriate technology. The same point can be made with reference to skyjacking, a favored mode of hostage taking several decades ago but impossible to carry out without an aircraft industry on which to inflict it.

Most technological innovations in advanced societies, moreover, are put in place with no special concern for their survivability under attack; the result has been an unsystematic accumulation of installations and systems that constitute "leveragable nodes of attack" (Kupperman, 1987, p. 573).

The advanced technology of advanced nations, then, is the first manifestation of the paradox that what makes us strong also makes us weak. It is a given with which we must live. No responsible policy maker could dream of recommending paring back our technological might as a defense against terrorism, even when faced with a truth that, in principle, might point in that direction.

Increased Interdependence and Vulnerability

One of the hallmarks of modernization is that both the economy and society become more highly differentiated and their units become more highly specialized (Smelser, 1959). In the economy, specialization involves an increasing division of labor, with the consequent proliferation of types of jobs and occupations, as well as commercial and industrial specialization. In other sectors, such as education, medicine, and government, social organization also become more complex through the processes of differentiation and bureaucratization. One corollary of differentiation is the growing interdependence among the specialized parts that differentiation produces. This is evident in the economy, where specialized suppliers of factors of production, firms, markets, and consumers stand in interdependent balance. This process has reached new heights in the globalized economy, in which extraction, manufacturing, and assembly are widely dispersed throughout the world, as are markets for products. Transportation systems are dependent on the production of fuels, which are in turn dependent on suppliers, often located abroad. The same interdependency applies to social institutions as well, with a democratic government dependent in part on families and educational institutions for the "production" of an informed and responsible citizenry, industries dependent on training, and institutions of public education dependent on governmental support for their ongoing work.

The implications of the world's vastly increased interdependency for the potency of terrorism is that if one point in the system of interdependency is destroyed, then many others are indirectly crippled. Disabling electrical supplies also disables mass transit, the health care system, many water-pumping systems, and electronic information systems, to say nothing of industrial production. A nuclear explosion in a single port will likely trigger the closing of all ports (out of repeated attacks), the consequence of which will be to paralyze economic life in general. In a word, the interdependence of parts increases the vulnerability of the entire system if one part is destroyed or disturbed.

Increased Permeability

One of the by-products of international interdependency associated with globalization has been the massive increase in the movement of products (through trade), people (through migration and tourism), capital, ideas, and information across national boundaries. One need only go through any international airport or become familiar with import-export and migration (including illegal migration) statistics to appreciate the magnitude of these flows. Globalization would not be globalization without such movements, and any diminution of them would have adverse economic consequences.

These massive increases in worldwide movements have made national boundaries more permeable and diminished the effectiveness of efforts to monitor them. The sheer volume of cargo shipments into ports and people into airports has overwhelmed systematic efforts of customs and immigration officials—themselves the products of nation-states in their earlier incarnations—carefully to monitor everything and everyone passing through. Even the definition of boundaries has changed. Every international airport is a port for incoming people and products, and most of these ports do not lie on the boundaries of a country. Many flows of financial resources, information, and ideas, being electronic, do not cross national boundaries at all but are transmitted without reference to them.

This pervasive permeability constitutes an asset for terrorist organizations, whose movements of people, information, and resources are much more difficult to track because they are likely to be lost in the flows of huge numbers and quantities, and because so many of their transactions are unobserved.

Democratic Societies and Vulnerability

Several treasured features of democratic societies, which arguably are their greatest sources of political strength and stability, are also points of vulnerability to infiltrating and to organizing and executing attacks. These are civil liberties, such as those defined in the Bill of Rights, especially rights limiting police powers and the intrusiveness of the state, legal due process, freedom of expression, and freedom of association. Especially important are institutionalized rights to privacy. The significance of these rights with respect to crime in general and terrorism in particular is that it makes secret planning and movements more difficult to detect and prevent, for the obvious reason that they make it more difficult for governments to secure information on and track the movements of their citizens. The freedom of the media, already mentioned as a resource for terrorists, is by the same token a source of vulnerability for target societies, in that without wide publicity, the effects of terror—to terrorize, to publicize, to make political points—would be crippled. The stress on civil liberties and its associated institutions is, then, another example of how a specific societal apparatus can simultaneously be significant as both a fundamental strength and a fundamental weakness.

A derived vulnerability of democratic societies, mentioned now but discussed in detail in chapter 5, is their almost predictable impulse, when attacked or threatened (as they are under conditions of war and terrorism), to roll back those civil liberties in the interest of increased surveillance, apprehension, and prosecution—the "terror of counterterrorism." The impulse to roll back, in its turn, triggers still another vulnerability, namely, the deep political divisiveness experienced in democracies when groups sensitive to threats to civil liberties rise in protest against the inroads on them.

The Final Transition: When, Where, and How Terrorist Groups Attack

This heading opens the final, culminating phase in detailing the causes of terrorism: the occurrence of one or more attacks. It poses simultaneously the question that political leaders, defenders, and citizens want most to know about and the questions about which we know least. It is to these questions, moreover, that most of our resources are dedicated as part of our effort to prevent, deflect, or minimize the effects of terrorism.

The first and most evident reason we know so little is that it is the essence of terrorists' intentions to conceal that knowledge. They thrive on uncertainty and live on stealth and surprise. The most effective counter to this ecology is to gain direct knowledge of their operations by constructing an effective system of multiple intelligence sources, including informants, which is an exceptionally difficult operation, especially in the case of that variant of international terrorism that is clandestine, "stateless," based on mobile and mutating cells, and dedicated to maintaining commitment, loyalty, and secrecy among the members.

There is a second reason why the task of gaining precise knowledge about attacks is so formidable. The decisions to attack are grounded in highly specific historical situations of the moment and often based on last-minute decisions to proceed or not proceed with an attack, even if it has been planned in advance. Among the considerations that enter these decisions are (1) the terrorists' reading of the political situation, including the likely symbolic and political impact of an attack, (2) the completeness of their plans, (3) the availability and training of their attack personnel, (4) their sense of immediate opportunity, and (5) their sense of immediate risk, which includes their perception of defenses against attack, the disposition of counterterrorist forces, and the likelihood of retribution (the deterrence factor). Each of these factors weighs differently in any given attack, thus adding to the indeterminacy associated with it and leading to the necessary but regrettable conclusion that it is impossible totally to predict or prevent actual terrorist attacks, much as we aspire to do so.

Conclusion

This chapter on the conditions and causes of terrorism has been a long one, and the discussion has proceeded along many avenues. It is worth summarizing where we have been and what has been accomplished.

The main informing assumption is that the causation of terrorist behavior is multiple in two senses: (1) many causes are operative, and (2) the various causes operate at different levels of generality and vary in their causal significance: some are permissive and encouraging, some are precipitating, some are inhibiting, some are preventive. It follows that the most fruitful way to conceptualize the issue of causation is to represent the issue as a combination of different causes, each of which "adds its value" to explanation.

This combinatorial principle yields a view of terrorism as the end point of a long funneling process, with the possibility that the accumulating sequence of conditions and causes will produce other kinds of outcomes all along the line. In delineating this process, I have identified, first, a wide range of conditions that come to be regarded as dispossessing or depriving; next, a transition to how these conditions are regarded by affected groups; a focusing of this dissatisfaction into an ideology, which becomes the basis for channeling individual motivation by recruiting and mobilizing groups; next, a series of structural conditions and short-term situations that simultaneously constitute blockages to certain kinds of political expression and opportunity structures for the expression of others, including collective violence; next, the availability of publicity, financial means, and weapons and technology as resources; and finally the vulnerabilities of target societies, which constitute a final set of opportunities but which may be reduced through defensive and preparatory measures. These various conditions and causes are the elements of a theory of terrorism.

An upshot of this line of explanation is the proposition that terrorism constitutes only one small subset of many possible outcomes in that its various conditions and causes may combine in different ways to produce different results, such as collective resignation and inaction, peaceful protest, or forms of violent conflict other than terrorism.

Emerging implicitly from the analysis in this chapter on conditions and causes is a special form of entrapment that arises in our dealing with terrorism. It is not a conceptual entrapment so much as a historical and political one. It may be expressed as follows:

Entrapment 1. Many conditions culminating in terrorist activity are products of centuries of colonial and other forms of international domination, the evolution of the nation-state form, and recent conditions associated with economic, political, and cultural globalization. Accordingly, many of these conditions are those that even the United States, the world's most powerful nation, cannot significantly alter, given the heavy heritage of history and the virtual impossibility of mobilizing political support to make the attempt. Efforts to ameliorate the contemporary effects of those conditions are possible and should be considered, such as aid and investment programs aimed toward making the world's distribution of wealth more equitable, and these measures should be listed in the repertoire of efforts to reduce the long-term probability of terrorist activity. Beyond those efforts, however, attempts to deal with terrorism must take many causal conditions for all realistic intents and purposes as given and beyond definitive solution.

To be aware of this entrapment means that foreign policy and counterterrorist policies must take these conditions largely as historical constraints and rely on means that are more nearly within our control. Analysis of the conditions and causes of terrorism dictates this conclusion, which will be elaborated in chapter 7.

CHAPTER 3

Ideological Bases of Terrorist Behavior

EARLIER I asserted that almost all behavior that has been identified as terrorist is associated with extremist social movements based on extremist ideological beliefs. Wilkinson went even further: "*every* internal terrorist movement or group requires an extremist ideology of some kind to nourish, motivate, justify, and mobilize the use of terror violence" (1988, p. 95). There are good social science reasons why such statements, strong as they are, have validity. In this chapter I sketch the anatomy of these beliefs and indicate how knowledge of them adds in our struggle to unravel the phenomenon of terrorism.

I use the concept of ideology comprehensively, and so differ from authors who employ the term to refer to secular political beliefs on the right and left of the political spectrum and distinguish them from religious justifications (Wilkinson, 1987, p. xiii). Without denying the usefulness of distinguishing between secular and religious for other purposes, I employ no such distinction, because I am seeking common vectors in *all* such belief systems. In this way I hope to bypass a lingering tension in the literature about similarities and differences among belief systems that are associated with terrorism. On one side of the argument, Horowitz (1983) has asserted that it makes no sense to distinguish between left and right ideologies because "terrorism is a unitary phenomenon in practice and in theory" (p. 48). On the other side, Hoffman refers to the differences between right and left (1986) and between religious and secular (1998). Whether one chooses one of these views or the other depends entirely on the analytical purposes one has in mind. Obviously, content matters, for example, if one is seeking to explain the appeal of different ideologies to different groups. However, in this chapter I try to identify the general cognitive and emotional ingredients found in the structure of ideologies; as a result, similarities will stand out more than differences.

An Unlikely Introduction

In 1889 and 1890 a religious movement known as the Ghost Dance spread rapidly through the Dakota Sioux and a number of other American Indian tribes. It was based on a messianic belief, the underlying principle of which was that "the time will come when the whole Indian race, living and dead, will be reunited upon a regenerated earth, to live a life of aboriginal happiness, forever free from death, disease, and misery (Mooney, 1896, p. 177). The movement was not new, having arisen among the Paiute in Nevada in 1870 with the assertion by a tribesman, Tavibo, that an earthquake would engulf and destroy the whites (and, it was claimed later, nonbelieving Indians), leaving their houses, goods, and stores for the Indians (La Barre, 1970; Du Bois, 1939).

The later version, as pieced together by Mooney, predicted an earthquake for the spring of 1891 (one variant specified July 4 of that year). A messiah identified with Jesus would appear. No human agency was required to bring this about. However, in preparation for the event, believers were admonished to practice honesty, peace, and good will, even toward whites (Mooney, 1896, p. 777). The doctrine took on a more hostile flavor among the Sioux, long regarded as very powerful and warlike, where Sitting Bull, the medicine man, became "the great apostle of the Ghost Dance" (ibid., p. 895). Among the Sioux the belief in white extermination rose to a high level of salience; "the white man would be annihilated and the Indian again reign supreme." The whites had been sent by the Great Spirit to punish the Indians for their sins, but by now those sins were expiated, and deliverance was at hand. In a mighty landslide the whites would be smothered, and the few that survived would become small fishes in the rivers. After the avalanche, the Indians would behold "boundless prairies covered with long grass and filled with great herds of buffalo and other game." Unbelievers and renegade Indians would also be swept away with the whites. Believers were asked to participate in various rituals, including sweating ceremonies, as well as the Ghost Dance itself, in preparation for the millennium. One feature of the ceremonies was the believers' use of a "ghost shirt," which was "firmly believed to be impenetrable to bullets or weapons of any sort" (ibid., pp. 787–790 passim).

All those who have examined the background of the Ghost Dance movement point to extreme conditions of dispossession and deprivation among the Sioux in the years before 1890. In 1868 the Sioux reservation was created. Subsequently railroads were run through the territory, and gold was discovered in the Black Hills. Both brought white immigrants and settlers, who killed off most of the buffalo herds within a few years. After the Custer war and massacre of 1876, the Sioux reservation was shorn to one-third the size of the land originally promised. A system of government rations (mainly beef) was instituted to replace the slaughtered buffalo herds. In 1888 the Indians' cattle were decimated by disease, and both 1889 and 1890 witnessed massive crop failures and epidemics of measles, grippe, and whooping cough. In 1890 the government also reduced rations by more than half.

This decade of broken treaty promises and extreme hardship left the Sioux very dispirited. Moreover, a "large and influential minority" had opposed the reductions in the Sioux reservations. Finally, the unrest included beliefs that the traditional Indian way of life was decaying under the dominant influence of the whites and their civilization (ibid., pp. 824, 829), thus imparting something of a fundamentalist ingredient to the movement.

In the title of his classic account, Mooney referred to the events of November and December 1890 as a "Sioux outbreak." It was much less than that. In 1890, when dancing ceremonies were sweeping the land, Indian police and white authorities became alarmed (no doubt because of the menacing imagery of white obliteration), and tried to break up the dances. The greatest centers of excitement were at Standing Rock (where Sitting Bull was the leader) and at Pine Ridge (where Red Cloud was the leader). The U.S. government sent in troops on November 17, and 3,000 Sioux fled to the Badlands. Dancing continued at the camp of Sitting Bull, and on December 15, when he resisted arrest at his camp, he was killed. A brief disturbance occurred in the Badlands on December 18, and on December 29 about 250 Sioux, including many women and children, were massacred at Wounded Knee. In the end, Mooney abjured use of the word "outbreak" (because only one white noncombatant was killed and no property was destroyed) and referred to the event as the "Sioux panic and stampede" (ibid., p. 891).

The Ghost Dance made its appearance in more or less identical form in many other American Indian tribes at the time, but less notice was taken because its expression was more passive. In a subsequent study, La Barre described not only these episodes but also similar ones in South Africa in 1856, New Zealand in 1934, and many in the Melanesian chain that went under the name of cargo cults (La Barre, 1970, pp. 233–48). All arose in the context of outside political domination, all envisioned the disappearance of the oppressors, and all had a vision of the dramatic creation of an ideal life. Recently, Winchester described a brief and failed uprising of fundamentalist Muslims in Java, long under the yoke of Dutch colonial rule, in the wake of the great eruption of Krakatoa in August 1883. The movement was given articulation by a local religious leader, Hajji Abdul Karim, who predicted the appearance of a messianic figure who would save the world from godlessness. After the volcanic eruption the belief spread that Karim had predicted it, as he had other events, and that it was thus a sign. The believers in this small movement launched several attacks against the Dutch and their installations, but these were savagely repressed (Winchester, 2003).

Movements of this sort have come to be grouped under a larger category, "nativism," studied mainly but not exclusively by anthropologists. Though differing radically in content, they all have the same impulses: explaining the suffering of a people, assigning responsibility for it to inimical agents or forces, anger at and punishment for the agent, and the vision of an ideal and often blissful future condition free from pain and suffering.

The reason why I have qualified this introduction as "unlikely" is because the phenomena described are remote from contemporary terrorist activity in time, place, and context, and as a result, direct and wholesale comparisons among them are likely to violate both historical reality and our comparative imaginations. However, if we limit comparisons to the structure of the ideologies, remarkable parallels appear, and we not only can discover a widespread human reaction to experienced dispossession and deprivation, we also appreciate can what these systems of belief contribute to the political situation of believers, to their motivation, and to their agendas for action.

Ideology as Invention and Syncretism

The ideology of the Ghost Dance religion of 1890 was a unique mix of ingredients from Christian theology, American Indian culture and practices, the historical situation in which the peoples found themselves, and similar movements in the recent past.

The principle of syncretism applies to all ideologies, both those that defend the status quo and those that protest against it, including those that inspire terrorist activities. Their development follows the logic of the formation of cultural products in general. In the search for ideational formulas that would explain their situations and give meaning to and motivate their activities, interested groups have at their disposal whole cultural traditions of their own and other societies, a range of legitimizing values (for example, freedom, equality, and justice), past ideologies of all stripes, a population of historical heroes and villains, recorded or living memories of past social movements, and perceptions of the contemporary economic, political, and cultural scene. The imaginative ideology (and the imaginative leader who espouses it) picks and chooses from this myriad of elements and forges a worldview that gives consistency and purpose to the faithful and their audiences. That is what is meant by syncretism.

Ready examples of syncretic ideologies are:

- The multitude of anticolonial ideologies, which borrow from indigenous sources and from the cultures of the colonial powers themselves (see, for example, Rutherford, 2005).
- Liberation theology, a mix of adopted Catholic and Marxist elements that inspired much political activity in Latin America in the third quarter of the twentieth century (Taylor, 1988).

- The ideology of the Shining Path movement in Peru, which included ingredients from Marx (class struggle), Lenin (imperialism and revolutionary leadership), and Mao (the role of the peasantry, the strategies of revolution), and the synthesis and adaptation of all of these to the contemporary scene in Peru by an articulate intellectual leader, Abimael Guzmán Reynoso (Palmer, 1995).
- The ideology of the Red Army Faction in West Germany in the 1970s, which was an amalgam of imagery of the armed struggle for liberation in the Third World (inspired largely by the writings of Che Guevara), indictment of the Federal Republic for harboring Nazism (derived from recent German historical experience) (Kellen, 1990), and condemnation of the consumer society of capitalism (borrowed largely from Herbert Marcuse's diagnosis) (Pridham, 1981).
- The contemporary religious ideology of Middle Eastern terrorism, which is a synthesis of selected elements of the Koran, the writings of modern fundamentalist radicals such as Sayed Qutb and the Ayatollah Khomeini, Saudi Wahhabism, as well as a continuously changing diagnosis of the domestic and international situations as perceived by the leaders of the movement. The emerging ideological portrait is one that identifies past and present enemies of Islam (both external and internal) and envisions the fusion of religion and polity in the restoration of a community based on pure Islamic principles (Williams, 2004; Martin, 1987).

The logic of syncretism applies not only to the current structure of a given ideology but also to its evolution over time. As a movement's political and cultural environment changes and its leaders engage in struggles for influence in the movement, the components of its ideology also change, as leaders, interpreters and followers strive to explain successes and failures and to make the essentials of the ideology consonant with changing conditions. This principle explains why any given ideological complex—individualism, capitalism, Marxism, anarchism, fascism—is not a single entity but has a distinctive history. Ideologies are forever being resynthesized to resonate with changing conditions and with changing readings of what is ideologically correct for the times.

The Professor and the Unabomber

Theodore Kaczynski—the "Unabomber"—who spent eighteen years as a terrorist, mainly in mailing bombs to selected persons of special symbolic significance to him, was arrested in his Montana hideaway on April 13, 1996.

Six months before the arrest, I was approached by a small delegation of representatives from the Federal Bureau of Investigation and the United States Postal Service, both of which were involved in the search for the Unabomber. His famous Manifesto, "Industrial Society and Its Future," had already been published in the *New York Times* and the *Washington Post*, as Kaczynski had demanded, but his identity was not yet known, and investigators had uncovered no decisive physical evidence that might have led to his identity. As a kind of last resort—at least in my estimation—they had decided to turn to a number of academics who they thought might make helpful if indirect suggestions that would generate more knowledge about the Unabomber and his past.

I agreed to cooperate. The investigators supplied me with copies of the Manifesto and the communications he had written after different bombings had occurred. They asked me to read all the material carefully and come up with anything I might infer about his age, personal background, major influences on his thinking, where he might have been during the time his views crystallized, and anything else I could think of.

After getting into the Manifesto, I almost came to regret my decision to help. It made very tiresome reading. I wrote to my investigators that the style of the manuscript was "heavy, pedantic, turgid, obsessional, haranguing, quarrelsome, sometimes arrogant." The effect of this style was to make the document "alternatively confused, tedious, repetitious, boring, and deadening." I declared it a failure as a revolutionary manifesto, "more likely to induce sleep than zeal in the reader."

That assessment, I realize, was not very helpful, and I now regard it mainly as a way of unburdening myself of my frustrations. Regarding the document more seriously, however, I could discern some definite patterns:

- The structure of Kaczynski's argument displayed every typical ingredient of ideologies that justify terrorism (see chapter 3). It included a negative harangue against an "enemy"—industrial society and its technology, networks of formal organizations and powerful media, all of which crippled individuals and diminished their freedom and sense of autonomy. Almost all social problems, including alienation, illegal drug use, political corruption, race hatred, terrorism, and many others, were products of this insidious domination. This negative utopia contrasted with a less explicit positive one, which involved the restoration through revolutionary change of a kind of simple community found in primitive and preindustrial societies. Though Kaczynski was a loner and not part of a social movement, his ideology had all the earmarks of protest movements that sometimes use terrorist methods.

- Many intellectual influences on the Manifesto could be discovered, including that of Karl Marx (though Kaczynski was also impatient with the contemporary left). He also was influenced by the thought of Rousseau and modern communitarian theory, both of which idealize the "natural condition" of the human being as originally innocent and uncontaminated by oppressive social organization. The most decisive influence, however, came from a sub-branch of sociological thought—the critical theory of Herbert Marcuse and Jürgen Habermas, especially their preoccupation with the oppressive character of technology, as well as democratic ideologies of "liberalism" and "toleration" (a Marcuse trademark), the notion of society in crisis, and the ennoblement of the small community (Habermas's "life-world").

- I came up with a number of his abiding preoccupations—the insidious controlling power of technology, the world as dominated by power and control, the difficulty of controlling emotions and passions, his need to debunk, and a thorough ambivalence toward academics. He assailed them for their social irresponsibility and their "insatiable drive for status." At the same time, his highly qualified, pedantic, and labored style was more academic than that of most academics.

On the basis of a reading of this content, plus a between-the-lines assessment of the likely psychoanalytic meaning of the language and symbolism of the manuscript, I came up with a number of conclusions for my investigators:

- Taking the omnipresence of critical theory in the Manifesto, knowing that the ideas of Habermas and Marcuse were the "in thing" among protest activists between 1968 and 1971, and making the operative assumption that the most decisive intellectual influences on him must have occurred in his late twenties, I told the investigators that he was between forty-five and fifty-five years old. As it turned out, he was fifty-three years old (born May 22, 1942) at the time I wrote my report.
- Knowing where the radical "action" was in those years, I posited that he was probably exposed to one or more of the politically active university communities at the time. I mentioned the University of California at Berkeley, Columbia, Brandeis, and the New School for Social Research, with the University of Chicago and the University of Wisconsin as more remote possibilities. As it turned out, he spent two decisive years in the late 1960s as a junior faculty member in the Department of Mathematics at Berkeley.
- I posited that he was a "failed academic or graduate student" in the social sciences. I did this because of his amateurish, immature, and undigested use of the social science literature. I was wrong on this count, but he was an amateur—a mathematician who adopted social science concepts in a somewhat wooden manner.
- I posited that he first embraced the left but then rebelled against it in disillusionment because of his sense of the left's oppressiveness. He was preoccupied with the hypocrisy and sham of both "mainstream" and left politics. I could not know what I later learned: that his doting parents were social and political liberals, but he had come to feel betrayed by everything they stood for as a long-term result of his unsuccessful coming to terms with the trauma occasioned by the birth of his younger brother. But what I had to say was not inconsistent with this.

I do not pretend in the least that this little exercise led the investigators anywhere, least of all to their discovery and arrest of him. That depended above all on his brother's identification of him after reading the Manifesto—an ironic twist of fate in a fraught brother-brother relationship. However, I would like to add that the exercise confirmed the idea that the language, symbolism, and preoccupations of terrorists can yield some knowledge that might be helpful in narrowing the search, to say nothing of generating understanding about what may drive the perpetrators to extreme actions.

Ideology as Diagnosis

Throughout the chapter I refer to "terrorist ideology" as those beliefs that have been inspirational to groups that have engaged in terrorist activities. Such ideologies, however, typically enjoy an existence beyond such groups and are not exclusive to them. It is more accurate to say that they are appropriated, adapted, applied, and activated by terrorist groups.

The first thing an ideology does is *identify and explain* what is wrong or threatened in the world of believers and hoped-for believers. In doing this it structures and makes concrete the more diffuse dissatisfactions experienced by a group and lumps the diverse reasons for these dissatisfactions into a single explanation. In the nascent Ghost Dance ideology, it was the erosion of traditional Indian ways since the domination of the white man. In the Nazi ideology as enunciated by Adolf Hitler in *Mein Kampf,* it was the humiliation of the German people by the provisions of the Versailles Treaty of 1918 and the activities of a conspiratorial cabal of international Jewry. In the ideology enunciated in communist writings, the contemporary ills of the world (and in particular its working classes) are assigned in highly elaborated ways to the contradictions and evils of bourgeois capitalism and its agents. Anticolonial and separatist ideologies typically identify suffering in the form of lack of independence, privations, and oppression forced on the indigenous group by another group, by a home state, or by a foreign nation. In radical black movements the trouble is invariably traced to the oppression and privations imposed by the dominant whites and their racist practices. White supremacist ideologies show much variation, but common elements in their diagnoses are the threats to whites and their welfare and culture from Jews, blacks, Catholics, and a government that taxes and attempts to deprive citizens of arms. The ideology of groups that have engaged in terrorism in Israel (many inspired by Rabbi Meir Kahane) rests on a radical diagnosis of rampant anti-Semitism in the world, including especially the designs of Arabs in and around Israel. The radical Islamic ideology that has most recently come to be associated with Islamic terrorism enunciates a long history of abuse and oppression of Islamic lands and peoples by crusaders, Jews, and imperialists (personified mainly by the United States), abetted by secular Arab leaders who have collaborated with them.

Almost all these diagnoses contain an indictment of the outside agents. I will turn to the ingredient of agency presently. It is important to specify what value these diagnoses add to the larger picture of extremist movements. First, they constitute an invitation to believe in this particular *account* of things, and not to accept others (correspondingly, other, competing ideologies typically become the objects of attack). They are also an invitation to experience the *affect* of outrage, and to search for specific outrageous situations and responsible targets. They give reasons why it is reasonable and legitimate—even obligatory—to experience that outrage. As such they involve an emotional as well as a cognitive structuring for potential believers. Extremist ideologies also contain an invitation to mobilize certain *defenses* against experiencing unacceptable aspects of affects. Post, a psychologist of terrorism, pointed out that the defenses most common for terrorists are externalization (locating the problem or threat exclusively outside oneself) and splitting (dichotomizing affect into unqualified hatred of a "them" and idealization of an "us") (1990, pp. 27–28). Thus, ideology is a (proto)-theory, a series of (usually simplified) empirical assertions, and an intelligible explanation for the asserted state of affairs. These elements bring people some distance from generalized dissatisfaction toward accepting specific cognitive beliefs about the reasons for their dissatisfaction, experiencing certain affects (typically anxiety and anger), and confronting these affects. In these ways an ideology, if accepted, becomes a key part of the motivational complex that may lead to action.

Ideology as the Assignment of Agency and Responsibility

Not all ideologies attribute human suffering and unhappiness to social agents. An ascetic mystical religion, for example, typically assigns suffering to a cosmic agency—beyond the influence of human action—and for that reason often induces a mode of passive acceptance or contemplation as a way of dealing with that suffering. Other types of religion assign suffering to unfriendly gods, the mysterious intentions of a friendly god, or the work of supernatural demons. These also encourage a posture of passive adaptation. Secular ideologies may achieve the same effect. More than a half-century ago, Chinoy (1955) interviewed automobile workers who were either unemployed or dead-ended in unrewarding jobs with little prestige. The main reason for their failures, they explained to Chinoy (and to themselves), was that they hadn't tried hard enough in life. They seemed to be resigned to that, and displaced many of their unrealized hopes to ambitions for their children. More recent research has revealed that many people living on welfare blame themselves for their unemployment and failure to succeed, believing that if only they had worked harder or pulled themselves together, they would not be in such circumstances (Wilson, 1987). Still other explanations of misfortune can be assigned to chance, or "the breaks" or "the way the ball bounces." In all these instances, the probability of collective protest against others is muted, because the causes of suffering are either assigned to nonhuman agency or internalized as moral failings of the sufferer.

Another equally pervasive human tendency, however, is to identify one or more target groups who are responsible for the dangers to and suffering in a given group. Negative affects accompany this identification, and the agents are typically portrayed as having distinctive characteristics, motives, and hostile intentions. These are the components of stereotypes, which invariably become attached to outsiders thought to be menacing. Such negative components may live comfortably, if not altogether consistently, side by side with other sets of beliefs (often religious) that depersonalize or internalize threats to the group.

Some of the deepest and most enduring historical antagonisms exist between religious groups—Christians and Jews, pagans and Christians, Catholics and Protestants, Christians and Muslims, Hindus and Muslims, and Jews and Muslims—and many subdivisions within them, often along modernist–fundamentalist lines. Conquerors and conquered also develop mutually antagonistic and blaming belief systems. Franz Fanon captured the extremist colonialist mentality vividly:

> Native society is not simply described as a society lacking in values. It is not enough for the colonial to affirm that those values have disappeared from, or still better never existed in, the colonial world. The native is declared insensible to ethics; he represents not only the absence of values, but the negation of values, and in this sense he is the absolute evil. He is the corrosive element, destroying all that comes near him; he is the deforming element, disfiguring all that has to do with beauty or morality; he is the depository of maleficent powers, the unconscious and irretrievable instrument of blind forces. (quoted in Cronin, 2002, p. 48)

Much of the content of modern Western racism derives from theories explaining the inferior civilizations and cultures of colonized peoples. The colonized, on their side, return the favor, selecting out the "white men" (in the case of Native Americans), the Dutch, the British, the French, the Germans, the Portuguese as oppressors and responsible for hardships and the loss of traditional ways of life. Such beliefs have survived into postcolonial ideologies (Kelly, 2001). In addition, after the wave of independence of former colonies in the decades following World War II, old communalisms, often submerged in hatred of and common solidarity against the colonials, reemerged as inherited racial and ethnic hatreds among them in the formerly colonized areas in Africa, Asia, and the Indonesian islands.

Secularized ideologies on the right and left have revealed a difference with respect to the identification of agents. In that general grouping of ideologies under the headings of socialism, Marxism, and communism, the main thread has been to blame the system of capitalism. Some spokespersons for those ideologies claim explicitly that it is the system, not its agents, that are responsible for the contradictions, exploitation, and suffering in the world. In practice, however, that distinction has tended to break down: capitalists, their apologists, politicians and police as agents of capitalism have been singled out for attack and, in effect, have been found themselves to be blameworthy. The environmentalist left identifies global capitalism as the devastating culprit, but this system also tends toward concretization, as multinational corporations and other agencies such as the International Monetary Fund and the World Bank are singled out. Radical right movements have been more straightforward in their identification of dangerous and hated social groups. The most vivid example is Adolf Hitler's elaborated characterization of the Jews, deemed responsible, through an intricate system of conspiracies and infiltrations, for the travails afflicting the German nation and peoples. American right-wing extremist movements have accumulated a picture of multiple enemies, including politicians, intellectuals, communists, antiracists, women activists, homosexuals, drug addicts, Jews, Zionists, ethnic and racial minorities, immigrants, asylum seekers, Muslims, and "foreigners" generally (Bjørgo, 1995, p. 7). Despite the pervasive differences between left and right, both end up with specific parties to blame.

Three further tendencies emerge in extreme ideologies. The first is to extend the negative stereotype of "the other" into an absolute. The other becomes the enemy. That enemy, furthermore, has no positive redeeming characteristics. Most important, that enemy comes to be regarded as less than human, a designation that is extremely important in justifying treating them inhumanely. These are Hitler's *Untermenschen* (lower beings)—the Jews, Slavs, Gypsies, and homosexuals. These are the colonial peoples depicted by Fanon. These are the Israeli "sons of monkeys and pigs" identified in the radical Hamas ideology in Palestine (Oliver and Steinberg, 2005, pp. 101–2). These are those classes—the Bosch, Geeks, and Gooks—that opposing armies call their enemies.

The second tendency is to include as enemies those in the "home" group that sympathize with or have become like the enemy. These are the renegades, the traitors within. Those who espoused the Ghost Dance religion identified renegade Indians as among those who would perish in the apocalypse. Right-wing McCarthyites identified communism and communists as the main enemy of the American way of life, but also included fellow travelers, "pinkos," and liberals in the camp of the dangerous. Contemporary Islamic fundamentalists have developed an ideology that identifies "Americans, Jews, and Crusaders" as the main enemy but include as traitors secularized Muslim and Arab leaders who not only are unbelievers but also cooperate with the enemy. In 1984 an Iranian Ayatollah, Mohammed Baqer Al-Sadr, proclaimed "all [secular] states are inalienably illegitimate" (quoted in Hoffman, 1990, p. 3). Osama bin Laden specifically identified a number of "apostates" among leaders of Middle Eastern countries—Anwar Sadat and Hosni Mubarak of Egypt, Hafez Assad of Syria, Ali Abdallah Saley of Yemen, and Muammar Qadaffi of Libya (Williams, 2002, pp. 98–101).

Third, extremist ideologies tend to develop an indiscriminate quality that includes not only the enemy but also everything that represents or symbolizes that enemy. Some international terrorism is a spillover from internal rebellion against a regime thought to be allied with or supported by an outside power, which becomes a legitimate object of attack. For examples, "when Westerners are kidnapped by the FARC (Fuergas Revolucionarias de Colombia) in Colombia or the Abu Sayyef in the Philippines, the political aim of the kidnapers is to target the policy of support by the West of the government that the terrorists wish to overthrow" (Addison and Murshed, 2001). In 2001, in a manifesto for the global Islamic jihad, Ayman al-Zawahiri identified, as agents of the enemy, the United Nations, secular rulers of Muslim societies, multinational corporations, international communications systems, international news agencies, and international relief agencies (cited in Sageman, 2004, p. 20). Osama bin Laden called upon his faithful "to kill the Americans and plunder their money wherever and whenever they find it" (cited in Cronin, 2002, p. 405), and identified "the enemy" as "every American male, whether he is directly fighting us or paying taxes" (interview on Al-Jazira, cited in Silvers and Epstein, 2002, p. 360). Finally, past wrongs inflicted by the enemy are put in the same category as present ones—atrocities to be avenged.

What do these ideological ingredients involving agency and blame have to do with terrorism? Earlier I described ideology as an apparatus that readies people for collective action. The ideology that diagnoses the nature of suffering provides concrete meaning for the diffuse and scattered experiences of dissatisfaction and its associated affects of anxiety and resentment. The ideology that posits agents responsible for this suffering supplies a further "readying" element. It gives anxiety greater structure by converting it into fear of specific others. It gives anger greater structure by converting it into hostility against those others. Like the identification of suffering, the identification of responsible agents invites potential believers to experience those affects. Especially if it takes on the three generalizing tendencies just identified—generating absolute stereotypes, including domestic enemies, and expanding symbolically—the ideology provides a comprehensive justification for engaging in aggression, including violence, against those singled out as enemies.

Ideology as Vision

Examination of the Ghost Dance movement reveals a vision, naïve in some ways but profoundly reflective of the plight of the American Indians at the time. It was a vision of a future that connoted plenty of what mattered to the Indians (land, buffalo, and other game); a community of happiness, peace, and freedom from suffering; the obliteration of the despised white oppressors; and a society in which the Indians would reign supreme. The envisioned utopia matched point for point—and offered a solution for every point—the pattern of suffering and oppression experienced by the tribes. It was a mirror for affects as well. While the diagnosis of their situation was an invitation to experience despair, anxiety, and rage, the envisioned future was an invitation to experience hope and anticipate bliss.

The ideology of the Ghost Dance religion was a syncretic version— tailored to indigenous culture and local conditions—of a messianic belief. This genre of belief traces to the Judeo-Christian tradition of the coming of the messiah and has appeared and reappeared in various episodes in Western and colonial history (Cohn, 1951; Tuveson, 1949; La Barre, 1970; Wilson, 1973). A recent manifestation of such a vision appeared in the proclamation of an Iranian cleric during the Khomeini regime that "the 12th and last of the Shiite Imams, or successors to the

Prophet Mohammed, is expected to appear eventually to institute the rule of God's law on earth" (quoted in Hoffman, 1990, p. 43).

Messianic movements belong to a subclass of movements that have been called regenerative, nativistic, fundamentalist, or revitalization movements in the social science literature (Wallace, 1956). The generic elements of messianism are a sense of imminence of a catastrophic event (often world destruction, accompanied by the arrival of the messiah); the guarantee of salvation and a perfect community; a call for preparations for the event, which may vary from passive purification to active struggle; the mobilization of "evidence" to demonstrate faith and belief; a belief in "signs"; the crystallization of a moral community with a "cause"; and, finally, some notion of divine intervention in the regenerative project (Rapoport, 1987).

The structural components of this kind of ideology constitute a template for all transformative movements. Very few of these movements eventuate in violence or terrorism (whether they do or not depends on the confluence of conditions outlined in chapter 2), but many movements that do engage in terrorism adopt this kind of ideological structure as inspiration. My analysis is not restricted to religious movements but is meant to include the whole range—religiously inspired movements, ethnonationalist struggles, left-wing and right-wing political movements, and single-cause movements (such as environmentalism and antiabortion). All express hope, and all have an ideal vision of a better society and a better life; accordingly, they become part of the motivational package that drives such movements. The different components of this generic ideology vary greatly in content as well as explicitness. Despite this variation, the general feature is hope and vision, which are an integral part of the ideological package that motivates extreme movements that may turn to violence.

I begin with the least likely ideological candidate, anarchism. Its very name connotes nihilism—the annihilation of all government, laws, and private property. The anarchist ideology crystallized in the work of William Godwin shortly after the French Revolution and occupied an extreme position within the spectrum of left-wing radicalism in the nineteenth and early twentieth centuries. It served as the legitimizing rationale for many assassinations and much revolutionary activity in tsarist Russia, Europe, and the United States. Its main enemies were state leaders and its representatives, who were to be "condemned immediately to death," and its general aim was "merciless destruction" (Nechaev, quoted in Laqueur, 1978, p. 70). The utopian side of anarchism is vaguer but nevertheless discernible. Godwin himself foresaw a future victory for the principle of "general welfare" and the emergence of a society in which "not a sword will need to be drawn, not a finger to be lifted up in purposes of violence." Accordingly, there will be no serious thought of resisting "the universal sense of mankind" (see Eltzbacher, 1960, p. 38). Michael Bakunin, the guiding spirit of much of Russian anarchism, also espoused a "constructive side," which involved a vision of a worldwide federation of producers' associations (in contrast to Marx's envisioned workers' state) in which complete economic and social equality would be realized (see Avrich, 1967, p. 25).

The classic vision of the communist ideology is found in the pages of the *Communist Manifesto* (Marx and Engels, 1954 [1848]). While sharply critical of "utopian" socialism, which emphasized the viability of small communities, Marx and Engels themselves envisioned a scientifically based utopia that would arise with the destruction of capitalism and the abolition of its institutions. With the concentration of power in the proletariat, "we shall have an association, in which the free development of each is the condition for the free development of all" (ibid., p. 37). Engels subsequently referred to communist society as a "universal emancipation" and "the ascent of man from the kingdom of necessity to the kingdom of freedom" (Engels, 1959 [1880], pp. 111, 109). Utopian elements also appeared in Engels' characterization of the life of preindustrial workers in England (Engels, 1993 [1845]). While the concrete depiction of life in the communist utopia has always remained elusive, the ideal of freedom from capitalist or capitalist-derived oppression has remained a constant element. The idea reappeared in altered form in the ideologies of terrorist movements in the United States and Western Europe in the 1960s and 1970s. Hoffman believes that these movements were disadvantaged because they "formulated the least clear and most ill-defined vision of the future" (1998, p. 172; see also Addison, 2002, pp. 64–65). Contrary to this view, one of the interviewers in the clinical study of members of the Red Army Faction in Germany concluded that the core was fundamentally visionary:

[The terrorists] want The Revolution, a total transformation of all existing conditions, a new form of human existence, an entirely new relationship of people to each other, and also of people to nature. They want the total and radical breach with all that is, and with all historical continuity. Without a doubt they are utopian. (Günter Rohrmoser, cited in Kellen, 1990, pp. 49–50)

Even though the visionary element varies along the continuum from vagueness to explicitness, it is invariably a part of the ideological package.

This same imagery of emancipation is found in many of the anticolonial, secessionist, and ethnonationalism movements as well, for example in the Marxist faction of the Palestinian Liberation Movement. In most cases, this imagery of oppression is accompanied by a relatively tangible vision, either the expulsion of the colonial power and the establishment of an independent homeland or, in the case of ethnic minorities within a state, an autonomous territory of their own.

Movements on the right often envision a return to an imagined traditional past of white supremacy and pure Christianity. The Nazi ideology envisioned a "Thousand-Year Reich" based on a revitalization of German values. The Aum Shinrikyo cult in Japan foresaw a cataclysm that would obliterate the international cabal of Jews, Freemasons, and financiers, and would usher in a thousand years of peace and "paradise on earth" (Hoffman, 1998, p. 124). Such formulations recapitulate the messianic religious impulse.

The Core of Ambivalence: Omnipotence
and Weakness of Other and Self

In passing, the National Commission on Terrorist Attacks made an observation about one set of ideological claims made by Al-Qaeda:

America had attacked Islam; Americans are responsible for all conflicts involving Muslims, Thus Americans are blamed when Israelis fight with Palestinians, when Russians fight with Chechens, when Indians fight with Kashmiri Muslims, and when the Philippine government fights ethnic Muslims in its southern islands. America is also held responsible for the governments of Muslim countries, derided by Al-Qaeda as "your agents." (2004, p. 76)

In this description, the commission pointed to a recurring theme of extremist movements: the characterization of the enemy as omnipotent (which typically includes omnipresence, omniscience, and conspiracy). Decades earlier the Ayatollah Khomeini, in announcing his intention to export the Iranian revolution "throughout the world," announced that "all the powers are intent on destroying us, and if we remain surrounded, ... we shall certainly be defeated" (Hoffman, 1990, p. 2). During the Iran-Iraq war in the 1980s, the Iranian media frequently treated the war as an imperialist plot devised by the "Great Satan," the United States, to destroy that country's revolution (Hyman, 1994). The same theme appears in the anti-Israeli pronouncements of the Hamas movement in Palestine: Zionism represents an all-out assault on the Palestinians "by promoting provincialism, alienating the nation from its cultural roots and clamping down on its economic, political, military and even intellectual hegemony" (Hamas Web site, cited in Cronin, 2002, p. 299). The Islam fundamentalist spokesman Al-Zwahiri spoke of "the tremendous increase in the number of ... enemies, the quality of their weapons, their destructive powers, their disregard for all taboos, and disrespect for the customs of wars and conflicts" (quoted in Sageman, 2004, p. 23). The theme of enemy omnipotence appears in rightwing fascist movements (notably the portrayal of international Jewry in Nazi ideology), in communist portrayals of the capitalist class and its agents, and sometimes in attacks on "the establishment" generally.

In the same ideological nexus, however, the theme of the weakness and corruption of the enemy appears. In the Marxist literature the capitalist bourgeoisie is regarded simultaneously as all-powerful and manipulative but also as beset with crises, on the defensive, and ultimately doomed to perish in its own contradictions. Regarding the ultimate triumph of the Palestinians in the "conclusive battle between Islam and the Jews," Ahmad Yasin, the spiritual leader of Hamas, announced "the battle to expel the Jews will take place between the faithful servants of Allah and the cowardly Jews" (cited in Oliver and Steinberg, 2005, p. 26). In contemporary anti-Americanism in some Arab countries, the

United States is described simultaneously as an all-powerful enemy and as a corrupt and vulnerable society based on materialism, consumerism, homosexuality, sexual permissiveness, the freedom and sinfulness of women, and, most important, secularism and godlessness. (The fact that these are points of ambivalence and conflict *within* Islamic societies as they struggle between modernism and traditionalism gives them even more affective bite [Fukuyama, 2002, p. 31]). America is also regarded as simultaneously mighty and weak. In the wake of September 11, 2001, a radical Lebanese journalist remarked, "The symbol of the free world and its greatest deity (the little U.S. god) has been broken and its legend has been smashed by the strikes against its three major pillars (globalism, political hegemony, and military hegemony)" (Åhmad, 2002, p. 291). Rubin and Rubin summarized themes emerging from dozens of radical Islamic sources as follows: "America is said to be an imperialist bully, but at the same time the revolutionary claims he possesses the secret of defeating the United States" (2002, p. 77).

Ambivalence also appears in the characterization of the righteous. On the one hand, themes of victimization abound. Most ideologies of the dispossessed contain themes of "chosen traumas" and derived "chosen glories" from the history of the righteous groups. Persecutions, injustices, massacres, and martyrs are the recurrent themes (Volkan, 2004). The corollary to this sad history is that the heroic group is portrayed as the weak victim of powerful oppressors and enemies. It is important for ideological and political purposes that the reference point is the group as such:

> [O]ne must see oneself as a representative victim, victimized only through one's membership of a group that is subject to unjust treatment. . . . [The individual] is victimized because of the unjust treatment of one's group. . . . So one acts as a representative of that group [and] expresses the indignation and apprehension of the group. (Gilbert, 1994, p. 78)

Out of that victimization of the weak, however, comes the power to resist, to fight, and to overcome. Extremist ideologies fill themselves out with a picture of the omnipotence—if not actual, then potential—to destroy even the most powerful enemies. The proletariat is the ultimate mighty crushing force of bourgeois society in Marxist ideology. And in contemporary radical Islamic ideologies, faith in the cause enables righteous fighters to bring down both Israel and the American giant, to drive enemies from Islamic lands, and to overcome ungodly forces in their own societies (Williams, 2002).

While the ambivalent interplay between themes of omnipotence and weakness in both friend and foe does not seem to meet accepted canons of cognitive consistency, it does resonate with the logic of affect, which pitches hope against despair, power against helplessness, and righteousness against evil. "Many terrorists define their role as that of sacrificial victim; whether or not this image accords with reality, the notion of being willing to die for a cause is important to the terrorist's self-perception" (Thackrah, 1987a, p. 25). Such beliefs, ambivalent though they are, also constitute a powerful force for mobilizing individuals and groups to violent action.

Ideology and the Strain Toward Consistency

In his pioneering work on the sociology of culture, Talcott Parsons tackled a series of difficult problems dealing with the functions of ideology in social life. Among these he identified the processes of "rationalization" that ideologies manifest as a result of the "strain to consistency" in belief systems (Parsons, 1951, pp. 348–59). "Man is a cognizing animal" (ibid., p. 350), he said, and strives to give more or less consistent meaning to his or her values, goals, and activities. He considered this a universal process, applying to the elaboration of institutionalized belief systems, such as free enterprise, as well as belief systems of "deviant" groups such as gangs. Clearly, the process is found in extremist ideologies that come to fortify and justify terrorist activities.

The term rationalization is an apt one because it carries two connotations, both relevant to the analysis of terrorists' belief systems and their dynamics. The first, more positive meaning is "making rational"—that is, rendering consistent—events, purposive actions, and situations in terms of the worldview of the believers and hoped-for audiences. Ideological elaboration is a way of making sense of the world by avowing that "things fit together." It is an altogether natural response, especially in a confusing or threatening environment, because it paves the way for making sense of *one's own activities* in responding to it. The second, more negative meaning of rationalization is to confirm as favorable "evidence" some events and situations that appear consistent with one's preferred worldview and to "explain away" events and situations that seem at odds or even contradict that worldview. Sometimes this process involves labored distortions of facts that might on their face be at odds with ideological tenets. Here are a few examples of this double process:

- Two "explanations" were circulated in Muslim nations shortly after September 11, 2001. The first was the assertion that it was Jews (or, alternatively, that it was a Jewish plot) to attack New York and Washington to create a pretext for the United States and Israel to wage further aggression against the Muslim world (Sharkansky, 2003, pp. 27–28). The second was the assertion, issued after the film footage of Osama bin Laden and his associates gloating over the attack, that the film was an American fabrication. Both assertions served to confirm the evil and devious intentions of Americans and Jews and to reinterpret what appeared to be a barbarous act of violence on the part of Muslims, a peaceful and humane people. Both stories complemented longstanding beliefs spread by Hamas faithful, for example, that the British Broadcasting Corporation, the U.S. Congress, and the world media are controlled by Jews (Oliver and Steinberg, 2005). Such are the rationalizing dynamics of ideology. More recently, the same logic of assimilation appeared in the wake of the tsunami disasters in the Indian Ocean on December 26, 2004, as rumors spread that the tidal waves were caused by an American underwater nuclear detonation designed to kill Muslims and destroy their communities.
- The very same events of September 11 were given consistency within the ideology of the American radical right in an announcement by the Reverend Jerry Falwell on September 22, 2001. He interpreted the events of September 11 as God's way of punishing secularist America for its immorality. Gays and liberals in particular were singled out as blameworthy. Falwell subse-

quently withdrew these comments under an onslaught of public outrage at the suggestion that America brought the attacks on itself (Ringstrom, 2002, p. 37). Parallel but also subdued expressions of self-indictment came from the left as well. Assertions such as "the United States had it coming," that we as a nation have been guilty of atrocities much worse than 9/11, and that "the Americans created bin Laden during the Cold War" (quoted in Judt, 2002, p. 18) appeared.

- When the May 1, 1985, attack by the Belgian Communist Combatant Cells on the Belgian Employers' Association building in Brussels inadvertently killed two firemen, the CCC "regretted" the killings, but in the end asserted that the "pigs" (gendarmarie) sent the firemen to their deaths as a contrived act so that the authorities could exploit the incident (Cordes, 1987, p. 329).

- In the bombing of the U.S. Embassy in Dar es Salaam on August 7, 1998, eleven people were killed, none of them Americans. In a subsequent interview about the deaths, Osama bin Laden was quoted as saying that "when it becomes apparent that it would be impossible to repel these Americans without assaulting them, even if this involved the killing of Muslims, this is permissible under Islam" (cited in National Commission on Terrorist Attacks Upon the United States, 2004, p. 102). The ideological dynamic seems apparent: the defensive interpretation of an embarrassing datum to make it less embarrassing and consistent with the larger purposes of the movement's ideology.

- On the American side of the ideological divide, it is appropriate to point out the ideological significance of the long insistence— on the part of the George W. Bush administration and others favorable to the 2002 invasion of Iraq—on the issue of the possession of weapons of mass destruction by the Saddam Hussein regime and on the links between Al-Qaeda's terrorism and Hussein's Iraq. More than facts were involved: the assertions proved to be unconfirmed in all subsequent investigations. The principle of ideological consistency, however, makes sense of the assertions: a drive to confirm the evil of the enemy and to strike back at political critics who were denouncing the invasion of Iraq as irrelevant to terrorism. Critics of the war, too, had reasons of ideological consistency for insisting on the falsity of the Bush administration's claims and for celebrating that falsity.

- Most ideologies associated with Marxist and neo-Marxist movements over the past one and one-half centuries have included some view of the motivations of a capitalist class with an insatiable drive to seek profits and to exploit the working classes. This view has been employed variably to interpret strikebreaking activities (consistent with the main view), compromises by capitalists (biding their time), and welfare and other reforms (avoiding a worse revolutionary fate or postponing the inevitable revolution). More recent left-inspired ideologies, such as that of the Red Army Faction in West Germany, reveal similar ideological elaborations about capitalist and capitalist-state strategies. In South Africa in the 1980s, interpreters within the African National Congress (with an ideology incorporating both anticapitalist and national liberation themes) interpreted the pragmatic reforms of apartheid by the administration of P. W. Botha as trickery designed to streamline the system of apartheid domination (Clifford-Vaughan, 1987, pp. 279–80).

The key to understanding such elaborations of the oppressors' motivation is that no event or situation escapes consistent interpretation within that particular worldview.

More generally, it can be observed that once we appreciate these flexible and elastic—"rationalizing"—elements of an ideology, we have in hand a number of categories that apparently can explain anything of relevance that happens. The portrayal of an enemy as simultaneously evil and cunning is the most typical formula. It is this ingredient that gives the ideology of extremism its frequently attributed "paranoid" character (see Robins and Post, 1997). This is not to say that those who believe in the ideology are clinically paranoid; it is to say, however, that the ideology has the apparent capacity, through elaboration, to claim that nothing is accidental or coincidental, that everything has a purpose, and that that purpose is part of a larger design. Such are the lengths to which the "strain toward consistency" goes.

With respect to terrorism in particular, the pressure to rationalize is especially pressing for one special and exceptional reason. Terrorism typically involves violence and killing (usually of innocents), a solemn taboo in most religions, generally forbidden in most cultures, and, when permitted, highly circumscribed legally and limited to specific agents (soldiers, law enforcement officers, executioners). The recommendation to kill comes immediately into conflict with these normative prohibitions. As a result, most terrorist ideologies seek justification for killing enemies. Most typically this is found in the simultaneous demonization of the enemy and glorification of the moral, political, or religious cause that is defined as so urgent and so holy that killing is justified. The utterances of Osama bin Laden, for example, make it a duty for believing Muslims to kill Americans and unbelievers. The nineteenth-century revolutionary Karl Heinzen put forth a secular, philosophical justification:

> Let us . . . be practical, let us call ourselves murderers as our enemies do, let us take the moral horror out of this great historical tool and just examine closely whether perchance our enemies may claim a special privilege in the matter of murder. If to kill is always a crime, then it is forbidden equally to all; if it is not crime, then it is permitted equally to all. Once one has overcome the objection that murder per se is a crime, all that remains is to believe one is in the right against one's enemy and to possess the power to obliterate him. (cited in Laqueur, 1978, p. 54)

Appreciating the dynamics of ideological elaboration also permits us to grasp its dynamic character. Ideology is not a thing, fixed in time, but rather a continuous process of development and rationalization, forever adding, forgetting, explaining, and adapting to the world as new events and situations—particularly unanticipated ones—arise.

This ideological dynamic manifests one additional notable feature. Once a party in conflict has enunciated more or less articulately the ideological essentials that guide it, that ideology takes on a life of its own and becomes something to which its advocates must pay direct attention. Put another way, ideology becomes interest. Its exponents must assure that it remains alive—by repeating it, by publicizing it, by honing it, and by protecting it from actual and anticipated criticisms. Furthermore, and ironically, the ideology becomes something of a prison for its believers. They must continuously examine their own plans and behavior to ensure that they are not blatantly inconsistent with the claimed ideological principles; they must try to protect it against those who point out apparent inconsistencies by denial, explanation, or some other defense. This particular dynamic assures that when some mission of conflict is undertaken in the name of a voiced ideology, it is virtually guaranteed that a large part of that mission will be the production of ideological spin designed to maintain the ideology in its most favorable light and to protect it from critical assault from within and without.

The Confrontation of Ideologies: Terrorist and Antiterrorist

Terrorism and the defense against it produces yet another paradox. As we have seen, one of the principal conditions that foster extreme ideologies is a shared sense of dispossession and suffering. With the right combination of circumstances (detailed in chapter 2), this kind of ideology can lead to campaigns of terrorist activities against designated enemies. For societies experiencing terrorist attacks or the threat of them, the sense of danger, uncertainty, and accompanying anxiety comes to constitute a very similar set of conditions and thus constitutes a favorable breeding ground for antiterrorist ideologies in the societies under threat. The paradoxical element is that these ideologies display similar vectors and structures as they build up a picture to confront the opposed content of the terrorist ideology. When this develops, a particularly rigid and uncompromising form of mutual distrust and confrontation between parties believing in absolutes is at hand.

This kind of confrontation in turn tends to restrict if not rule out many conflict-resolving possibilities and to encourage others. If enemies regard one another as antagonists in the totalistic terms that emerge in their respective ideologies, the following possibilities arise:

- Mutual trust is minimized, for who can ever trust an evil and devious schemer?

- Honest communication is also minimized, because even friendly words by a demonic enemy are regarded as a feint or a front for deeper demonic motives.
- If the antagonists are mutually portrayed as fanatics bent on destruction, then appeals to reason are fruitless.
- One's supposed friends or neutral parties who might not be enemies of the enemy may not be trusted either; this circumstance reduces the likelihood of helpful intervention by third parties in the conflict.
- Because the mutual enemies are portrayed in such extreme terms, the belief that they can be defeated only by resorting to force may become the dominant assumption.
- Because enemies portray one another as subhuman or nonhuman in the universe of good and evil, they resort to killing and destruction, because the ideological polarization endows these measures with legitimacy.

In sum, combining the typical attribution of absolute evil intent of the enemy (and absolute good to oneself), along with a projected picture of systematic scheming on both sides, contributes to an escalation of mutual distrust and overreaction.

Perhaps the most vivid illustration of absolute ideological polarization is found in the beliefs generated in the communist bloc and the Western powers during the prolonged period of the cold war between the end of World War II and the collapse of the communist system in 1990. This was not the kind of terrorist situation the world now confronts, though the threats of mutual nuclear destruction were terrifying, and both sides supported terrorist groups with varying degrees of explicitness and directness. One facet of this sustained conflict was an extreme ideological confrontation. This was fed in the communist bloc by an amalgam of beliefs deriving from the Marxist-Leninist-Stalinist traditions, which included a diagnosis and vilification of capitalism and its agents as oppressors of the world's workers and its poor. It was fed by the West with the portrayal of bolshevist-communist forces as correspondingly inimical to Western economic and political values and threatening to our civilization ("the evil empire"). Both ideologies took on a menacing character, and each legitimized feelings of deep hostility and toward the other. As a commentator on terrorism in 1986 noted, "The Reagan administration firmly believes that the USSR is the mastermind of world terrorism, and the Soviets believe the United States is aggressive and determined to expand its sphere of influence—through terrorism if necessary" (Adams, 1986, p. 2). In the end these ideologies were tempered by deterrence and mutual fear of massive loss of lives and destruction in nuclear attacks, by establishing international lines that each side came to learn could not be crossed, and by waging smaller conventional wars that communicated big messages. This more realistic drama developed, however, in the context of mutual hatred based on opposing absolute ideologies. Similar patterns of vilification and polarization developed between enemies during World War II, though, like the capitalist-communist antagonisms, these tended to weaken or even dissolve when the period of conflict ended and new alliances and power relations emerged.

While the United States and other target powers did become concerned about international terrorism and took some measures to deal with it in the last decades of the twentieth century, only in the 1990s, after the end of the cold war, did this threat move toward becoming *the* identified danger to these nations. However, on September 11, 2001, the sense of threat and vulnerability magnified instantly, as a dramatic response to the suddenness, drama, immediacy, destructiveness, and horror experienced in the wake of those attacks. In the months that ensued, the nation witnessed, among other things, the emergence of a full-blown antiterrorist ideology, voiced and fostered mainly by national leaders but shared by many others. This ideology, moreover, according to form, manifested a point-by-point structural correspondence with the Islamic fundamentalist ideology in the name of which the attacks were made. These are the main ingredients:

Vilification. The language of response, enunciated mainly by President Bush, identified the perpetrators as "outlaws," "murderers," "barbaric criminals," and "killers of innocents" (address, October 27, quoted in Whittaker, 2002, p. 49). The response also focused concretely on Osama bin Laden and Al-Qaeda. President Bush also identified the "axis of evil" as inimical forces in Iraq, Iran, and North Korea, thus paralleling bin Laden's identification of "evil [in] the Peninsula of Muhammad" in a statement made shortly after September 11 (quoted in Prados, 2002, p. 13). The international dialogue is also marked by a search for negatives, including the symbolic struggle over who should be called a terrorist and who should not. As Crenshaw observed, "calling adversaries 'terrorists' is a way of depicting them as fanatic and irrational so as to foreclose the possibility of compromise, draw attention to the real or imagined threat to security, and promote solidarity among the threatened" (1995a, p. 9).

Opposition of absolutes. In an address to a joint session of Congress on September 20, 2001, President Bush said, "Every nation, in every region, now has a decision to make: Either you are with us, or you are with the terrorists" (quoted in National Commission on Terrorist Attacks Upon the United States, 2004, p. 482). A few weeks later he proclaimed, "in this conflict there is no neutral ground" (quoted in Whittaker, 2003, p. 49; see also Domke, 2004). Shortly afterward Osama bin Laden said, "I tell [international infidels] that [events] have divided the world into two camps, the camp of the faithful and the camp of infidels" (quoted in Prados, 2002, p. 13). The symbolic battle that has subsequently evolved involves a continuous search for and defense of negative, stigmatizing symbols (Gerbner, 1990, p. 93).

Exaggerations of the agency of the other. In the 1960s, in Berkeley, when I was simultaneously an observer of student activism and a member of the university administration confronting it, I noticed a consistent tendency. Those in the administration were obsessively concerned with the strategies and tactics of the free speech movement and its derivatives, and forever assigning intention and motive to almost anything that happened. The activists, on their side, regarded the administration as equally purposeful, never doing anything without a plan, and systematically organized in its campaign against the activists. These assignments were very remote from the true state of affairs. Both sides were engaged in a somewhat clumsy game of guessing, making mistakes, changing their minds, and generally coping day by day in the midst of confusion. Consistent with this regularity, a full reading of the report of National Commission on Terrorist Attacks reveals both the confusion, vacillation, inaction, uncertainty, and failures of coordination of various American agencies with antiterrorist responsibilities and the tenta-

tiveness, mistakes, near mistakes, and close calls as the terrorists developed and executed the September 11 attack. Ideologies and counter-
ideologies consistently defy this truth, however, in their effort to understand and simplify by attributing design to the enemy.

One of the by-products of ideological polarization is the development of a game that might be called ideological "last tag." By this is
meant that opponents engage in propaganda, interpret events, and pro-
voke or take actions that constitute "proof" that the opponent deserves
the negative labels assigned. Both sides also gauge their behavior so
that they can avoid being labeled in those negative lights. The constant
struggle between protesters and police to fix or avoid, respectively, the
label of "police brutality" is a prototypical instance of this game. In
many manifestations of terrorism, perpetrators try to avoid being labeled criminal killers by not taking innocent lives, or, when they do,
explain why they are not really doing so or why it is justified. Governments try to avoid labels that picture them as oppressive, or when they
are evidently oppressive, to explain why it is necessary in light of the
dire threats they face. All this is carried out with an eye to real or imagined audiences that may give or withdraw political support. On the part
of political authorities, a motivation in the game is to isolate terrorists
from public support on account of their excesses; on the part of terrorists, the motivation is to drive authorities to overreactions and the commission of atrocities, which cost the authorities legitimacy and enhance
support for the victimized among some audiences (Post, 1990; Berry,
1987, pp. 294–96). Sometimes the strategies and tactics of the game
itself come to overshadow the substance of the political conflict itself.

This game of last tag was a vivid feature in the period of protest
and terrorism and quasi-terrorism—and the response to it—in West
Germany from the late 1960s into the 1980s. The heavy-handed treatment of the antiwar protesters in the late 1960s left the government
vulnerable to the accusations of protesters that it was democratic in
name only and fundamentally a continuation of the Third Reich. Widespread political controversy developed over empowering legislation and
the government's enforcement of it. When the protest turned visibly
toward extreme terrorism in the 1970s, however, the government's
hand was strengthened through lack of public support for the movement's excessive violence. One former member of the Red Army Fac-

tion assessed the turn of the movement toward "cowardly murder" as completely counterproductive: "We thought with our political actions to overcome the exploitation and domination and in reality, were only used [by the interested authorities] to make the conditions ... uglier yet" (Klaus Jünschke, cited in Merkl, 1991, p. 192). The emergence of such a game appears to be a regular feature of political conflict, and probably an inevitable accompaniment of conflict involving extremist ideologies, terrorism, and counterterrorism. It is certainly a conspicuous element in the contemporary international face-off between religiously based terrorist groups and the United States.

Rhetorical reaffirmations of symbols of legitimacy. The ideological output of radical fundamentalists who represent and support violence on the part of terrorist groups is replete with justificatory references to the Muslim cause, affirmations that Allah is on the side of the terrorists, and glorification of the purity of Muslim religious life. The attacks on the United States on September 11 excited a spontaneous burst of American nationalism, with great displays of the flag and reaffirmation of American principles of freedom, justice, and democracy. The rhetorical battle of symbols continues in what Derian has described as a "mimetic war of images"—an ideological symmetry in an asymmetrical power situation (2002, p. 109).

The imagery of war itself, frequently invoked in the current scene, is an aspect of the search for legitimizing symbols. On the side of the terrorists themselves, one need only recall the self-adopted military labels of Irish Republican Army, the Red Army Faction, the Japanese Red Army, and the Red Brigades (Crenshaw, 1995a, p. 11), and the adoption of words such as "commandos" (Merkl, 1991, p. 183). A basic ingredient of radical Muslim ideology is the idea of a holy war (Juergensmeyer, 2003), against, interestingly, the memory of Western crusaders, themselves so engaged. The counterterrorist imagery invokes the idea of a "war on terrorism," which has become a feature of everyday language. The positive symbolic reference is to the idea of a just or righteous war—an all-out belligerence against an unjust war (Gilbert, 1990, pp. 19–22; see also Miller, 1991)—or "the American way of war," as one critic put it (Falk, 2003, p. 108). Those who point out the misguided nature of the "war against an abstract noun"—with no government to defeat, no territory to conquer, no way to validate the disappearance of the threat, and no way to gain full "victory" (ibid., p. 8)—have valid points to make, but they miss the ideological power and legitimizing significance of the imagery of war.

The inverse of the contest over the appropriation of legitimizing military symbolism is the reluctance of parties to endow their enemies with it. Governmental and media accounts of international violence lean toward terms used by the press in reporting, such as "rebels," "insurgents," "terrorists," "guerrillas," and "revolutionaries," all of which connote opposition to the status quo (Picard, 1993, p. 98).

My identification of the parallels between terrorist and counterterrorist ideologies should not be misread. There is no claim whatsoever that the parallels connote a moral equivalence. To conclude that is to fall into a trap. Assessment of the morality of parties involved in conflict is a matter separate from understanding ideologies, and all of us arrive at our respective moral judgments. There is no contradiction, however, between arriving at a moral preference and analyzing and understanding what is going on in a situation, even though a moral stance sometimes constitutes a protective shroud for not understanding. What I have been seeking is the structural equivalence that develops when opponents are involved in what they regard as a mortal struggle. That these ideologies should develop on both sides is completely understandable as an aspect of deep conflict. The consequences of such polarized ideologies, however, are mixed. On the one hand, they serve as resources for mobilizing the faithful. On the other, they lead to the drawing of "battle lines on both sides . . . in an abstract, totalizing rhetoric" (ibid.; see Barber, 2003, for a savage critique of dominant American antiterrorist ideology) and sanction deadly and destructive actions against opponents who despise one another.

Without joining the ranks of those who embrace totalistic antiterrorist ideologies or those who reject them, it is nevertheless possible to point up an entrapment in the struggle against terrorism, which can be phrased as follows:

Entrapment 2: Democratic polities under threat of terrorist attack are likely to accept extreme and absolute counterterrorist ideologies, because they simplify a complex situation, because they appeal emotionally to a citizenry under threat of attack, and because political authorities can shore up their support by adopting or voicing them. Yet such ideologies, at the very least, tend to narrow the range of strategies available to deal with terrorism, and more seriously may spawn overreactions and forms of aggression that may be counterproductive from the standpoint of dealing with the terrorist activities and their potential supporters.

Summary: Ideology as Structure, Invitation, and Weapon

In concluding this account of the ideological bases of terrorist groups, it is important to reiterate that this chapter, along with chapter 4 on recruitment, group process, audiences, and the media, should be read as dealing with the large and complex topic of motivation. In this complex of factors, what explanatory value does the consideration of ideology add?

The ideal typical *content* of ideologies associated with extremist movements—some of which turn to terrorism—has displayed the greatest variation, and from that standpoint, every ideology and subideology can be said to be unique. With respect to *vectors*, however, a commonality emerges. All ideologies begin with the diagnosis that the world, or some aspect of it, is fundamentally out of shape—usually unjust, inequitable, and oppressive. Some agent—person, group, nation, culture—is identified as responsible for the world's troubled state and blamed as an enemy in the process. The ideology also contains a vision of a more perfect world—sometimes looking toward the past, sometimes toward an idealized future, sometimes a mixture of both, but in all events better. A way is foreseen, moreover, to fight the enemy, to effect change, and to move toward the vision. As part of the realization of the vision, the enemy will be punished or even obliterated. Specific exhortations as to right conduct are often present, including purification rituals, keeping the faith, and fighting the enemy directly. Lastly, ideologies tend toward polarization into systems of good and evil, deification and demonization. It is this package of beliefs that commands the moral engagement of terrorists in the cause. The "moral disengagement" from violence and murder, cited as one of the necessary conditions for committing them (Bandura, 1990), is the mirror reflection of the moral engagement of terrorists in their cause.

This assertion of commonality is, I realize, a controversial one, and it should be pointed out legitimately that these vectors vary greatly in the degree to which they are explicit or implicit in different ideologies. Nevertheless, there is a certain tendency for ideologies to "fill themselves out" by developing the several common ingredients I have identified. This is not the result of some mystical cultural tendency but the result of the tendency of both espousers and believers of the ideology to represent their viewpoints as coherent and consistent within the framework of their first assumptions. The internal logic of ideology is such, moreover, that they produce a certain internal cross-justification: hatred is justified by referring to the miserable state of affairs a group suffers under, positive actions are justified by appeal to the vision, and so on.

The first service that ideologies of all sorts serve, then, is to structure the complex world of reality for the believer and potential believer. It is an existential fact of life that everyone is exposed to a vast array of personal experiences, influences from others, orally presented and written materials, the media, and, through all these, an inconsistent if not chaotic view of the world, morality, and oneself. Ideology, as well as other kinds of beliefs, selects from history and flow of experience and structures the world in an equally selective way. The ideologies of social movements, including those that inspire terrorist activities, are put-together syncretic views of reality, a mix of history, tradition, literature, religion and contemporary events. Ideologies put these ingredients together in meaningful packages, identifying what is important and what is not important in the world, and above all what is amiss with and what is right about that world. Ideologies crystallize confusion and vagueness into structure and certainty.

There is a second, equally important ordering function. Throughout the analysis I have been sensitive to identifying the specific emotions that each and all of the ingredients of extremist ideologies are intended to activate. An ideology provides a structure for the affects of anxiety, despair, indignation, hope, anticipation, and elation, and weds them to its selective existential picture of the world. Thus, an ideology constitutes an invitation to believe and an invitation to feel. This service of ordering the world both cognitively and affectively for leaders and followers of extreme social movements is an essential for persuading others and for securing sympathy, recruitment, loyalty, and action.

This combination of belief and affect gives extremist ideologies their exceptional power as part of the motivational complex. This power derives from another combination: the match between its message and the situations of potentially supportive audiences and possible recruits to the cause. Such ideologies derive even more power when they find listeners whose situation is uncertain, confusing, threatening, desperate, and seemingly overwhelming. Ideologies are thus powerful weapons in mobilizing both those who may ultimately turn to terror—when other conditions are present and the time seems right—and those who are threatened by terror.

I add, finally, that ideology is in the end a cultural resource, and therefore it is a mistake to assume an identity between the formal structure of an ideology and the internal motivation of those who associate themselves with it. Ideologies are not simply and automatically internalized. From the individual psychological point of view they should also be regarded as a resource to which the individual refers periodically as justifying his or her actions, as reinforcing relations of solidarity with others, and generally as giving coherent accounts of the world.

CHAPTER 4

Motivation, Social Origins, Recruitment,

Groups, Audiences, and the Media

in the Terrorism Process

THE FOREGOING CHAPTER on ideology focused on a key
variable essential for understanding the motive forces for terrorism. A
core feature emerged: ideology is simultaneously cultural and psychological in significance. It is above all a cultural construction that both
invites and shapes individual motivations as it becomes accepted or
appreciated by members of terrorist groups and their surrounding body
of sympathizers and supporters.

Ideology, however, must be regarded as only one factor in the motivating process. In this chapter I identify a number of others that contribute to actors' becoming committed to ideologies and acting in the
name of those ideologies. Among these factors are (1) psychological
motives, including personality traits and types of inner conflicts that
actors bring with them and that press toward extreme or violent behavior; (2) the social backgrounds of terrorists, or locations in the
society's social structure that predispose individuals toward extremist
movements that may turn in a violent direction; (3) avenues and
mechanisms by which leaders and other members persuade or coerce
recruits into accepting the ideological cause and joining a group that
pursues it; (4) group processes that foster commitment, conformity,
and loyalty (this factor includes the vulnerabilities of such groups);
and (5) audiences for terrorists and terrorist groups, a topic that includes the role of the media.

In turning to this line of analysis, it is necessary to stress from the
outset that, important as these factors are, information about them

is among the least reliable. In the process of accumulating applicable knowledge, the following problems present themselves:

- Within the context of collective actions in general, terrorist episodes are very rare events, and it is almost impossible to know the nature of the larger population of events (extreme group behavior in general? social protest in general?) of which they are a subclass.
- Terrorist episodes are often carried out by clandestine groups and through networks, which adds to the problem of identifying representative numbers.
- Terrorist activity by its nature shares the quality of secrecy with other behavior such as crime and corruption. Those who engage in it are instructed and motivated not to reveal information about almost all aspects of their behavior (with the exception, perhaps, of after-the-fact taking of credit for episodes, with the aim of influencing audiences). Those who infiltrate terrorist groups (spies and intelligence operatives) do gather firsthand information, but this also is kept secret, and in any event it is highly selective with respect to the interests of their agencies.
- When terrorists are apprehended, imprisoned, and questioned, the information gathered suffers from the motivation of prisoners to misrepresent, out of ideological considerations, memory distortions, and the desire to avoid self-incrimination (Sageman, 2004, p. 68). Often, too, interrogators are interested in seeking legally relevant information for purposes of criminal trial, which may or may not be enlightening in explaining terrorist behavior.
- In press conferences and other public statements, publications, and biographical reflections, in which terrorists give accounts of their motives and aims, they have reason to distort information about their motives in the interests of ideological consistency, self-justification, and intended effects on audiences.

The quality of information on the motivational aspects of terrorism, then, is the product of inferences drawn from fragmentary and often unreliable direct data about terrorism. Correspondingly, it is often necessary to rely on our knowledge of kindred types of phenomena such as extreme social movements in general, mind control processes

("brainwashing"), religious conversion, pilgrimages, and initiation rituals. When we do turn to these other phenomena, we encounter methodological difficulties in generalizing from processes that resemble terrorism in only limited ways.

Individual Personality Variables and the
Inclination to Terrorism

Terrorist behavior is extreme behavior, often involving killing innocents, destroying property, and creating social mayhem. One
immediate and irresistible line of inquiry is to ask why people would
be motivated to do these things. One answer that appears from time to
time is that there is a distinctive personality type corresponding to the
designated kind of behavior. The explanatory effort is not a new one.
The early criminological literature produced different accounts of the
"criminal personality"; Lasswell (1960) described a "political personality" as one with an obsession of power derived from feelings of personal
inadequacy, and Wolfenstein (1967) attempted to depict a "revolutionary personality" driven by hostility toward authorities and derived from
Oedipal relations with fathers. Beginning in the 1960s, the literature on
terrorism has also revealed a search for the typical terrorist personality
(McCauley, 2004) and for clinical types such as narcissistic, paranoid,
psychopathic, and schizoid.

Some psychoanalytically informed accounts of terrorists are very
specific. In a composite account, Akhtar (2002) painted the following
picture of the "terrorism-prone individual":

> [M]ost major players in a terrorist organization are themselves
> deeply traumatized individuals. . . . As children they suffer chronic
> abuse and profound emotional humiliation. . . . They grow up mis-
> trusting others, loathing passivity, and dreading the recurrence of a
> violation of their psychological boundaries. . . . To eliminate this fear,
> such individuals feel the need to "kill off" their view of themselves as
> victims. One way to accomplish this is to turn passivity into activity,
> masochism into sadism, and victimization into victimizing others.

Hatred and violent tendencies toward others thus develop. The resultant "malignant narcissism" renders mute the voice of reason and morality. Sociopathic behaviour and outright cruelty are thus justified. The narrowed characteristic of paranoid mentality ... along with a thin patina of political rationalization, gives a gloss of logic to the entire psychic organization. (p. 90)

In a similar exercise, Pearlstein (1991) attempted to locate the core of the terrorist personality in the dual traits of "narcissistic injury" and "narcissistic disappointment," through which the individual's ego is unable to measure up to its ideals and is punished by the superego. The resulting "narcissistic rage" paves the way to violence. Pearlstein examined the available biographical materials of ten known terrorists and concluded that in all cases except one (Ilych Ramirez Sanchez, known as Carlos the Jackal), "narcissistic injury or narcissistic disappointment plays a critical psychobiographical role" (ibid., p. 7). He did qualify his conclusions by acknowledging that narcissistic personality disturbances are not necessary psychological requisites for becoming a political terrorist (ibid., p. 39).

Other versions of this line of reasoning could be presented, but these two accounts reveal its theoretical and methodological vulnerabilities. The psychological complexes appear to be neither necessary conditions (because other motives may lead ultimately to terrorist behavior) nor sufficient conditions (not all narcissistically wounded individuals become terrorists) for that behavior. Furthermore, it is an error to assume that terrorist behavior is an undifferentiated expression of personality variables; multiple motives are activated at different stages of the process (inclination, recruitment, socialization, and ongoing group membership). Finally, the empirical bases on which such accounts are based are limited or unavailable, and this makes the accounts largely speculative.

It is not surprising, therefore, that the search for a terrorist personality as a distinct type has been more or less abandoned. Basing their claims on interviews with terrorists and inferences from their behavior, various investigators have denounced the idea. Long asserted that "a generic terrorist personality does not exist" (1990, p. 18). Taylor challenged all assumptions that terrorists are ill or fanatic (1988, p. 73). Post concluded that "comparative studies of terrorist psychology do not indicate a unique terrorist mind" (1987, p. 92), adding that the level of skill and adaptive needs required are incompatible with psychotic or deranged states. Hoffman argued that "most terrorism is neither crazed nor capricious . . . indiscriminate or senseless" (2002, p. 63). Whittaker went to an opposite extreme and characterized terrorists as "rational in their beliefs and in their behavior"; they calculate risks, choose options, and think about when and where to strike (2002, p. 73). In his study of 172 international Muslim terrorists, Sageman (2004) found no systematic support—though his data were, as usual, woefully incomplete—for any of the favored psychological variables of narcissism, paranoia, and authoritarianism.

The literature on terrorist motivation thus breaks down along the lines of stressing either the rational or the irrational—a tension that has characterized most of the history of the study of social movements. On the one side, terrorists are regarded as impelled toward violence by psychological forces that are at some level beyond calculation, and the reasons they give for their actions (including explaining them as "calculated") are treated as justifications of the acts they are compelled to commit. On the other side, terrorists are seen as basically strategic if not entirely rational, and for that reason their behavior cannot be assigned to irrational or nonrational personality types or drives. These positions were articulated in a dialogue between Crenshaw (1990) and Post (1990), and the tension continues to cast a shadow on the literature. In my assessment, the opposition is an unfortunate and nonproductive one. There is every reason to believe both that deeper psychological forces must be involved in the commission of deliberate violence and that, given the political and psychological goals of terrorism, calculation of opportunities, costs, and benefits must also be a part of the picture. The analytical challenge is to develop a psychology that provides berth for both.

Despite the largely justified rejection of single personality types and typical psychopathologies, the search for psychological variables has not disappeared altogether. After declaring the nonexistence of a terrorist personality, Long did single out "low self-esteem" and a "predilection for risk-taking" (1990, p. 18). Borowitz (2005) built a case for a sense of self-glorification in an unjust world as the core of terrorist motivation. Post suggested that the glamour of publicity and its implied exhibitionism are important ingredients (1990, p. 36), and Sprinzak identified a type of megalomaniac hyperterrorist (2001). Crenshaw turned to an entirely different facet of terrorism, group solidarity and discipline, which imply "a range of motives associated with conformity and dependency on the group" (1988, p. 37).

Careful empirical work on left-wing German terrorists of the 1970s and 1980s (summarized in Merkl, 1991) revealed high proportions of young men and women from broken homes, a high incidence of past major clashes with parents, schools, or employers, and records of criminal or juvenile offenses—all relating to the thread of rebelliousness against authority suggested in some psychoanalytical accounts. It should be remembered, however, that those terrorists were recruited from primarily middle-class backgrounds and in a historical setting in which the citizenry was very preoccupied with Germany's authoritarian past (Wasmund, 1986). Neo-fascist groups in Germany in the same general period were recruited more from the lower class and *lumpen* origins (Merkl, 1986). Right-wing Italian terrorists, like those from the left, however, were primarily middle class and well educated (Weinberg and Eubank, 1988). In still other historical instances, notably when terrorists are children of radical parents ("red-diaper babies"), and in other historical settings in which kinship solidarity plays a role in recruitment (for example, in Italian terrorism and the Basque and Palestinian liberation movements), anti-authoritarianism may play a role, but in these cases it is likely to be fused with obedience and guilt toward parents and siblings as well (Post, 1984).

From the foregoing, it appears that the literature on individual motivation is in a tangle and begs for sensible resolution. The following lines of thinking come to mind. First, it is imperative not to drop the issue of individual motivation altogether, for it appears that disturbed individuals with chaotic personal pasts are susceptible to the meaning, comfort, and rewards that extremist groups have to offer. Second, terrorism should not be regarded as having a single motive. Religious martyrdom and suicidal enterprises excite different (if overlapping) motives from defensive, right-wing hate groups. Different motives are at work in first generations of terrorists, where groups band together out of a common sense of deprivation and grievance, than in the later generations, where motives come to be shaped around responding to counterterrorism, revenge, and keeping the organization viable (Crenshaw, 1983). Third, and most significant, terrorism should be regarded as a significant synthesis of cognition, meaning, and affect. Post's characterization of motivation as a process of "consolidating psychosocial identities at a time of great societal instability and flux" (1990, p. 31) seems closest to the mark. Motivation for extremist, including terrorist, protest is a meld of (1) social circumstances that are experienced as adverse, (2) personal and sometimes chaotic life histories, and (3) an ideology that provides a coherent cognitive and emotional framework for achieving that meld.

Social Origins and Recruitment

So diverse are the manifestations of what we classify under the heading of terrorist activities that no single, universal principle of recruitment appears to be universal. Certainly no specific psychological drive or personality offers much explanation. Nevertheless, some general themes in the social process of recruitment have emerged, both in the terrorist literature and in analyses of other phenomena that may be comparable to terrorist recruitment.

Let us begin with the instructive description given by the National Commission on Terrorist Attacks on the origins of the team of terrorists that engineered the September 11, 2001, attack on the World Trade Center and the Pentagon. They came from different social backgrounds, a circumstance almost dictated by the fact that at least a few of them had to speak enough English to communicate with passengers and crew. As for the "muscle" hijackers—those who were to keep the passengers at bay—twelve of the thirteen came from Saudi Arabia. Most of these were young (twenty to twenty-eight years old), unmarried, unemployed, and with no more than a high school education, though some had university experience. Clusters of them came from specific communities. They did not come in from the streets; Al-Qaeda recruiters, clerics, and in some cases family members were "levers" for recruitment, and contacts were made through local universities and mosques. There was also some attrition of recruits along the way. A few were judged to be unsuitable, others dropped out, and still others confronted obstacles in securing travel documents (National Commission, 2004, pp. 334–41).

The general themes in this account are the use of networks and personal ties, including kinship ties, to locate and influence potential candidates for recruitment, a hint of some tenuousness in the integration of candidates in solid occupational and family roles, and a suggestion that some of them were in a state of drift in their own societies. It should be added—though the commissioners did not make this point—that Saudi Arabia is a country in which the culture of fundamentalist Islam is especially strong, both because of the presence of the holiest of mosques in Saudi territory and because of the extensive spread of the fundamentalist ideas of Wahhabism in that country. This last factor falls into the category of a "readying" influence that does not guarantee recruits to extremist groups but makes a higher likelihood that they will be found in that region.

Sageman (2004), relying on a sample of 172 international Muslim terrorists—a sample larger than but not unlike the 9/11 group—attempted to gather information from the public domain about their backgrounds and characteristics. Leaders originated mainly from Egypt and had bonded together in the Afghan operation against the Soviet Union in the 1980s, then had become full-time terrorists. Most of his sample came from upper- and middle-class backgrounds, with occupational and educational levels appropriate to these classes. These findings on occupation and education match an earlier study (1983) of 350 known terrorists (reported in Twenlow and Sacco, 2002). Several findings relating to the recruitment processes, however, are relevant to the general understanding of joining extremist movements. First, more than two-thirds of those recruited into a jihad were residing in a county other than where they had grown up. Second, though all were highly qualified for employment, few were employed at the time of recruitment. Both these facts suggest a lack of attachment, perhaps alienation. Third, most joined the jihad by stages of growing progressively closer (though many dropped out along the way), and those who joined appeared to have become more devout religiously in the period preceding their recruitment to the jihad.

One of Sageman's most striking findings concerned the role of social affiliation in the recruitment of terrorists. Of the 150 international Islam terrorists on which he had admittedly incomplete information, friendship and kinship (mainly the former) played a role in three-quarters of the cases. Most joined the jihad as clusters of friends. The urging of immediate family members and in-laws also played a role (2004, pp. 111–13). Discipleship in schools was less important, and its effect was noticed mainly among Southeast Asian recruits. The role of mosques was complicated. Mainly they appeared to be places where interested young men were drawn and met one another and where friendship groups formed. The mosques and their leaders, however, helped provide the religiously based ideological frame for the groups, thus assuming a supplementary rather than simply indoctrinating role. By virtue of this pattern, religious ideology and group affiliation served to supplement and reinforce one another and work toward the kind of commitment that would propel young men into lives of righteous battle, exposure to danger, and sometimes suicide.

Sageman cited evidence of the importance of social affiliation in the recruitment into (nonterrorist) religious cults, left-wing German and Italian terrorist groups in the 1970s, and radical Egyptian Islamic groups (ibid., pp. 125–35). Other research has underscored the centrality of kinship ties in recruitment to the Basque independence movement and to Al-Qaeda itself (Post, 2002). Kinship relations have also been shown to pervade the Palestine Liberation Organization (Schiller, 2001).

As recruits to the Islamic terrorist groups move into active involvement, definite measures to ensure loyalty and conformity come into play. This also involves group dynamics, described by McCauley (2004) as the "psychology of comrades." Deliberate strategies insulate the recruits from outside influences (Crenshaw, 1988). Demands may be made for abstinence and frugality, meditation and prayer, loyalty and devotion (Azzam, cited in Gunaratna, 2002, p. 4). Promises of salvation through martyrdom are held out, and worldly rewards for the surviving families of martyrs are offered. In extremist groups such as Hamas, a full cult of martyrdom has developed, with elaborate ideological encouragements (heroism, rewards in heaven), a proliferation of posters, graffiti, videos, and folk legends extolling specific martyrs, and public torture and even killing of accused collaborators (Oliver and Steinberg, 2005). For the recruits into the 9/11 attack group, Osama bin Laden required a personal oath of loyalty for a suicide operation, and the training period itself involved further indoctrination and devotional exercises (National Commission, 2004, p. 340). Such mechanisms of social control have long been familiar to scholars of secret societies (see Fong, 1981) and extremist groups in general.

Examination of the social and psychological elements involved in recruitment suggest that joining terrorist groups—especially but not exclusively religiously inspired ones—resembles a number of other phenomena. These are religious and cult conversion, initiation ceremonies, the social isolation experiments, psychotherapy, coercive persuasion or thought reform ("brainwashing"), and religious pilgrimage. The suggested comparisons are selective and tentative, given the status of knowledge about all of them. Great care should be taken in claiming literal or wholesale parallels, for none of these is identical to another, and the recruitment process of none of them parallels precisely recruitment into terrorist groups. At the same time, common social and psychological elements make their appearance and suggest that recruitment into terrorist groups may be a subtype of a more general process.

The similar processes I have in mind range all the way from those that are in no sense voluntary (brainwashing prisoners of war) to those that are largely voluntary (joining a college fraternity). In practice, most of these processes involve a mix of both. For example, in fraternity initiations, joining is clearly a voluntary act, but the initiation ceremonies themselves involve many coercive ingredients (Leemon, 1972). A similar mix can be observed in the process of bringing an individual into a religious cult. The above account of the transition into terrorist organizations also reveals a mix of voluntary and coercive elements, suggesting that the imagery of passivity and coercion sometimes invoked to explain brainwashing is not applicable (Sageman, 2004, pp. 124–25), as is the idea that terrorists are mainly self-propelled by psychological forces.

An influential revision of the nature of religious conversion was developed in the 1960s by Lofland and Stark (Lofland, 1981; Lofland and

Stark, 1965). Their interpretations were generally confirmed in a number of subsequent studies (Downton, 1979; Galanter, 1999; Stark and Bainbridge, 1980; Whitehead, 1987). The essentials of the process are the following: first, a social and psychological history of recruits marked by personal dissatisfaction with oneself and one's life, often accompanied by psychic pain (not reducible to specific psychopathologies, however), and a sequence of unsuccessful experimental identity-seeking efforts, followed by a gradual, step-by-step evolution of a view of oneself as a religious seeker; second, the importance of friendships, social networks, and personal influence in the recruitment process; third, the incorporation of recruits into an extremely close, cohesive, and supporting group as the conversion process proceeds, with new rounds of group-centered activities; fourth, a process of redefining oneself as a new or reborn person, often involving a renunciation of the past; and fifth, taking on the new faith as a more or less totalistic way of life. The entire process is characterized by a fusion of group relations and ideological commitment, which are complementary and mutually reinforcing. The process is consistent with the imperfect knowledge we have about recruitment into terrorist organizations.

The general psychological transformation involved in this process is a certain destructuring of the individual's former conception of self (also sometimes called renunciation or "stripping") (Clark et al., 1981), a transition period, and then a restructuring process, with a new sense of self-commitment. The transformational process is a general one. In their characterization of the coercive persuasion (brainwashing) process, Schein and colleagues (1961) described it as one of unfreezing, changing, and refreezing of a person's outlook (pp. 119–20). Using different words, Lifton (1969) identified the themes of renunciation and guilt, reeducation and confession/rebirth, all in the context of a mix of threats and leniency (pp. 67–82). Parallel processes have been identified in the typical process of religious ritual and pilgrimage (Turner, 1979), group psychotherapy (Foulkes, 1964), and psychoanalytical psychotherapy (Whitehead, 1987). To reiterate: none of these processes is identical to recruitment into terrorist organizations, and comparisons have to be carefully and selectively drawn. Furthermore, individual and situational differences give variability to all of them. However, all appear to involve social-psychological sequences that are more or less consistent with what we know about joining a terrorist organization. Viewed in this light, the process of terrorist recruitment is not something entirely new under the sun but is a subspecies of radical personal and ideological reorientations achieved under special kinds of group influence and solidarity.

A special word must be said about suicide terrorism, which has been part of the Hezbollah resistance to the Israeli invasion of Lebanon, the stock-in-trade of subsequent episodes of Palestinian terrorism, a weapon of the Liberation Tigers in Sri Lanka, part of Al-Qaeda's terrorist operations, and an ingredient in the anti-American insurgency in Iraq. History has produced similar manifestations, including the organized kamikaze operations by Japan in World War II, self-immolation as a mode of protest, and many episodes in the history of martyrdom (for an exhaustive contemporary survey, see Shai, 2004). Suicide is widely regarded as the ultra non plus of the terrorist enterprise because it extends the principles of loyalty and commitment to some kind of logical end point: the willingness to end one's life. Especially in the West we are likely to experience shock and disbelief as we think about this practice, committed as we are to the values of individualism and the sanctity of life. Given such a commitment, we are inclined to regard all kinds of suicide as products of the profoundly suffering or deranged life.

We should not deny the role of past individual hardship as one factor in recruitment of suicide terrorists. Many males who join come from that mass of unemployed or underemployed individuals with apparently hopeless futures, and at least some female terrorists in Palestine had been shamed and dishonored in Muslim society on account of infertility, divorce, and other sources of degradation (for examples, see Victor, 2003). Examining terrorism in comparative context, however, should lead us to qualify this exceptionalist view of suicidal terrorism. We should recognize, first, that terrorist activity in general—to say nothing of joining an army of a nation at war—heightens the probability of one's death ("to die for one's country") and differs from actual suicide only in degree. Second, suicide has a number of tactical advantages over other violent methods, including greater difficulty of detection, low cost, and no fear of subsequent interrogation of those captured (Sprinzak, 2000, pp. 67–68). Most important, however, examination of the recruitment and actions of suicide terrorists in-structs us that is not a special thing in itself but the end point of a continuum of the recruitment and commitment-inducing process, with the salient role of groups and primary ties in the process (Silke, 2003). This is consistent with the theory of suicide as learned behavior, which results in different rates and patterns in different cultures (Lester, 1987). If we bring to mind the Palestinian cases described by Oliver and Steinberg (2005), suicidal behavior associated with terrorism can also be described legitimately as conformist if not enforced behavior.

The Decline of Terrorist Groups

For a variety of historically specific reasons, we think less about the decline and failure of terrorist movements than about their toughness and durability:

- Terrorists themselves supply us with one reason. In many of their ideologies we find statements of how patient they must be and how their victories over their enemies will be realized only over time. In addition, the most spectacular of attacks have scarcely been impulsive but have taken years of planning and mobilization for execution.
- We tend to skew our thinking toward their successes, such as the kidnappings at the U.S. embassy in Teheran, the defeat of Russian forces in Afghanistan, and unprevented attacks on American targets. We remember the successes rather than the failures because they are more threatening.
- More generally, most of our current thinking has focused on Al-Qaeda, one of the best-financed, well-organized, and most reso-lute terrorist organizations in history, with continued vitality de-spite its partial obliteration in the Afghan War.
- Finally, and perhaps most telling, our own counterterrorist ideo-logical inclinations lead us not only to regard contemporary inter-national terrorists as morally evil but also to exaggerate the strength of their motives, power, cunning, resolve, and intelli-

gence. This exaggeration is a generic feature of ideological polarizations that accompany deadly conflict between parties who regard one another as mortal enemies.

In fact, the accumulated historical record of terrorist activities gives the lie to these perceptions. Most terrorist groups not connected with social movements have tended to be "small, short-lived and responsible for only a handful of incidents" (Hewitt, 2003, p. 61). Many movements that have turned to terror have, after a season, been discouraged or repressed out of existence or have lost their steam; the most notable of these are the majority of Caribbean (Cuban and Puerto Rican) protest movements of the 1950s and 1970s and the radical left movements in the United States and Europe in the same period. Right-wing movements, with the notable exception of the Ku Klux Klan, have also come and gone. Most of the state-sponsored terrorist groups of the 1980s weakened as the states in question withdrew support from them in the face of international pressure and sanctions. Some groups have quit terrorism to become political parties, for example, the Irgun in Israel, which was transformed into a political party after Israeli independence, and the Muslim Brotherhood in Egypt, which was severely repressed and reemerged as a small quasi-party (Weinberg and Pedahzur, 2003). Those movements that have enjoyed a longer existence, such as the Basque nationalist movement, the Irish Republican Army, Hezbollah, Hamas, and Al-Qaeda, have done so for a combination of historically specific reasons, including robust financing (IRA, Al-Qaeda), engagement in an especially bitter ethnic-religious conflict (ETA, IRA, Hamas), or involvement in multiple activities, of which terrorism is only one (Hezbollah).

Why do terrorist organizations fail or decline? In raising this question in a chapter on motivation, I should acknowledge immediately that the answer is only in part a matter of terrorist motivation. External circumstances also play a role. Consider, for example, the influential statement of reasons for decline put forward by Ross and Gurr (1989) on the basis of their study of North American terrorism. They listed four:

- Preemption, or making it impossible for terrorists to carry out their activities, by hardening targets or imprisoning or killing leaders.
- Deterrence, or increasing the risks for terrorists or those who might join or support them, by enacting antiterrorist laws and increasing the severity of punishment.
- Burnout, or the decline of commitment to the group and its purposes, occasioned, for example by factionalization, rank-and-file resistance to leaders, and defections.
- Backlash, or declining political support among "previously neutral and disinterested groups" as well as "many of the people on behalf of whom they claim to act" (ibid., p. 409).

The first two are mainly external to the terrorist group (that is, the result of counterterrorist actions on the part of authorities), and the last two are more nearly motivational in character. In fact, however, both preemption and deterrence, if effective, alter the motivations of terrorists; burnout is primarily motivational, though it is also related to how terrorist groups fare in their environment; and backlash refers both to the motivation of terrorist groups and to the disposition of constituencies external to them. In fact, the path toward decline is invariably an interaction between motivation and external circumstances.

On the basis of a comparative study of seventy-seven terrorist organizations, Crenshaw produced a different but overlapping list of interacting causes of decline: "the government response to terrorism (which is not limited to preemption or deterrence), the strategic choices of the terrorist organization, and its organizational resources" (1991, p. 80). The principle of interaction between circumstance and motivation applies to her classification as well.

Another word should be added about the internal dynamics of terrorist groups. Earlier I developed the principle that terrorist activities almost always emanate from extremist social movements with extremist ideologies (see chapter 3). A corollary of this principle is that terrorist organizations must be especially concerned with maintaining the ideological commitment of their members, which means internal surveillance of their loyalty and efforts to contain backsliding (Della Porta,

1992). In addition, extremist movements are especially prone to internal factional disputes over first principles, strategies, and tactics (Schiller, 2001). Another ingredient of these movements is that in periods of organizational inactivity, boredom and ennui are likely by-products, because extremist ideologies invariably include a sense of urgency and the need for action. Lack of action increases the likelihood of second thoughts, backsliding, and internal disputes. Group commitment to an extreme ideology thus constitutes both a strength and a weakness for terrorist organizations. The same double-edged quality applies to the need to maintain extreme secrecy. On the one hand, secrecy is a necessary ingredient of success. At the same time it consumes a great deal of the energy of an organization, and discourages some otherwise efficient modes of communication, such as relying on written instructions and using telephones that may be under surveillance.

We do not possess very sound knowledge about the causes of decline and failure of terrorist movements. Even the scientifically perfect list would have to be accompanied by the disclaimer that there is no single formula for decline, and that different combinations of causes apply to each historical case of decline. The decline of American black militant groups in the 1960s, for example, seemed mainly the result of effective and aggressive actions on the part of police authorities. The decline of the radical Italian left resulted from a combination of more effective policing, a policy of amnesty for cooperating terrorists, and public disaffection with terrorist violence. The dynamics of decline may be different for secular and religious movements. And finally, the coordinated action of political authorities is more difficult to attain in dealing with international than with domestic terrorist movements. Despite the limitations of our knowledge, an understanding of the dynamics of decline should be an essential component of informed counterterrorist policies.

Audiences and the Media

In the 1870s, Italian anarchists coined the term "propaganda by deed" to refer to terrorist activities (Fleming, 1982). Terrorism in general has been described to as "a propaganda tool" (Adams, 1986,

p. 7). As a matter of consensus in the literature, terrorist incidents are referred to as "symbolic." That is to say, the main point of terrorist attacks (targets of violence) on innocent civilians (or even military installations) or property is not the attacks themselves. They are meant to coerce enemy governments (targets of demands) to act politically, or to create instability and mayhem. Access to the targets of demands is thought to be gained by affecting the public (targets of attention and targets of terror), who will bring the pressure of public opinion to bear on governments (see Schmid, 1998, p. 48).

These formulations are generally if not universally applicable. Furthermore, they entail a corollary: a necessary component of terrorism is that it relies on audiences. Its intended effects simply cannot be realized if it cannot reach those audiences. A further corollary is that, because they are typically small, local, and secret, terrorist groups do not have direct access to audiences and therefore must rely on institutions and organizations that mediate between them and their activities and the intended audiences. These are the media (appropriately named in this context, because they lie between and communicate, back and forth, between terrorists and their audiences). Another twist on these relationships is that the media themselves, having their own independent interests, must be counted as both audience to be influenced and communicator of influence to other audiences. Finally, as the media have progressed over time from town crier through print and radio to mass television, they have become an ever more potent component of terrorist activities and are now capable of transmitting radio and television accounts and images of terrorist events deemed newsworthy around the world more or less instantaneously.

Audiences and Motives

The foregoing statements about audience and media are beyond controversy. What do they have to do with the motivation of terrorist activities? Stated simply, terrorists must rely on publicity as an essential component of any success they might hope for, and this reliance becomes an interest and thus a motive on their part. They cannot ignore either audiences or the media if they are to communicate their message and affect the attitudes, emotions, and behavior of those they intend to influence. They must influence audiences through the media, and they must consider the best ways to do so as one of the ingredients in their planning and execution of activities.

This position is at odds with some accounts. The author of one of the best general treatments of terrorism (Levitt, 1988) makes an effort to distinguish religious terrorism from other types of protest in several respects. First, compromise is ruled out in religious terrorism because it would mean "acquiescence in the dominance of the ungodly, and . . . thus tantamount to defeat." Second, the religious terrorist is indifferent to audiences; "[l]oss of popular support is of little concern to the religious terrorist, since the act is done for God, or God's clerical proxy, not public opinion" (p. 185).

We may give qualified support to the first observation but reject the second. Absolute ideologies—of which religious ideologies are usually instances—tend to identify goals as principles, not interests, thus making compromise appear as a sacrifice of principle. Yet even strongly religious terrorist movements, such as Hamas in Palestine, have flirted with compromise with respect to the political status of the Palestinian territory or state, and Palestinian groups have shown a history of disagreement over violent terrorism versus peaceful negotiation and have continuously jockeyed with one another in the internal struggles for power within the umbrella organization of the Palestine Liberation Organization. With respect to audiences, it is an axiom that all social movements, including religious and terrorist ones, are aware of and to some degree responsive to support (or loss of it) from one or more audiences.

There is a second, more personal motivational aspect to terrorists' relationship with the media connected with audiences and media. This concerns the psychological effects of publicity and its excitation of tendencies to grandiosity and narcissism. (This formulation is very different from saying that, as a matter of individual psychology, terrorists are driven by megalomania or narcissism.) Post (1990) made the relevant observation about a youthful recruit to a terrorist organization:

Before joining the group, he was alone not particularly successful. Now he is engaged in a life and death struggle with the establishment, his picture on the "most wanted" posters. He sees his leaders as inter-

nationally prominent media personalities. Within certain circles he
is lionized as a hero. (p. 36; see also Sprinzak, 2001)

The public idealization of martyrdom in the name of a cause, a prominent feature of radical Palestinian terrorist groups in Palestine (Oliver
and Steinberg, 2005), complements this effect of media seduction. To
make the point more generally, the glitter of media success constitutes
one of the ingredients of all contemporary social movements, and an
undue preoccupation with media glamour and media effects may constitute a major component of (and sometimes a diversion for) a movement (Gitlin, 1980).

Multiplicity of Audiences

Like all social movements and political groups, terrorists and
terrorist organizations must address a diversity of audiences in their
environments, and this complicates their lives politically. While the
number and kinds of relevant audiences differ by historical setting, the
following composite can be suggested (see Smelser and Mitchell, 2002b;
Irwin, 1989):

- Already active terrorists. Care must be taken to ensure the loyalty
  and conformity of those already on board. Points of vulnerability
  in their commitment were reviewed in the previous section.
- Potential recruits. The usual message to be communicated is that
  the terrorist organization remains viable and effective, remains
  committed to a legitimate cause, is viable and effective, and is
  deserving of self-sacrifice.
- Actual and potential supporters in the relevant host societies.
  These are the larger "sentiment pools" in the societies out of
  which terrorists operate, as well as their national governments.
  This concern applies both to domestic terrorism, in which terrorists occupy a certain (usually radical) place in the larger polity,
  and international terrorism, which, while often "stateless," must
  take into account the disposition of the societies in which they
  base their operations.
- National governments of target societies. These are the "enemy"
  societies, and the message is to maximize the sense of danger, un-

certainty, and confusion in their ranks, with an eye to effecting some political response or change.

- National majorities of the target societies, which are typically fearful of and hostile to terrorist attacks but whose beliefs and sympathies can be influenced at least marginally by their perceptions of the terrorists and by political responses on the part of their home governments that are perceived as misguided.
- National minorities of the target societies. Sometimes such groups do not exist, but when they do, they are typically immigrant minorities from the societies from which the terrorist activity appears to be emanating. Examples are the Irish-American population courted by the IRA and the Muslim and Arab minorities in the contemporary United States.
- Actual and potential allies and opponents of the target society. This evidence is particularly salient in international terrorism, in which one of the aims is to isolate the target society by alienating others. The most conspicuous example is the attack on trains in Madrid in 2004 on the eve of the Spanish election as "punishment" of the government for its support of the United States in the Iraq War and to place pressure on the electorate. The same logic of punishment figured in the July 2005 attack on the London underground, which also coincided with the meetings of the G-8, a symbol of wealthy, "imperialist" countries.
- World opinion. This is perhaps the most elusive and most nearly imagined audience of all, but it is nonetheless a very important arena in the minds of terrorists in establishing their legitimacy. It is addressed through the worldwide media and organizations such as the United Nations.

The critical feature of these audiences is that they are multiple, internally diverse, and different in their outlooks and interests. The political problem created for terrorists and counterterrorists alike is a juggling act: how to tailor their messages in order to maximize their support and minimize opposition in as many audiences as possible. (Exceptions to this rule are enemy governments, whom terrorists hope to frighten, shock, enrage, and spur to political overreactions, which in turn are believed to alienate many other audiences and thus generate support for terrorists among them.) The audience dynamics involved in terrorism are not significantly different from those of political contestation in general.

Insofar as terrorism is simultaneously a struggle over images and symbols and a struggle for audience support, all these audiences for terrorists perforce become audiences for target societies as well, and a component of counterterrorism activities. In fact, the various audiences constitute the relevant background for the real wars and symbolic verbal contests between terrorists and counterterrorists. There is reason to argue, moreover, that the role of audiences has become progressively more salient as the history of terrorism has evolved in the past half-century. Domestic terrorism, emanating from local grievances and directed at national governments, is oriented mainly toward domestic political audiences, though other groups and nations may register reactions of sympathy, apprehension, or outrage in different mixes. International terrorism as it has developed since the 1960s is aimed at influencing the fortunes, policies, and sympathies on an international scale (much of the history of Palestinian-based international terrorism, for example, has been oriented to calling attention to and legitimizing the plight of the Palestinians to international audiences). The escalation of the ideological dimension of international terrorism since September 11, 2001, has meant an even greater salience of international audiences, as radical terrorist organizations have striven to divide opinion in the United States and to court favor with or punish third parties who respectively oppose or cooperate with American policies toward terrorism and American international interventions. The United States, on its part, has aggressively defended democracy and mounted a heavy ideological assault on the evils of terrorist extremism. Moreover, insofar as the rhetoric of terrorism has evolved toward a polarized ideological opposition between radial Muslim and radical American counterterrorism, the entire world has become a stage for courting public opinion through propaganda and actions. In this instance the resultant "clash of civilizations" is not so much a product of an autonomous, "almost global resurgence of religion," as Huntington (2004, p. 356) argued, as it is the precipitate of strategic appeals to world audiences by parties who regard themselves as locked in a world political struggle with one another.

The Literature on Media and Terrorism

In combing over the literature on terrorism, I have found the treatment of the media to be among the least satisfactory from the standpoint of scientific soundness. Paletz and Boiney (1992) laid out the accusation in unqualified terms:

> [T]he bulk of the literature on the relationship between the media and terrorism is dismaying. Some of it is blatantly propagandistic, consisting of shrill jeremiads, exhortations, tendentious examples, and undocumented assertions. Unexamined assumptions abound, terms go undefined, and arguments are untested. Works suggesting solutions to perceived problems place overwhelming responsibility on the media. (p. 23)

The indictment is extreme but not unjustified fifteen years after it was written. It suggests that the literature has incorporated the largely normative and partisan tone of the larger political concerns about the media, and has not been immune from the dynamics of scapegoating and defending against it.

It is a small step from acknowledging the role of the mass media as a link between terrorists' actions and their intent to induce terror to asserting that the media are acting in complicity with terrorists and are blameworthy for this. The Right Honorable Lord Chalfont (1990) cited the "depressing fact" that "newspapers, radio, and television have probably done more than the terrorist organizations themselves to make organized political violence glamorous and successful" (p. 18). Davies (2003) claimed that modern communications "have done more than anything else to promote terrorism as an effective way of waging war" (p. 25). Wardlaw (1989) specified this by arguing that media are an avenue for expressing and overdramatizing terrorists' views, and that media permit contagion of destructive methods, hinder police operations, increase terrorists' sense of power, and provide technical information to terrorists. In these ways, the media become participants in terrorism itself.

The next extension is to advocate some kind of regulation or control of the media. Lord Chalfont argued that such control is regarded as normal and acceptable in wartime (1990, p. 19). The historical record has revealed efforts to muzzle the press by the Spanish government in its struggle against the Basque movement, the Anti-Constitutional Advocacy Act in West Germany in the terrorist era of the 1970s, and the Irish government's ban on state radio and TV from carrying interviews with IRA representatives and sympathizers (Wilkinson, 1990; see also Schaffert, 1992). By and large, however, democratic governments have been reluctant to impose censorship or otherwise restrict freedom of the press, and have relied more on appeals for self-regulation. After the hijacking of the Trans World Airlines Flight 847 in 1985, Prime Minister Margaret Thatcher, in an oft-quoted phrase, said that television should "find ways to starve terrorists . . . of the oxygen of publicity" (cited in Alexander and Latter, 1990). Earlier, Ronald Reagan had framed the issue dramatically in a complaint published in a journalism trade magazine in 1977:

> If the nation's television assignment editors and radio news directors would take a collective deep breath and declare a moratorium on live coverage of terrorist events during the commission of the crime, they would be cutting off the source of inspiration for an untold number of loose nuts who harbor crazy ideas. (quoted in Terrell and Ross, 1992, p. 87)

In the 1980s, in response to government pressure, a number of news agencies, including the United Press International, the Columbia Broadcasting System, and the *Chicago Sun Times*, adapted self-regulating guidelines, some of which were very specific (for example, not undermining police and first responders' efforts) and some of which were vague and difficult to apply to specific situations (for example, avoiding sensationalism). Furthermore, such guidelines, like many self-retraining codes of ethics for professionals, were short on mechanisms for interpreting, adjudicating, and enforcing the proposed guidelines.

Efforts to limit the media meet with opposition from both the media (which condemn censorship and defend their historical independence and their objectivity, as well as "the public's right to know") and from civil libertarian groups. Such conflicts tend to repeat themselves and run along familiar and well-warn paths. A recent example is a report in the *New York Times* (2005c) on May 2, 2005, citing the statements of the chairman of the Corporation for Public Broadcasting (CPB), a Republican, accusing government-supported public radio and television of a "liberal bias" and calling for "balance." This item excited a flurry of letters to the editor, almost all antagonistic to the CPB, and a minor Internet campaign proclaiming that PBS was under attack and citing the opposition of organizations such as Free Press, Consumers Union, and Common Cause.

This line of argument leads us to pinpoint another conundrum that the era of terrorism has accentuated:

Entrapment 3. Solutions regarding the media's role in the terrorist process, are apparently unavailable; this produces a recurrence of vigorous controversies in which preset partisan and ideological postures are activated and for which stable solutions are not forthcoming.

This snarl is closely related to the "civil liberties entrapment" to be discussed in chapter 5. Its essence is that existing institutional and cultural arrangements, which are highly valued in a democracy, become the focus of repeated controversies when confronted with the complex of terrorism, with all its ambiguities and generalized threats. These controversies do not lend themselves to solutions because to intrude on those arrangements appears to compromise sacred ingredients of the democratic process. By way of contributing modestly to understanding and perhaps moving beyond this entrapment, I offer a brief sociological account of the dynamics by which it has arisen and why it remains a running sore in the polity.

A Sociology of the Media: A Crucible for
Conflicting Interests and Imagined Audiences

The media, as institutionalized in democratic societies, have a function that is directly relevant to the democratic process itself: to provide citizens with news and interpretation of events, with the presumed effect of contributing to an informed citizenry. This function is a principal basis for the media's legitimacy as an institution. At the same time, they do not perform this role in a straightforward way. They are implicated in a complicated network of interested actors, including themselves, which places conflicting demands on how they perform that role. What follows is a generic analysis of this network of forces, phrased with special reference to the issue of terrorism.

The main actors on the stage in the media drama are:

- The media themselves.
- The reading, listening, and viewing publics.
- Business and commercial organizations that advertise in the media and sometimes own them.
- Political actors, notably the political party in power and the opposition party, as well as issue-oriented groups, both hostile to and protective of the media.
- Terrorists.

Each of these groups has its own values and interests. As an institution, the media are committed to presenting the news fairly and accurately, and under the constitutional provision of freedom of the press, they are free to do this without the formal intrusion of outside agencies, especially governmental ones. In practice, however, there are constraints on this activity. The media themselves do not wish to go unread, unheard, or unwatched. Consequently they are constrained by their perceptions of what they imagine their publics want to hear. The interest of these publics is sometimes informed empirically by audience surveys, but it is also informed by a certain amount of imagining and guessing. Moreover, different media appeal to different audiences. Some elite newspapers and public radio and television, for example, cater to what they imagine to be a serious, educated, intellectual audience, and they look down on and deliberately play down the sensational. Much of commercial radio and television (for example, the personal talk shows) and tabloid rags highlight sex, conflict, violence, intrigue, and anything else sensational. The rest of the media fall somewhere in between.

Beyond this concern with audiences, the media have other values and interests. They do not simply wait for the news to come to them. Given their priorities, they seek it out. Reporters and staff have beats—

police, federal, and so on—where news is made. Furthermore, the media are deeply motivated by the real and imagined value of the scoop—getting the news and reporting it first, thereby reaching their audiences sooner, increasing their readership or viewership, and accruing at least short-term status in the journalistic world. This interest applies less to most of their audience, who attend more to the news itself and less to where they learned of it first. In addition, the media have become increasingly committed to investigative reporting, which is always present to some degree but has been elevated to very high salience beginning in the 1970s with the dramatic uncovering of the Watergate scandal by the *Washington Post.* Investigative reporting means taking an initiative and targeting specific kinds of activities, often those that one party or another may not want publicized. When carried to extremes, the principles of scoop and investigative reporting push the media toward two kinds of irresponsibility: hastily reporting inaccurate or harmful news in the interest of getting it out fast, or emphasizing disproportionately the dirt they have uncovered. Partially offsetting this tendency, the media have an interest in protecting themselves against accusations of irresponsible journalism. In addition, a number of watchdog agencies and groups, including the Federal Communications Commission and associations of journalists themselves (for example, the Washington-based Committee of Concerned Journalists), act as counterpressures.

Most media depend heavily on commercial advertising to survive, and as a result, advertisers form one of their key audiences and sources of influence on them. The primary interest on the part of advertisers is to maximize sales of their products. Derivatively, they are interested in the level of readership, listenership, or viewership that their preferred medium enjoys, on the theory that the larger the audience, the more likely their advertisements are to be seen or heard. The corresponding pressures on the media are two. One is to put out the kind of news that draws large audiences—in a word, to sensationalize. The other, occasionally real but often imagined, is not to alienate commercial advertisers by publishing news, interpretations, and editorials that run counter to their political or ideological interests. The tension between conservative business interests and the liberal values of the journalistic profession is a constant one, and occasionally flares into open controversy.

A side comment on the idea of freedom of the press is in order. As specified in the Constitution and treated in the courts, it refers almost exclusively to freedom of the press from intervention on the part of government. It is political freedom, much as academic freedom is a safeguard against political interference with free expression. The issue is different with respect to the economic dimension, however. The media are beholden to advertisers for income. They are also beholden to their subscribing customers, both for income from subscriptions and because advertisers are interested in advertising to large audiences. By virtue of these relationships, the freedom of the press is compromised by the press's vulnerability to real and imagined economic pressures from these constituencies. Moreover, this economic pressure can spill over into the kinds of news the medium decides to highlight and the kinds of editorial opinions it espouses.

Formal political interest in the media is further complicated in a democratic society that lives by competitive party politics. Since the media are the main sources of citizens' knowledge, it may be assumed that the interest of the party in power is to maximize positive perceptions about itself by encouraging favorable news and commentary and minimizing exposure that will lead to embarrassment, adverse criticism, and scandal. It is similarly interested in the unfavorable exposure of political opponents. The opposition is motivated in precisely the opposite direction—to maximize the embarrassment of the party in power and to have itself portrayed in the most favorable light. Both parties are so motivated because they are forever making calculations and assembling support for public support for future electoral battles. Running against these contrary interests to control the news, however, is the principle of freedom of the press, which interdicts censorship and direct efforts on the part of government and political groups to dictate what the media will make public. The resulting set of conflicting forces leads to the following: (1) political groups who want to see, selectively, favorable and unfavorable news; (2) media that, as often as not, are looking for unfavorable news of all sorts; and (3) the formal inability of governments and parties to muzzle the press, even though politicians routinely criticize the press, accuse it of bias, and sometimes intervene directly in the reporting process (Dadge, 2004), thus introducing an informal political influence in the context of its formal prohibition.

An appreciation of these contradictory forces, moreover, yields a sociological account of political spin and why it is such a conspicuous feature of political life in a democratic society with a system of universally available media. Governments and parties cannot guarantee or control the news that the media print or air. They can, however, influence it by trying to make that news appear as favorable (or as unfavorable) as possible—twisting facts, assigning motives, reframing by referring to positive or negative frameworks or values, and so on. Spin is a way of making or remaking the news when news cannot be dictated.

This account of the forces influencing the media leads to an appreciation of their role in the relation to terrorism and terrorists. On the one hand, almost all who write about terrorism have perceived and acknowledged that terrorists want maximum publicity of their actions in the interest of influencing their various audiences. On the other hand, terrorism has all the ingredients of newsworthiness. It is frightening and violent, and for that reason alone it catches immediate attention. Furthermore, it is in the interest of media, in competition with one another, to "get inside terrorism"—to provide facts and explanations about it that will further excite audience interest (Nacos, 2003). More remotely, terrorism strikes at the heart of social order. If it is domestic terrorism it kills, destroys property, and constitutes a challenge to the government and keepers of the peace. If it is international terrorism, it does all these things and also threatens the nation's safety from without. Because terrorism produces publicly visible events with which federal, state, and local governments are obliged to deal responsibly, these governments immediately come under scrutiny as to how effectively they are dealing or have dealt with such events. Their behavior appears immediately in the processes of assigning blame and identifying scapegoats. Furthermore, while both the party in power and the opposition may share a fear of, antagonism to, and abhorrence of terrorist actions, they inevitably develop partisan interests in how effectively or how ineffectively the government is dealing with the threat. The result is a continuous process of monitoring how well the government (and how presumptively effective or ineffective the opposition) is doing in the "war on terrorism."

All these considerations guarantee that terrorism will be at the top of the news. In that sense, it can be concluded that the media are friends of and conspirators with the terrorists, simply because they afford terrorists the publicity they want. But that is not the end of the story. The question that ensues beyond their portrayal of terrorism is how they portray it. On this score, those who write about media and terrorism—and no doubt the public as well—are in continuous disagreement and disarray. In that sense the writers are also actors in the drama played out in the entrapment.

Is there a productive exit from the entrapment involving the (presumptively) adverse effects of publicizing terrorism and the principle of freedom of the press? It is difficult to envision one without the sacrifice of some fundamental democratic principle. Perhaps the most helpful path would be for a consortium of leaders in the worlds of journalism and law to adopt a systematic code of responsibility—in contrast to the ad hoc responses of the media to governmental pressures in the past—with respect to the reporting on terrorism (and perhaps on crime and violence in general). This effort would be carried out separately from interested governmental parties. The code should be as explicit and practical as possible. In addition, journalists—perhaps through their professional associations—should establish concrete administrative, quasi-judicial machinery for assessing specific cases of violation of the code and meting out sanctions of censure of media and reporters. Such an arrangement would preserve the freedom of the press from political intervention but would complement it with a systematic, formal, professionally generated code for responsible conduct for those guaranteed such freedom. Such a path is not a sure solution; one need only regard the self-regulating machinery of the medical, legal, and academic professions to appreciate its limitations. Nevertheless, such an effort would be a more productive tack than the continuous and insoluble struggles involving the government, the media, and interested political groups.

Conclusion: The Motivational Complex

for Terrorism

Like the accumulating social conditions that underlie the proclivity to terrorism as a form of conflict, the process of motivation and mobilization involved in generating terrorist groups and activity is a "value-added" process. Given the presence of general predisposing conditions, there must be a convergence of ideological articulation of dissatisfaction, dovetailing with the motivational dispositions of potential recruits, leadership, persuasion, recruitment, involvement of networks of personal ties, and continuous exercise of pressure and sanctions within groups committed to terrorist activities. These are the factors that combine to constitute the motivational complex. To recognize this combinatorial principle is an advantage because it avoids the pitfalls of arguing directly from remote causes (such as dispossession) to specific outcomes, and it spares us the simplified single- or few-cause explanations. As we will see in chapter 6, moreover, these motivating factors for terrorist activity are also points of vulnerability. Consequently, knowledge of the motivational complex constitutes an asset for discouraging terrorism.

PART III

CONSEQUENCES AND CONTROL

CHAPTER 5

Anticipating, Experiencing, and

Responding to Terrorist Attacks

AT THIS JUNCTURE we turn the analysis around. In the first four chapters we looked at terrorism from the standpoints of its conditions, causes, and ideology, as well as the several additional forces that motivate terrorist individuals and groups. Now we shift to the targets of terrorism—groups and societies under attack. We will consider, sequentially, what it means to be vulnerable to or fearful of attacks; what it is to be attacked, and what immediate responses are to be expected; and what are the medium- and longer-term consequences of terrorist attacks (and the threat of them) from the psychological, economic, political, social, and cultural points of view.

Such a multifaceted view is essential, because expecting, experiencing, and responding to terrorism pervades every facet of a society. This might be said to be the genius of terrorism: it keeps—if successful, should keep—defending societies both on their toes and off balance, disoriented at all times, whether anything is happening or not (Thornton, 1964). The mechanism by which that effect is achieved, moreover, is through exploitation of the cognitive experience of ambiguity and the affective experience of anxiety. Both of these experiences reflect uncertainty about the nature of the threat of terrorism and about ways to fear it. The dread of terrorism is not unlike that of crime, accidents, disasters, and wartime fear, but it is the peculiar combination of lethality, ambiguity, and anxiety that makes it the pervasive virus that it is.

The Nature of Anxiety about Terrorism

What is it like to live in a society threatened with terrorism? Any answers to this question must be based in the first instance on the experienced salience of the threat itself. The response differs with the degree of salience, as follows:

- When the threat appears remote. In this case terrorism is scarcely in the public consciousness. Although U.S. society has had a history of regularly occurring domestic terrorism on both the right and the left, its fear of unanticipated attack from foreign sources has been notably absent until very recently. This historical sense of luxury, of an absence of fear, has conditioned many of our reactions to international terrorism.

- When terrorism is an actual threat—mainly because of recurrent incidents—but when public consciousness is not aroused. The 1980s seem to represent such a period, when terrorist attacks on American targets were evident and national leaders, including President Ronald Reagan, were proclaiming such attacks a national crisis (Simon, 1987). Public consciousness remained low, however, largely because all the attacks occurred abroad and the cold war dominated the headlines. The 1993 attack on the World Trade Center was dramatic, but the fact that it failed in its most important aim of bringing down a tower probably hastened the public forgetting of this otherwise salient event.

- When terrorism is regarded as a real and present possibility. September 11, 2001, was the dramatic culmination of a number of attacks by Al-Qaeda on American targets. After that event, fear of terrorism became something of a way of life for government, first responders, and many citizens, even though no additional attacks on the American mainland have occurred. The universality of fear should not be exaggerated, however. It is geographically concentrated in likely urban target centers (New York, Washington, D.C., and Los Angeles, for example), and experienced only subliminally in smaller communities. The level of apprehension also varies over time as well, for example, at moments of heightened warnings before political conventions and elections, and at times of major attacks abroad, such as the London Underground attacks in July 2005. Even under these circumstances, the principle of rapid public forgetting asserts itself. Public opinion polls showed that immediately after the anthrax incidents in October 2001, 59 percent of

Americans polled reported that they were worried that they or a family member would become a victim of terrorism. Six weeks later that figure had dropped to 35 percent and was continuing its downward trend (Schoch-Spana, 2003).

- When terrorist actions become repeated and routine events over a period of time, as has been the case in Israel and Northern Ireland. In such circumstances, public anxiety is surely salient, but attitudes harden, and many citizens become defiant in their commitment to maintaining daily rhythms and employ defensive postures such as denial of danger and gallows humor (Sharkansky, 2003, pp. 115–16). Ironically, the more routine occurrence of terrorist events may be less productive of generalized anxiety—and more productive of adaptive behaviors—than the imagined and feared occurrence of events of unknown dimensions.

It is essential to keep these lines of variation in mind to avoid stereotyping in our thinking about the relations between terrorism and public anxiety in potential target societies. It is worth dwelling on the third type of situation, however, if for no other reason than that it is the dominant one in the United States at present with respect to international terrorism and promises to remain so for some time to come. What are the social-psychological characteristics of this high-salience situation?

First, attacks are likely to be, and to be perceived as, rare events. This assumption makes realistic sense, given what we know about the long periods of planning that went into past attacks, their periodicity, and the fact that the nation's defenses have become more systematic and probably more secure (to an unknown degree) as a result of the nation's efforts since the September 11 attacks. Rarity produces a number of consequences. Anxiety can jump at moments of dramatic events, such as the 1995 germ gas attack in the Tokyo subways—the first of its kind (Sprinzak, 1998)—and at times of alarm and warning. As a general rule, however, it is psychologically uneconomical for people to sustain a high level of worry about extremely rare events. The dynamics of rapidly fading memory and worry about earthquakes and other natural disasters—except for really catastrophic ones—confirm this rule. The typical course of events is for moments of high anxiety to give way to periods of denial and a return to routine, which may be counterproductive with respect to maintaining readiness and preparation. It is also likely that authorities' efforts to keep the population at a high level of preparation for rare events not only adds to the anxiety level but also generates indifference (the "crying wolf" syndrome) or impatience with authorities for issuing unexplained false alarms (Dow and Cutter, 1998). Ironically, this rarity places authorities in a no-win situation. If they are diligent in keeping the population constantly prepared for attack and no attacks occur, they invite criticism for overreacting. If they are not so diligent and an attack does occur, they are the first targets in the season of blame that ensues.

Second, potential attacks are uncertain with respect to target, as well as to kind and extent of damage. Anyone who has attended a conference of experts on defense against terrorism knows that the list of targets is practically endless—cities, electrical systems, computer systems, transportation networks, postal and monetary systems, food and water supplies, dams, buildings, and large public assemblages. Furthermore, current technological potentialities make possible an array of weapons, from thrown rocks to nuclear blasts, as well as a multitude of biological and chemical toxins, poisons, and infecting agents (see Manning and Goldfrank, 2002). The difficulties of mounting an attack that employ some of these weapons are formidable and the realistic probability of such attacks is low, but imagination, fed by anxiety, typically defies the rules of probability. Two consequences follow. (1) Under conditions of uncertainty, it is possible (and probable) to imagine the worst, because with a lack of reliable information, no stable limits to thinking are available. As harmful and counterproductive as are the games of "if I were a terrorist I would . . . ," they seem to be the inevitable product of uncertainty. (2) As a result of such limitless fears, it becomes impossible to defend against all imagined dangers and contingencies without paralyzing or bankrupting the entire society. The affective ramifications of these consequences, moreover, are heightened anxiety, a sense of hopelessness, and pessimism. The literature on terrorism stresses repeatedly that its main weapons are psychological. To make that assertion more precise, the psychological consequences are those that are generated by the factors of extreme but uncertain danger and rarity of occurrence.

Vulnerabilities of Agencies of Defense

By agencies of defense I refer first of all to domestic organizations that are in place to prevent terrorist attacks from occurring. These organizations include intelligence organizations that operate abroad and at home, armies, law enforcement agencies, and immigration authorities. The problems facing these agencies are considered in chapter 6. Second, I refer to those agencies that are geared to prepare for attacks and swing into action when they occur—the first responders. These agencies include police and the military (National Guard), fire departments, public health officials, relief and charity organizations, and, as it turns out, the media, informal neighborhood associations, networks of friends, and families, even though they are not explicitly and primarily geared to defensive priorities.

For formally designated agencies of response, a distinctive set of vulnerabilities stems from the dimension of uncertainty about when, where, and in what form an attack will occur. Potential attacks using weapons of mass destruction pose special difficulties. First, since, with one exception, these weapons have not been (but realistically may be) employed by terrorists, knowledge about their consequences must therefore be derived from related types of events, from scenarios, and from general knowledge (McGlown, 2004). Second, many chemical and biological attacks (especially the latter), unlike bombings and kidnappings, can be covert, that is, introduced secretly and perhaps not discovered until later, and gradual rather than one-time in their effects (Noji, 2004), and for these reasons they are more difficult to discern and contain. This range of possibilities makes planning for the occurrence of terrorist events more complicated than planning for specific kinds of natural disasters (earthquakes, tornadoes, hurricanes, floods), the damaging dimensions of which are generally known even if they are variable in occurrence. In principle, agencies should be prepared to respond to everything, but this ideal cannot in any remote way be realistically achieved.

Given these multiple possibilities, the fact remains that, as far as we appreciate them at the present time, terrorist attacks in and on the United States are likely to be rare events. This circumstance, however, creates an additional problem for agencies of response. Although some of them (police, fire, and relief agencies) have ongoing responsibilities that keep them occupied, the readiness skills for addressing terrorist activities are never exercised, except when renewed in various kinds of scenario exercises. The "sleeping sentry" effect always remains a possibility when events never or rarely happen, even though those anticipated events are likely to be deadly.

Preparing and Warning the Population

Warning of Attacks

Disaster research in the past half-century has produced a great deal of knowledge about warning a population at the time of an approaching disaster. The essence of this research is that warning is a social process in which not everybody hears, understands, or gives credibility to the warning. Warnings are also endowed with personal meaning. Furthermore, deciding how to react is often a collective process, involving seeking information, accepting it, interpreting it, and acting—or not acting—on it (Lindell and Perry, 2004). To be successful, warnings should be experienced as coming from a credible source and should be consistent, accurate, and clear. They should also be relatively definite and certain as to what people should do. Even when all these elements are present, responses to the warning will vary according to whether people are with kin and friends. Demographic characteristics such as age and gender also affect the reception of and reacting to warnings, as do personality characteristics such as an individual's sense of personal control (Fitzpatrick and Mileti, 1994).

This knowledge has accumulated mainly in connection with disasters—floods, storms, fires—for which warnings are possible. Terrorist attacks render advance warnings moot in most cases, because terrorist strikes, to be effective, should be planned in secret, should be of unknown nature, and should be executed without warning. In most cases, specific warnings cannot be issued. The most that can be given out is a "risk communication" (ibid., p. 71) rather than a warning. This places responsible officials in a precarious position, adding another element to the no-win situation in which they find themselves; if high risk is indicated and nothing happens, or, more critically, if low risk is indicated and an attack occurs, the finger of blame is likely to be pointed at officials and their agencies.

In this connection it seems appropriate to assess the principal terrorism warning system in place for first responders and the public generally—the color-coded system, which is regarded as a signature item of the tenure of Secretary Tom Ridge of the Department of Homeland Security. Introduced early in 2002, the system is meant to communicate a level of risk of terrorist activity. The levels of warning are:

- Blue: "low risk"
- Green: "guarded" or "general risk"
- Yellow: "elevated" or "significant risk"
- Orange: "high risk"
- Red: "severe risk"

The system is intended to notify first responders as well as the public (usually daily on television news) of the level of danger. Secretary Ridge linked this system of communication to preparedness: "[f]or every level of threat, there will be a level of preparedness" (Ridge, 2005, p. 86). During most of the time since its installation it has remained on yellow, but from time to time the system has been temporarily elevated to orange (for example, on the first anniversary of September 11, 2001, at the time of the Muslim Hajj holiday in February 2003, and at the beginning of the Iraq War). Secretary Ridge described the system as "effective" (ibid.). However, it reveals a number of limitations as a warning system:

- When changes in these levels are made, they are usually explained by referring to indefinite background information, with some indication that more is known but cannot be divulged for security reasons. Unfortunately, such messages serve mainly to communicate a level of alarm if elevated and perhaps relief if lowered, but very little else. They provide no guidance as to how citizens should structure their thinking cognitively, and certainly no guidance for behavior. First response agencies have reported that the information accompanying the color-code changes is inadequate as a guide for their actions (United States General Accounting Office, 2004).

In a dirty-bomb scenario sponsored by the Department of Homeland Security and the National Academies in Chicago in July 2004, Secretary Ridge presented some opening remarks and entertained questions. As a member of the audience, I had occasion to raise this limitation with him. His response was that the warning system was mainly a means of communicating with preparedness agencies. This response underscored rather than answered the difficulty: although it may convey definite messages to first responders and mandate procedures to be activated, the warning system cannot be regarded as an effective communication device for the general public because it is minimally informative.

- The information conveyed is ambiguous. How, for example, does a hearer discern a meaningful difference between "elevated" and "high" (Peña, 2005).
- The system is based on an erroneous assumption of an undifferentiated public that reacts automatically and uniformly to a risk communication (Aguirre, 2004).
- In practice, the system has devolved into a simple two-color scheme, yellow and orange, with the extremes avoided. At the lower end, no official or agency wishes to be caught having issued a blue or green warning on the eve of an actual attack. Red is tantamount to a very extreme warning and carries the danger of exciting extreme reactions, which also leaves the authorities vulnerable if nothing happens.

Although the warning system carries definite messages to first responders and mandates procedures to be put in place, it is severely limited as a public warning system. It is not surprising that it has drawn cynical attacks for "announcing today's level of risk to determine how safe [Americans] are supposed to feel—and feeling deeply unsafe precisely because their level of fear is now color-coded for them" (Barber, 2003, p. 25).

Apparently, the decision to go public with the warnings was based on the agency's apprehension that they would be leaked to the media and the public anyway, even if communicated only to the first-responding agencies, so why not make them public (Brill, 2003)? In the end, however, the scheme, while understandable from political and public relations points of view, seems to have created an unhelpful, alarm-without-information system.

Cognitive, Emotional, and Behavioral Responses
When a Terrorist Attack Occurs

The ambiguities and uncertainties that characterize the period in advance of possible terrorist attacks also characterize the situation immediately in the wake of an attack. As a result, we may expect a scramble for information on the part of all parties—government and public officials, first responders, and the general public—when an attack occurs. Depending on the information available and how it is framed, different affective reactions are aroused. Finally, these cognitive and emotional reactions impart a definition to the situation and frame individuals' and groups' behavioral responses. In this section I concentrate on the public, but I will refer to responsible agencies from time to time.

Because terrorism involves multiple threats, it is necessary to anticipate a multiplicity of types of public reactions. In this respect, terrorism contrasts with more specific kinds of disasters, such as tornadoes and earthquakes, for which more or less scripted programs of response are available. Because of this feature, planning, preparation, and training for responses to terrorist attacks are more complicated. The possibilities are not infinite, however, and decisions can be made as to the greater or lesser likelihood of all possible scenarios, and priorities for planning and preparation can be graded according to these judgments.

The following are the main dimensions of variation of attacks that determine variations in reactions:

- The *locus* of the attack—an urban center, an electrical grid system, transportation station or depot, a dam, agricultural fields, a sports event. If the event is evidently geographically contained, such as a bomb explosion in a shopping mall, reactions are less extreme the farther away people are from the event (the major concern is whether a similar event might be repeated elsewhere).

If the attack is less localized, such as poisoning of food supplies, anthrax sent in the mails, or contamination of the currency, the response will be generalized. In this connection, the potential terror of the small and amateurish mailing of anthrax following 9/11 was greater than the dramatic events on that day (massively shocking as they were), because the latter were localized and the former was generalized (everybody is exposed to the mail). The main immediate "terror" caused by 9/11 was in the vicinity of the attacks and at airports.

- The *type of weapon* used. This is closely related to the issue of locus. Obviously, the detonation of a nuclear device or a dirty bomb in an American city, or the dissemination of infectious or poisonous agents, will excite more extreme reactions than an attempt to blow up a dam, airplane, or stadium.
- The *number* of attacks. If single, we may expect and dread of more of the same, but reactions will focus on recovering; if multiple, the alarm will be much greater, for it will elevate the menacing question of where next.
- The *timing* of the attack. If an attack occurs in the daytime hours, news of it will spread very rapidly, but if it comes in the middle of the night, its spread will be attenuated as night owls hear about it immediately and perhaps telephone others to pass it on; others will hear the news only as they arise to meet the day. If the attack and news of it are in the evening, nighttime, early morning, or weekend hours—that is, when families are likely to be together— the response is different from the response to an attack occurring during weekday daylight hours, when families are dispersed to workplace, school, and home. Disaster research shows that the first impulse in situations of extreme danger is to join or protect loved ones.

All these factors point toward the likelihood of differentiated responses on the part of the public. It is also important to stress that there is no such thing as a single public and no single expectation of a uniform public response. There are differences in hearing about and responding to news of a terrorist event along familiar sociological lines—rural-urban, social class, knowledge of English, education, race, neighborhood, and gender (see, for example, Fothergill, Maestas, and Darlington, 1999). For example, almost any type of terrorist event occasions a stronger reaction in urban centers, since these areas are typically on the highest alert for terrorist attacks in any case. In addition, the more educated are more likely to hear about an event earlier, and are more likely to possess appropriate contextual information for interpreting it.

We turn now to an account of the likely immediate responses to a terrorist event, keeping in mind the differences along the dimensions just reviewed. Much of what we know about these responses derives from studies of natural disasters and major accidents. Some of this knowledge is applicable to terrorist-inflicted disasters. However, many points of difference emerge, stemming in large part from the fundamental fact that terrorist acts involve human agency and natural disasters do not (though, as we will see, some similar responses, such as a search for the responsible and blameworthy, typically follow the latter as well).

Immediate Cognitive Reactions: The Quest for Meaning and the Reduction of Uncertainty

In the immediate aftermath of a terrorist incident, a series of questions and concerns rise to salience. In combination, the "answers" that are generated help explain the kinds and levels of emotional responses and behavioral reactions. Because terrorist attacks are feared as extreme threats to life and property, the cognitive questions are simple but absolutely basic and existential. The principal questions are the following:

(1) *What happened?* The intensity with which this question is asked varies with distance from the attack, but it is always the first priority. The quest is for knowledge about an attack that concerns its location, its nature (blast, poisoning, disruption), its seriousness, its victims, its closeness, and the likelihood of its being repeated. In the first instance the concerns are framed with reference to the personal safety and welfare of the seekers of the information themselves, and secondarily but immediately (hereafter with reference to the fate of others. The answer

to "what happened" is a necessary cognitive preliminary to both emotional and behavioral reactions.

(2) *Who did it?* The possibilities are an act of nature, an accident, or the deliberate act of a person or group. For those in the immediate vicinity, this does not matter, because any one of the three constitutes a disaster situation. For those more remote, emotional reactions will be muted if the account indicates a natural disaster or accident has occurred. If it appears to be a deliberate act of violence, this ignites collective feelings of shock, fear, and rage. In this respect, reactions to a perceived terrorist attack differ sharply from reactions to an event perceived as an act of God or an accident.

In the absence of definite information, the assignment of responsibility follows the fault lines of public suspicion or prejudice (many who heard the news of the 1995 Oklahoma City bombing, for example, first attributed it to Muslim agents). Needless to say, authorities play a crucial role in this assignment of responsibility, and their behavior will shape public perceptions and reactions. For example, responsibility for the 9/11 attacks was assigned immediately to Osama bin Laden, Al-Qaeda, and the Taliban, which immediately introduced a note of intense anger and revenge into the emotional mix. After the subsequent anthrax episode the authorities indicated they had no idea who did it, and they could not initially say much about the nature of anthrax. This triggered anxiety more than anything else, and in the absence of knowledge many people came to their own conclusions about the identity of the perpetrator.

(3) *Are we vulnerable to further attack?* The framing of public response to this question varies according to both the nature of the attack (what was it), those responsible for the attack (who did it), and the degree of geographic proximity to the attack. The "we" includes a range of references—me personally, family and friends, and the home community. Fears tend to spread by analogy—for example, if the attack was directed against an urban center, then anxiety will be highest in other urban canters. The psychological principle involved is that in moments of perceived danger, people fear most a recurrence of what has just happened; for example, after the bomb explosion at Cairo's central bazaar on April 6, 2005, the U.S. State Department warned American tourists to stay away from the bazaar. The London Underground explo-

sions on July 7, 2005, led to heightened security precautions mainly in the mass transportation systems in the United States.

(4) *Should we do anything?* The response to this question is the end point of the structuring process that takes place in relation to the first three questions. If the attack is of a known type and if citizens have the information about how to respond, most responses will be directly consonant with that information—for example, remain inside in the case of radiological attacks, do not handle mail if the attack involves contamination of the mails.

Such responses are analogous to following structured and rehearsed routines for responding to natural events such as storms and earthquakes. Because of the diversity of possible attacks associated with terrorism, however, because of the incomplete dissemination of information, and because anxiety may overwhelm any programmed responses, a great deal of unanticipated behavior must be expected—mainly movement from imagined danger spots and efforts to join loved ones. In issuing advice for "personal preparation" for attack, the National Strategy Forum (2004) recognized these possibilities by recommending that, in advance, people determine multiple evacuation routes from home and office and designate meeting places with friends and loved ones.

All of the circulating answers to these questions are also subject to a degree of "credibility scanning," or some effort to establish their authenticity and plausibility (Perry, 1994).

A Scare at the San Francisco Airport

On a January morning in 2002, I was in the San Francisco airport waiting to board a plane to attend a meeting of the Committee on Science and Technology in Countering Terrorism (National Research Council) in Washington, D.C. I had arrived in plenty of time for the 8 a.m. departure, but as I neared the boarding gate a sudden announcement greeted me: The airport is being evacuated, take your belongings and exit to the street. I, along with about 3,500 other passengers, dutifully obeyed these instructions, without, however, having a clue about what was going on. We went outside and formed a milling crowd, in front of the airport on that chilly winter morning.

The mood of the crowd was ugly at first. Here we were, evacuated from the airport without explanation. The airlines and airport authorities were saying nothing, no doubt because of their fear of being held liable if they communicated too much or the wrong kind of information. Furthermore, there were no other authoritative sources of information. Speculative rumors about the reason for our evacuation began to spread from person to person. The crowd was very far from anything like rioting, but the mood of confusion, fear, and irritation was not unlike that which can set some kind of collective crowd action in motion.

Interestingly, technology came to the rescue. Many people in the crowd had cell telephones, and they were phoning home to tell families and friends about the incident or calling the East Coast to tell people they were going to be late. As these callers conversed, they began to receive information about what was happening at the airport. That information came from radio stations that were airing news bulletins about the evacuation. From these calls and from the face-to-face circulation of information through the crowd, we learned about the cause. A man had taken off his shoes to run them through a security scanner, and had retrieved them and walked away before the scanner revealed some nitrate substance that suggested the possibility of an explosive. (Shoes were on the mind of everybody, because Richard Reid, the notorious "shoe bomber" on a transatlantic flight, had been apprehended only weeks earlier, on December 22, 2001.) The security authorities, however, couldn't find the departed man, so they had to resort to the extreme of evacuating everybody, searching every corner of the airport, then sending the thousands of evacuees back through the security system again. This took a long time, created long waiting lines at the security stations, and taxed the patience of the people again. My own 8 a.m. plane finally left for Washington at 1 p.m.

The whole episode had a comical, Jacques-Tati-movie twist about it, but in the last analysis, of course, no terrorist warning is very funny. What struck me most of all was the rapid and extreme change of mood that occurred in the crowd as the correct information about the reason for the evacuation began to circulate. People were greatly relieved, took pleasure in passing the information on to others, and a temporary intimacy with others in the crowd—mostly strangers to one another, of course—developed, and friendly, excited chatter replaced the apprehension and anger.

When I went to the meeting of my committee on terrorism the next morning, I reported the incident to and claimed that I had been doing firsthand fieldwork on our topic of terrorism. All were amused, at this great distance from the event, and I took some good-natured ribbing about being the guilty party who had taken a walk through my newly fertilized garden before coming to the airport and setting off the scanner.

The episode, minor in itself and by now probably lost in the memory of those who experienced it, does, however, carry an important message. When people are subjected to an alarm signal without accompanying information about how to think about the event and its cause, much less how to organize their behavior, this results in feelings of confusion, anxiety, and a readiness to blame. When, however, authoritative information is forthcoming—in this case, the radio broadcasts were enough—those feelings dissipate and the comfort level rises, even though the initial situation was regarded as threatening and conceivably remained so. Warnings and warning systems should always have some cognitive structuring to them, should come from authoritative sources, and should contain some indication about what to think, feel, and do about the situation.

These four questions—and the framing of responses to them—are the general if not universal psychological responses to the occurrence of a major threatening event. From the way the answers are framed, we can make conditional predictions about what kind of emotional reactions and behavioral responses will follow. Use of the word "psychological," however, should not suggest that these responses is a matter of individual psychology. The development of information, interpretations, and affective responses is grounded in a social process. People will first seek information from relevant sources—public announcements by authorities, media reports, and information relayed by friends, relatives, and even strangers. The National Strategy Forum (2004) also instructed people to be prepared for the fact that phone lines may be tied up after an attack; such a search for information and emotional assurance is a universal postdisaster effect. As a result of this process, responses to a terrorist attack—with which people are less likely to be familiar than with natural disasters that recur periodically—will be correspondingly more diversified and less well controlled. Responses to terrorist events are forged from a mélange of official information, media interpretations, and interpersonal communications, including rumors.

In the immediate dissemination of information and interpretation—that is, in providing at least provisional answers to the four questions identified—both political authorities and the media play important and delicate roles. Political authorities—because they are authorities—face a special dilemma. In the aftermath of an attack, authorities cannot remain completely silent or else they lose control of the situation altogether; neither can they simply say that they know nothing, because that is another way of losing control. The dilemma arises because in the postattack atmosphere of uncertainty, authorities themselves may in fact know little and have nothing definitive to say. Interviews with reporters, a government spokesman, and a scientist after the anthrax attacks in September 2001 revealed that "[they] agreed on one thing—they were operating in the dark" (Hess and Kalb, 2003, p. 125). In addition, authorities are forever looking down the political road toward public excoriation for things they should (or should not) have said or done in the aftermath of an incident. Even in the wake of bombing attacks in World War II, victims often blamed not the countries responsible for bombing but their own governments for failing to protect them (Janis, 1951). This dilemma is a recipe for paralysis of authorities in times of crises of unknown dimensions. The most reasonable behavior in such extreme situations appears to be one of honesty—for authorities to report what they do know, however minimal that is, to urge calm, and to promise further information to the public as soon as it becomes available.

The media face a similar dilemma. On the one hand, they are interested and feel obliged to report all news, especially the electrifying news made by a terrorist attack. At the same time they may not know what happened, either. Under these crisis conditions, they are torn between issuing immediate reports of unverified information and their self-imposed constraint to publish only what is verified. As media they are under pressure to report—and want to report—sensational news, but they are also under constraints not to sensationalize it. The pressures to report quickly and to sensationalize usually win out in situations of disaster. Yet the media also face the prospect of criticism down the line for misreporting and misrepresentation. The upshot of these dynamics is that both political authorities and media face the prospect of a no-win situation, and both may be expected to muddle through on the basis of quickly made, ad hoc decisions as action unfolds.

Immediate Emotional Reactions

Decades of study of natural disasters and accidents have revealed a range of emotional reactions that are general if not universal (for a summary, see Hodgkinson and Stewart, 1998). These include the following:

- Psychic numbing, which involves a combination of disbelief, denial, suppression of affect, and refusal to assimilate the meaning of the event—as though it did not happen.
- Immediately thereafter, a mix of intense emotional reactions, including fear, anxiety, and terror, as well as rage and guilt. In the case of attacks believed to be terrorist, anxiety will be especially high (largely because of the dread of immediate recurrence, which does not accompany most natural disasters such as earthquakes, fires, floods, and storms). Rage will also be salient, because terrorism immediately suggests a responsible agent (even if unknown), whereas natural disasters are experienced in more depersonalized ways.
- If it is supposed that the attack is a terrorist one, that is, one inflicted by an enemy, feelings of solidarity will surge, generated by the high level of personal interaction that accompanies the collective search for meaning and the general in-group response to dangers from outside. This response resembles that to a threat or outbreak of war more than that to natural disasters, which do excite sympathy and feelings of community, though these feelings are directed toward the afflicted, not toward a suspected enemy perpetrator.
- If the attack results in casualties, an outpouring of sympathy for the dead and the bereaved. This has been termed "survivor guilt," which inevitably raises questions of "why others, not me," along with the existential connotations of that question.

The extent and depth of these emotional reactions vary with the degree of proximity to the attack. Furthermore, they vary with different levels of preexisting psychological frailty that survivors and witnesses bring to the event; this is the main reason why there is a distribution of emotional reactions from minimal to totally overwhelming (Hodgkinson and Stewart, 1998, p. 10; see also Wolfenstein, 1957).

Immediate Behavioral Reactions

The diversity of the impacts in different parts of the population and the diversity of cognitive structuring and emotional reactions implies a corresponding diversity of behavioral reactions. The following are the most typical:

- The immediate scramble for information and assurance, including a massive tie-up of telephone systems, as well as a groundswell of television watching and radio listening in the quest for news and interpretation. In this process, rumors inevitably play a role as part of the set of information-seeking and information-receiving activities (Turner, 1994).
- Most people in a population will remain immobile. This is especially true if an attack is localized and does not pose an immediate threat to more remote communities. The lack of movement results from a combination of fascination with the event, personal shock, and not knowing what to do. This generalization becomes shaky, however, in the event of truly catastrophic attacks—for example, radioactive devices set off simultaneously in a number of cities—in which case we would expect more random motion and escape behavior.
- Depending on the nature of the attack and the cognitive and emotional responses to it, there may be a great deal of geographic movement in the population, if avenues of movement are not blocked off either by the attack itself or shut down by authorities. The most obvious movement is evacuation or flight from perceived danger (for example, from the path of a moving radioactive plume). Less obvious but possible are movements on the part of populations in analogous areas, for example, flight from other

urban centers after one urban center is attacked. Decisions whether to evacuate typically are a complex process involving the perception of danger, interpersonal influences, and the availability of places to go (Gladwin, Gladwin, and Peacock, 2001).

The issue of outright panic flight arises in connection with the movement of populations. Panic connotes a pell-mell rush to exit, accompanied by a distinctive psychological component, namely, out-of-control fear and the sense that if I (or we) do not make a dash for it, escape is impossible. In fact, panic reactions are extremely rare in dangerous situations, as shown in studies of populations' reactions in World War II (United States Strategic Bombing Survey, 1947), the Three Mile Island crisis, (Clarke, 1999), the evacuation of the World Trade Center on September 11, 2001 (Glass and Schoch-Spana, 2002), and in many other studies (Dynes and Tierney, 1994). The reason for the rarity is that the cognitive and emotional structure that generates panic is highly specific; it consists of extreme fear, *combined* with the perception that exits are not yet closed but are closing. These precise conditions do exist in case of battlefield panics, when troops believe they are being surrounded, or in theater fires, when it is perceived that the exits are jamming. If exits are perceived to be open, then orderly withdrawal or flight occurs; if exits are perceived to be completely closed, then a number of other reactions (paralysis, resignation, prayer, drawing together with loved ones) but not panic are likely.

• A second movement of population, more likely to approach panic, is the effort on the part of individuals to join loved ones. In one sense this movement diminishes the likelihood of evacuation panic; few people leave an area without their families or loved ones. In some circumstances, however, it may produce a panic-like situation. If an attack in an urban center occurs in the daylight hours of a working day, when families are dispersed to work, school, and home, this may precipitate a mass movement within the city, as people try to unite with their families before leaving. The result would be blockages of all streets in the city as people attempt to dash to and fro. If families are together at the time of an attack—for example, on weekends—mass exit is a more likely possibility. The importance of kinship and other close social ties cannot be overestimated. It has been observed everywhere in postdisaster responses, from predicting how people behave in trying to escape in nightclub fires (Johnson, Feinberg, and Johnston, 1994) to how they evacuate threatened regions, as in the instance of the Three Mile Island accident (Cutter and Barnes, 1982), and where they prefer to go for shelter when made homeless (Bolin, 1994).

- A third possible population movement is what has been referred to as the "convergence effect"—the movement of people toward the scene of the crisis (Fritz and Mathewson, 1957). This is a recurrent feature of disasters. This movement obviously includes first responders such as police, firemen, and health personnel, but it also includes the movement of people out of motives of rescue, help, curiosity, and perhaps looting. Convergence often creates problems of congestion, interference, and safety for designated responders. Convergence behavior might characterize reactions to some terrorist attacks as well, but if an attack involves radioactivity, chemical toxins, or biological agents, warnings by authorities and fear of contamination would mute or reverse the convergence effect.

- A final effect is the emergence of what has been called a therapeutic community, characterized by the development of altruistic norms and activity, a feeling of unity, an expanded sense of citizenship, a diminution of community conflict, and heroic behavior on the part of first responders and ordinary citizens (Abrams, Albright, and Panofsky, 2004; Dynes, 1970).

Reactions in the Days and Weeks Following an Attack

Individual and Social Reactions

The first few days after a terrorist attack—assuming it is of significant proportions—will produce a range of behaviors that are familiar to students of disaster: locating and accounting for the dead and

removing from them from the scene; rescuing and giving medical attention to those who have been injured, poisoned, or sickened; and repeated airing of the event itself on television, including interviews with
survivors, and continuing coverage in all the media, with many reruns
and meticulous attention to any new detail that may seem newsworthy
(the "CNN syndrome"). Recent history and public attitudes also play
a role in how the population reacts. The reactions of fear, shock, and
outrage in the media and public were especially extreme following the
World Trade Center bombing, the Oklahoma City bombing, and the
events of 9/11. By the same token, because those events diminished the
country's "innocence of terror," much of the news and interpretation
of future terrorist events will be cast in the context of those responses,
and for that reason, other responses in both media and public will likely
be less extreme.

The first days after an attack also bring a period of mourning.
Mourning entails above all a process of coping for the immediate survivors. It is also a collective drama, with eyewitnesses, survivors, first
responders, and political and religious leaders—all orchestrated by the
media—as the principal actors. Because the mourning process is so
public on these occasions, it is subject not only to the emotional exigen-
cies of those suffering but also to certain norms as to how to mourn,
including the appropriate ways to express sadness and a taboo on expressing happy emotions and hinting that the attack and its toll of victims were in any way deserved.

The immediate sense of shock and mourning is part of the phenomenon of individual trauma that results from psychologically destructive
events such as battlefield experiences, physical assault, sexual abuse, and
natural disasters. Terrorist attacks fall into the same category. Most of
the damage to the mental health of the population can be and has been
assimilated to the idea of trauma, as it has been codified under the
heading of Post-Traumatic Stress Disorders in the American Psychiatric
Association's *Diagnostic and Statistical Manuals of Mental Disorders*.
PTSD has come to include a very wide variety of traumatic events.
Among them, exposure to terrorism comes closest to a combination of
criminal assault, disaster, and war (Hills, 2002). From the vast range of
symptoms associated with experiencing terrorism, Miller (2002) has
stressed the effects of grief, despair, personal loss, avoidance/protective

behavior, disturbances of memory and concentration, and a subsequent "fear of everything." Research reported in the clinical literature appears to confirm in general that deep and significant traumas do result from exposure to terrorism and that children and the elderly are especially vulnerable (Raphael, 1986). However, it is also realized that reactions vary in severity from "no particular reaction at all" to severe chronic symptoms (Hodgkinson and Stewart, 1998). The disaster literature indicates that in most cases, catastrophic disasters excepted, negative psychological consequences are mild and short-lived (Gerrity and Flynn, 1997; for the modest impact of earthquakes, see Siegel, Shoaf, and Bourque, 2000). Large-scale quantitative effects are hard to come by, because most studies are based on limited samples taken after disasters or other events with idiosyncratic characteristics (for example, Webel, 2004; Danieli, Engdahl, and Schlenger, 2004). The characteristics of the traumatic situation that appear to determine the severity of the symptoms are the following:

- Preexisting clinical vulnerabilities and symptoms, including previous traumas
- Proximity to the locus of attack (Schenger, 2005)
- Being an immediate survivor
- Witnessing death and injury firsthand
- Additional traumatic experiences after the event
- The effectiveness of care strategies, such as immediate crisis intervention

A variety of therapeutic strategies for traumatic reactions have been recommended as antidotes for terrorist-induced trauma, including on-the-spot crisis intervention, talking through, support groups, and professional longer-term therapy (Miller, 2002). Like the distribution of traumas themselves, however, the effectiveness of different treatments for trauma has not been firmly established.

I should mention one additional element of postevent traumas, in part because it is likely to escape our attention in light of the emphasis on trauma as an individual psychiatric condition. Trauma, like the mourning process, has social and normative dimensions as well. The traumatized person assumes or is encouraged by others to assume the role of victim, which carries with it normative expectations about how to express and conduct oneself. Sometimes the role of victim carries an expectation that an individual is entitled to financial compensation (as in the case of those wounded in war and in the case of the survivors from 9/11) or legal recourse (as in the case of those sexually abused). If so, the role of victim not only involves the individual's condition but also becomes the focus of tangible interests, which may crystallize into some kind of social movement (Smelser, 2004a).

Another predictable response in the wake of terrorist attacks is a wave of solidarity in the affected population. This is reflected behaviorally in the increased communication about and common focus on the event as a source of outside threat. This response is variable. The effect will be relatively stronger according to closeness to the vicinity of the attack. It will be stronger as the attack increases in magnitude. It will be stronger if the attack is on American soil than if it occurs abroad (even though the target might be American). It will also be stronger (and more patriotic) if the identified perpetrator is foreign rather than domestic (the Unabomber did not stimulate much community unity but rather more fear, anger, and fascination). It should be noted also that to an unknown degree, solidarity responses in the United States in the future might be muted in light of the country's catastrophic experience on September 11, 2001. The long "honeymoon period" (Raphael, 1986) generated by that crisis will not likely be repeated. The solidarity reaction will be shorter and less intense, and the political repercussions, including group divisiveness, will begin earlier.

Political Reactions

The immediate political consequences of a terrorist attack, particularly if it is a major one, are a surge of solidarity and unity in sympathy for the victims, outrage at the known or suspected perpetrator, and an increase in support and trust in political leaders. These are general wartime reactions, and they were never more vivid than in the post-9/11 months. However, not long after a terrorist assault, a season of political ferment emerges. This involves above all the assignment of responsibility and blame, and falls under four headings:

- Responsibility for perpetrating the event.
- Responsibility for not having prevented it from happening.
- Responsibility for responding to it once it has happened.
- Responsibility for ensuring that it will not happen again.

These are the fault lines along which immediate political reactions accumulate. The result has been called "blame assignation" by students of disaster behavior (Drabek, 1994).

The first and most immediate political development is a strong negative reaction and a demand for retribution against the perpetrator. The lines of this reaction depend largely on the specificity of the answer to the "who did it" question. If that target is identified, and that identification sticks as a publicly accepted belief, the reaction is direct and passionate (the bin Laden–Al-Qaeda–Taliban–Afghanistan effect after September 11); if the agent is not and cannot be known, there will still be an effort to identify the culprit(s), though this process will be more diffuse, running along established lines of national and international suspicion, itself generative of political controversy.

The impulse to blame is quick to spread symbolically to other groups believed to be related to or sympathetic with the identified perpetrator. That is one of the effects of crises posed by international threats in our own history—the identification of German-Americans in World War I, suspected Bolshevik and anarchist groups in the reactionary period following the Russian Revolution, Japanese-Americans in World War II, communists, "pinkos," and fellow travelers in the McCarthyism scare after the Chinese communist revolution and the Soviet development of nuclear capability, and Arab-Americans during the Gulf War. In the wake of 9/11, there was significant intrusion, including detainment, of Muslim immigrants in New York City, a pervasive fear in their communities, and subsequent political mobilization to resist and defend their rights (Minnite, 2005). Sometimes the blaming extends to political discreditation along existing ideological and political lines of cleavage. For example, after 9/11 a politically conservative group, the American Council of Trustees and Alumni, founded in 1995 by Lynne Cheney, wife of the (subsequent) vice president, launched an attack on American faculty and universities for their "blame America first" response to the terrorist attacks, for "failing America," and for fomenting disunity in a beleaguered nation (Silberstein, 2002). The intensity of this symbolic generalization of blame will be greater if the government and the media participate actively in it, diminished if they discourage it. Whether and how to distance themselves from this political tendency poses a dilemma for both.

Second, the political reaction is a scanning process—at first informal, later more official—for agents who might have failed in their responsibility to prevent the attack. This is a near-universal consequence of any kind of disaster. This scan varies according to the nature of the attack but typically include intelligence, security, warning or defense agencies, and political authorities. This search is especially salient in the case of terrorist attacks because these attacks, unlike many natural disasters, originate from human design and execution, and are therefore more subject, in principle, to prevention or control by responsible authorities. The scan is a public one, because the identification of responsibility is meat for the media as well as the public. It will have an even sharper edge if the presumed failure of responsibility seems traceable to failures on the part of the political party in power (for a sample of a host of recriminatory investigations by the American government after the Khobar Towers bombing in Saudi Arabia in June 1996, see Cohen, 2005).

Third, there is a scan for incidents of failure and ineptitude (as well as citations of heroism) on the part of first responders as part of the general search for responsibility and culpability. That such failures will have occurred is almost inevitable, both because of the fact that not all aspects of any attack can be anticipated in advance and because first responders invariably reveal failures of communication and coordination in their efforts to cope with the death, injury, and damage occasioned by an attack. The media lead the way in this search as well, out of their interest in uncovering what is newsworthy for a disturbed and news-hungry public. Class, ethnic, and racial conflict lurk behind the scenes, ready to surface, because in the aftermath of disasters, those with fewer resources (poor, minority, women) are typically more vulnerable (see, for example, Perry and Lindell, 1991) and less well treated

(Cutter, 1995)—for example, in the postdisaster sheltering of those made homeless (Bolin, 1994).

A parenthetical assessment of the reactions to Hurricane Katrina, which struck the Gulf Coast in late August 2005, is apt at this moment. While not a terrorist episode, its property destruction (though not its fatality rate) was comparable to the damage that would have occurred in a nuclear explosion. The event also afforded tragic (and magnified) confirmation of all the regularities of response following a disaster— a convergence of national attention on the area; a rush to aid, mal-coordination, conflict and paralysis of federal, state, and local re-sponse agencies; a season of blame and scapegoating; and the appear-ance of issues of racial and class conflict. The relevance of the chaotic response for terrorism was not lost, as evidenced when Senator Susan Collins (R-Maine), head of the Senate Homeland Security Committee, commented:

> If our system did such a poor job when there was no enemy, how would the federal, state and local governments have coped with a terrorist attack that provided no advance warning and that was intent on causing as much death and destruction as possible? (*New York Times*, 2005d)

Other critics raised the question of whether the fight against terror— especially the Iraq War—was not a misguided national priority, and whether excessive funding and a drain on resources because of the war on terrorism had left us wanting in the capacity to deal with cata-strophic natural disasters (*San Francisco Chronicle*, 2005).

The final political reaction to terrorist events involves two more positive political demands, each shaped, respectively, by the identifi-cation of the perpetrator of the act and assignment of culpability for not preventing or not responding properly to it. There are immediate demands for revenge against proven and suspected perpetrators, and simultaneous demands for the improvement of defense and the hard-ening of targets. It is a near axiom that the latter follow the logic of the attack itself (if biological poisoning, then the bolstering of detection devices and public health authorities, if an air attack, then the bolster-ing of airline security), on the general principle that the most urgent defense against terrorism is against the most recent type of attack.

Because of the immediacy and stridency of these demands, there is corresponding pressure on the opposition party not to oppose those measures of revenge and defense, both out of patriotic impulse and out of a desire not to be discredited in the eyes of a public angrily demanding action. This dynamic, moreover, plays into the perpetual cat-and-mouse game between target societies and terrorists, the former attempting to defend against what has just been attacked, the terrorists seeking new lines of attack.

Out of this dynamic of terror of future attack there also arises an inevitable tension between the hunger for security and safety and a democracy's tradition of civil liberties. This is a universal problem in societies subjected to terrorism (Wilkinson, 2001), and there seems no way for a democracy to avoid it. In the heat following a terrorist attack, particularly a major one, all the pressure is on surveillance, apprehension, imprisonment, and deportation (Sidel, 2003). So the impulse is for government to be aggressive and the opposition not to oppose. Equally surely, however, as time goes on, deep political divisions on the issue of security versus liberty will develop, if for no other reason than that this issue strikes at an aspect of democracy that is perhaps its most sacred item of political commitment. This tension is yet another instance of a kind of entrapment situation that is created for a democratic society under threat of attack. It produces:

Entrapment 4. The inescapable and apparently irresolvable tug-of-war between ensuring security against attack and preserving a sacredly regarded civil liberties. This issue will be treated in greater detail in the next section.

Longer-Term Economic, Political, and Cultural Consequences

Economic Consequences

The economic consequences of terrorism stand somewhere between the effects of disasters and the effects of wartime, including ingredients of both but not identical to either.

With respect to the locality affected—depending on the nature of the attack, and its degree of localization, and whether it is immediate or gradual in its effects—the economic effects of terrorism can be grouped under three headings: immediate postdisaster, recuperation, and longer-term recovery. These phases do not differ appreciably from those observed after disasters in general (Dacy and Kunreuther, 1969). The first concentrates on casualties and property damage. The second is characterized by rescue, caring, and cleanup activities and involves the inflow of funds from government relief agencies, humanitarian organizations, insurance companies, and private persons, many of whom offer free but nonetheless economically significant services, such as sheltering the homeless. The third phase, melding with the second, involves an inflow of capital and labor to rebuild and reconstruct the community. In contrast to the first two phases, in which the community suffers and responds to serious economic loss, recovery may be an economic blessing in disguise (ibid., p. 168), because, like all investment projects, it stimulates employment and local spending and improvement and modernization through replacement. In the wake of several disasters in the United States, subsequent research showed that growth of the share of the local Gross National Product was higher than previous forecasts had indicated (Hewings and Okuyama, 2003). This effect has been challenged, however, by the argument that local gains are offset by losses incurred outside the community as voluntary and government agencies channel resources into the affected locality (DeVoe, 1997). All these findings relate to more or less focused disasters. New and staggering economic scenarios emerge when we envision mass biological and chemical attacks (see Kaufmann, Meltzer, and Schmid, 2004).

As a rule, terrorist attacks are simultaneously local and national (and often international) in their ramifications, in contrast to many other kinds of disasters, whose most effects are mainly local. (An exception is the gigantic tsunami disaster of December 2005, which became instantly international.) Correspondingly, the spread of economic effects is wider. In the wake of September 11, New York City experienced "serious short-term dislocations on . . . workers in low-wage occupations" (Parrott and Cooke, 2005), which, however, restabilized; in addition, the insurance costs for the city and its business rose to sometimes prohibitively high levels (Swabish and Chang, 2005). More generally, economic hardships were experienced for a time by foreign and domestic airlines, tourist industries (including hotels, restaurants, and conventions), and entertainment industries. Energy prices rose. Corporate debt and bankruptcies increased. Compensating for these were economic improvements for passenger transport other than airlines, expenditures to build up the "security business," and profits in minor areas such as sales of flags and other patriotic symbols and souvenirs (Alexander and Alexander, 2002). Most of these reactions are explicable on the same principle that people react in fear of another disaster like the most recent one. Most of the economic effects, moreover, tend to abate as public apprehension subsides. A subsequent attack or series of attacks, however, may be expected to produce a similar pattern of selective economic distortions.

If the threat of terrorism elevates to the level of a national crisis of indefinite duration, then the resemblances to a wartime economy become more evident. The United States did not experience these effects in the last four decades of the twentieth century, despite the increasing seriousness of international terrorism and spectacular events such as the bombing of the World Trade Center in 1993 and the Murrah building in Oklahoma City in 1995. The September 2001 attacks, however, did create such a crisis. It brought with it more lasting economic effects, such as higher government expenditures for the military, financing a sizable security force for the airline industry, beefing up immigration and border control operations, spending on hardening targets by the Department of Homeland Security and other agencies (see Alexander, 2004), and a general acceleration of the security and surveillance economies (Organisation for Economic Cooperation and Development, 2004). Not least, finally, the country initiated two significant and costly military campaigns in the name of the war on terrorism and created a quasi-wartime economy. At the same time, the increase in overall defense spending did not reach the percentage of gross domestic product realized in the cold war, and contributed less to the federal deficit than the downturn in the economy and the tax cuts did (Lenain, 2004).

One consequence of this economic skewing, especially in public expenditures, is the likelihood that the drain on the public purse will downgrade other government commitments to a lower priority. Medical and welfare expenditures, education, and environmental budgets are likely to feel the squeeze. Wartime in general is notable for postponing social reforms in the interest of maximizing the war effort, and terror-threatened societies are no exception, as endless possibilities and pressures for defense and security spending build. Such skewing inevitably spills over into political conflict, deepening the political fissures along guns-butter and conservative-liberal political lines.

More remote long-term economic effects can also be anticipated. To mention only one, one of the by-products of heightened sensitivity to movement across the borders has been to create obstacles to the participation of many international scholars and students in the academic and scientific life of the country, to which internationals have contributed much in the past. The impact on recruitment to science and industry is not known precisely but is likely to be adverse. The same development has stimulated competition for recruitment on the part of European and Australian universities to capitalize on the political difficulties of entering the United States and to improve their scientific and human capital. As is the case with political ramifications, the remote and indirect economic impulses stimulated by terrorism and the fear of it are subtle and endless.

Political Consequences

Some of the longer-term political processes involve an elaboration of the search for responsible parties. The new tone that enters is one of partisan divisions over all these issues and over the issue of how to deal with the threat of terrorism. Among the manifestations as they appear in American polity (but also to some degree in all democracies) are the following:

- In the wake of attack, the party in power is almost compelled by the sweep of public outrage to become the official party of revenge. It cannot be passive. This impulse arises both from the pressure of immediate public opinion and from expectable partisan expectations that if the government does not act aggressively, it will lose public favor. This point applies to both political parties—whichever is in power—though partisan differences clearly put their stamp on the response. It is difficult to imagine, for example, that a Gore administration, established in power in January 2001, would not also have taken an aggressive international response to the events of September 11. It is not difficult to imagine, however, that that response might not have included an invasion of Iraq, because that administration would have been more distant from that issue than the Bush administration, given the special entanglement of the Bush family history with Iraq and Saddam Hussein.

- The opposition party is placed at a disadvantage in this circumstance, because to oppose toughness, which smacks of weakness, opens the opposition to suggestions of disloyalty and to constituency anger. As a result, the opposition party cannot comfortably oppose the impulse for revenge. Over time, however, divisions appear over issues of effectiveness of the execution of the response, misconduct, accusations as to which party is more diligent or "softer," criticism of side effects (neglect of health, education, and welfare), and profiteering.

- The tension between security concerns and civil liberties continues, dividing the polity along hawk-libertarian lines. Both major political parties contain both hawks and libertarians, so the division is not exactly partisan, but the struggles nevertheless take on partisan overtones. These and other forms of partisan conflict in a period of prolonged terrorist threat are rooted in two circumstances. First, the fact that national elections occur either regularly or in a constitutional rhythm means that the political parties seize on whatever issues they can to gain electoral advantage, and these issues include national security. Second, because the terrorist threat is a general and unknown one, manifesting itself in attacks only from time to time, the urgency for bipartisan solidarity tends not to be as great as it is in all-out war.

Solutions to bitter political divisiveness as an inevitable component of the politics of terrorist fear are hard to come by, and some might argue that solutions are not wanted, because they would diminish political opposition and government accountability. One could imagine, however, bold initiatives, both in Congress and the Executive branch, to institutionalize preparation for and response to terrorist threats as fully bipartisan enterprises, insulating those activities, to a degree, from the daily rough and tumble of partisan politics. Imperfect models of this insulation might be found in the long-term British response to terrorism emanating from Northern Ireland and in Israel's approach to its own security. I will return to the issue of partisanship in the final chapter.

A quick look at pre-9/11 political history. Because September 11, 2001, escalated the attention of politicians, policy makers, the media, and the citizenry to an unprecedented level, and because we still live daily with the repercussions of those events, it is tempting to treat the present as a new world, to which the previous history of terrorism and efforts to deal with it are not relevant. This is an error. Many nations have a history of defending against terrorism, and a reading of that history reveals that little is new in our contemporary responses, with the possible exception of the salience of American unilateralism, bred by the extremity of the historical events of 2001.

In 1994, shortly after the bombing of the World Trade Center, a number of scholars attempted to step back and assess the twenty-five years of political response to terrorism on the part of several of the countries most directly affected by it—the United Kingdom, Germany, Italy, France, Israel, and the United States (Charters, 1994b). Their declared purpose was to analyze the effect of national responses on civil liberties, but in effect they also included consideration of the nature of the terrorist threat each country faced and touched on all the major governmental and public responses to it. The following general points emerged from their analyses:

- Each country undertook some "restructuring of the organization chart" (Wilson, 1994) for dealing with terrorism. This meant a mix of redefining responsibilities for some agencies, creating new agencies, and creating new coordinating machinery. Every country experienced turf wars of varying severity (for example, among different police and military branches in all countries, between the central government and the *Lnder* in Germany, among different federal agencies in the United States). In some instances decisive action was delayed or deflected by jurisdictional rivalries and jealousies.
- Each country redefined the responsibilities of or created new military and paramilitary organizations for fighting terrorism.

- Each country introduced legislative or administrative measures that strengthened the hand of intelligence, security, and military agencies, particularly with respect to investigation, arrest, and detention.
- Each country pursued or agreed to join in a diversity of bilateral and multilateral international agreements to counter terrorist activity.
- Each country pursued some policy of hardening targets—arguably the easiest line of action for governments—that were thought to be most vulnerable to terrorists (important personages, airports, train stations, and publicly significant buildings).
- Each country experienced public demand for strong governmental action to protect the lives of its citizens, which led in turn to pressures to curtail civil liberties in different ways. However, "international terrorism did not prove to be the major destabilizing threat to liberal democracies . . . neither did the responses of those states realize the worst fears regarding the demise of civil liberties" (Charters, 1994a, p. 223). Citizens were subjected to the daily harassments of inspection and search associated with target hardening; Great Britain in particular imposed restrictions on the press. In some cases overzealous interrogation and arrest were recorded. In the United States, mainly because most of its terrorist experience consisted of attacks on American installations abroad, there was very little terrorist-related political intrusion domestically (Wilson, 1994). This situation changed dramatically, however, in 1996, when after a period of stalled efforts to legislate, the Oklahoma City bombing precipitated the passage of the Anti-Terrorism Act, which made it a crime to support terrorist activities and strengthened the government's power in a number of areas (Cole and Dempsey, 2002). Again, in the wake of September 11, 2001, the hastily passed Patriot Act extended federal arrest and interrogation powers, authorized greatly increased surveillance and more aggressive sanctions against foreign nationals (Farnam, 2005), and permitted a number of intrusions on the privacy and traditional rights of citizens. Both pieces of legislation have proved controversial and of unknown effectiveness in diminishing the threat of terrorism.

- Aggressive policies toward terrorists were often the source of political opposition and partisan division. This was least true in Israel, the most beleaguered of the nations, and perhaps most true in West Germany, which was living with the memories of the Nazi era (Sobiek, 1994).
- Almost all counterterrorist measures were reactive, that is, selectively introduced in the face of some major incident or in the face of terrorists' choices of new targets. Even in Israel, thought to be the most comprehensive and forward thinking in its counterterrorism, the pattern showed evidence of responding selectively to new sources of danger (Gal-Or, 1994). Terrorists, on their side, were also opportunistic. When the United States moved to improve airport security in the early 1970s, hijackers turned to less secure airports, mainly in the Third World. When airport security made hijacking more difficult, they turned to the sabotage of aircraft. When embassies were converted into garrisons in the 1980s, terrorists turned to other targets (Wilson, 1994) Two games were consistently played—catch-up by countries under terrorist attack, and cat-and-mouse on the part of terrorists.

Great differences among countries' strategies were observed. France was slow to develop antiterrorist measures at all, in part because it was wed to its historical role of providing asylum for political refugees (Harrison, 1994). Italy relied on compromise and partial amnesty, and its response was also limited by its continuing ties to Arab countries (Evans, 1994). Because of the constancy and seriousness of the IRA presence, Britain's antiterrorist measures were perhaps the most extreme (Warner, 1994). Differences in level of politicization over terrorism also were seen. The West German government was pummeled alternately for its aggressiveness and its passivity. The embarrassing American failure in the rescue efforts of the Iran hostages in 1980 is thought to have cost Jimmy Carter a second term (though other factors, such as soaring interest rates, also contributed), and the subsequent Iran-Contra arms-for-hostages scandal was a serious blight on the presidency of Ronald Reagan, whose shrill antiterrorist rhetoric of "no concessions" was undermined by the event.

Finally, it is almost impossible to assess unequivocally the overall effectiveness of the various nations' responses to terrorism. Some spectacular successes occurred, especially in the rescue of hostages; some targets of terrorism were made safer, and some statistical analyses showed periods of decline in terrorist activities. However, so many determining causes were at work that it is impossible to isolate and assess the general effects of the counterterrorism efforts (Charters, 1994a, pp. 214ff.).

Cultural Consequences

Terrorist events and episodes, however minor, are psychologically traumatic to varying degree for those affected directly—the wounded, the survivors, and the intimates of victims. These results, however, vary greatly in their collective significance for target societies. Some events, such as one-time assaults on an abortion clinic, make news for a moment but disappear from consciousness until another occurs. Some, such as the World War II bombing of Hiroshima and Nagasaki and the era of lynching of blacks in the American South in the late nineteenth and twentieth centuries, become a scar on the national conscience but remain largely latent. Some, such as the prolonged periods of violence in Northern Ireland and Israel, become "normalized" and are assimilated into the ongoing life of the affected population. Some, such as natural disasters that severely disable an entire community, may shape that community's life permanently and become a landmark that defines its cultural outlook indefinitely (Erikson, 1976).

It is worth commenting on recent terrorist events in the United States from the standpoint of cultural impact. Those that have been minor or that have failed (such as the attempted bombing at the Atlanta Olympic games in 1996) make big news but recede relatively rapidly. However, the bombing of the World Trade Center in 1993 and the bombing of the Murrah building in Oklahoma City in 1995) stand out, the first because it was the first foreign attack on American soil since the War of 1812 and nearly succeeded, the second because it was of such magnitude and was a product of home-grown terrorism. Both implanted themselves in the national consciousness and raised apprehensions about terrorism to new levels.

The destruction of the World Trade Center and the damage to the Pentagon on September 11, 2001, dwarfed all other events. It was and remains of such magnitude that it is likely to stand as a cultural demarcation comparable to the Civil War or the attack on Pearl Harbor for generations to come. A few comments on the cultural significance of 9/11 conclude this chapter.

In contemplating this cultural significance, it is helpful to refer to the notion of *cultural trauma*, a framework that has gained currency in studies by historians, anthropologists, sociologists, and psychologists in the past two decades (for a recent psychoanalytic view, see Wirth, 2005). Based originally on an analogy to psychological trauma, the ingredients of cultural trauma are its shocking and tragic character; its perceived assault on the cultural fundamentals of a society; its indelibility, that is, the incapacity of the affected society to forget it; a compulsion to remember and commemorate it; and periodic, politicized contestations over how it should be remembered. Historical illustrations of cultural traumas are the Holocaust in Nazi Germany and other major episodes of ethnic cleansing, the Great Depression in the United States, the Reign of Terror in revolutionary France, and the assassination of President John F. Kennedy (see Alexander, Yonah, and Pluchinsky, 2004).

September 11 and its aftermath reveal all the elements of cultural trauma:

- The immediate aftermath was a reaction of shock, disbelief, emotional numbing, and an incredible violation of the nation.
- Widespread and collective mourning, both spontaneous and official, occurred.
- There was an immediate sense of the indelibility of the events, along with the sense that it would not be forgotten, could not be forgotten, and ought not to be forgotten.
- An indefinite period of national brooding over the events followed, akin to a repetition compulsion.
- There was a collective endowment of the events with a sacred quality, not exactly religious in character, but a recognition that the events were supremely monumental.
- Deliberate efforts to remember September 11 emerged in the form of commemorative monuments and the formal noticing of anni-

versaries. This included a great deal of contestation and negotiation over how best to remember the events (Abrams, Albright, and Panofsky, 2004; Young, 2005; Smelser, 2004b).

Although the immediate effect of the trauma of September 11 was to stimulate solidarity and collective resolve, an inevitable element of politicization became apparent, focusing in particular on how the United States ought to respond (and has responded), and a sustained contestation among interested parties (including political parties) over the issues of national revenge, national loyalty, and ownership of the meaning of the trauma.

It remains to be seen whether September 11—and international terrorism in general—will be a major part of the national agenda, say, fifty years hence (for a discussion of contingencies, see chapter 7). In the shorter run, however, it is essential to acknowledge the events' traumatic essence, because they constitute a defining backdrop that will frame how other terrorist events will be assessed, how foreign policies will debated and adopted, how wars will be waged, how politicians will defend themselves and attack others, and how elections will be contested. In a word, the nation's history to come in the next several decades will not be understood without reference to the pervasive cultural trauma of September 11, 2001, and its evolving memory.

CHAPTER 6

Discouraging Terrorism

DISCOURAGING terrorism, the subject of this chapter, overlaps with the idea of responding to it, the topic of the previous chapter. Proper preparation and training of the population for attacks and equipping and training first responders help make terrorist attacks less damaging, thus indirectly discouraging them. It is appropriate, however, to treat the topic of discouragement in its own right, because it includes so many additional facets. I take up the subject as systematically as I can in this chapter, concentrating not so much on logistics and technology as on the human dimensions of discouragement—the psychological, social (especially the organizational), economic, and political aspects.

In many respects this chapter is written as a mirror image of the results reported in chapter 2 (conditions and causes), chapter 3 (ideology), and chapter 4 (motivation and group processes). This strategy is based on the axiom that all the determinants of contemporary terrorism are simultaneously aspects of its vulnerability and points of potential intervention to discourage it. Knowledge of those determinants, moreover, can inform us about the relative fruitfulness of different strategies of discouragement.

Introduction: An Excursion into the Semantics of Defense

Just as the semantics of terrorism are fraught with ambiguities and conflict, so are the corresponding defensive strategies against it. It is useful, by way of introducing this chapter, to sketch some of the territory and to reveal how the semantic differences only partially conceal policy preferences. The language is that set of terms used to describe the adaptive posture of target societies. From the standpoint of domestic terrorism, target societies include all societies that have experienced terrorism, and the long list would include the United States, many European countries, Egypt, Saudi Arabia, Indonesia, and many others. The main counterterrorist strategies against domestic terrorism have been surveillance, police powers, and the exercise of criminal law. With respect to contemporary international terrorism, the target societies are mainly the economically developed Western democracies, along with their presence in other countries. In this introductory section I concentrate on the language of contending with international terrorism.

- *Defending* against terrorism is perhaps the most reactive of the terms used, because in its minimum meaning it takes the threat of terrorism as given and works to control the borders and other points of entry, to intercept weapons, and to harden targets in foreign lands and in the home country. It could be extended to include disruption of terrorist activities at their source, but that is not the main connotation. *Maintaining homeland security* is the term activated in the legislation after September 11, 2001, and embodied in the cabinet department of that name; its connotations are much the same as those of *defending*, with international operations considered as separate issues and consigned to other agencies.
- *Preventing* is a broader term, subsuming *defending* but extending to intervention in terrorist operations abroad through intelligence, disruption, and possible intervention by special forces or military units. *Preventing* also connotes the possibility of invulnerability; that is if properly prevented, terrorist events will not occur.
- *Countering* is also a more inclusive term, encompassing multiple lines of adaptation, but like any term that uses *counter*—counteraction and counterintelligence, for example—the term implies acting to contain the effects of terrorist actions by employing defensive means against them.
- *Deterring* is a more specialized term. It refers to inducing fear or placing at risk things that terrorists hold dear. The concept was honed and applied in the cold war and referred mainly to West-Soviet relations. It is partially, but only partially, applicable to con-

temporary terrorism because of the peculiar motivations and cultural factors infusing terrorist movements (Davis and Jenkins, 2002; Friedman, 2004; Smelser and Mitchell, 2002a).

- The term *war on terrorism,* a concept activated from time to time in the past several decades and made the more or less official language of the administration of President George W. Bush since September 11, is the most proactive term, suggesting going after terrorists at their source before they come after us, and shrouding itself—as did the "war on crime," "war on poverty," and "war on drugs"—with legitimizing military symbolism, a sense of urgency, and advocacy of direct attacks, including preemptive strikes.

In my estimation, none of these terms is adequate to the realistic situation of international terrorism in our times. Each selects out—most often implicitly—a limited causal model of what terrorism is and what its threats are, and correspondingly points to only a limited repertoire of adaptive responses.

For reasons that will become clear in the analysis in this chapter, I prefer the word *discouragement* to capture not only the essence of terrorism but also the task of taking adaptive actions against it. There are several reasons for this preference, but the main ones are the following: (1) the term acknowledges the need for a struggle against terrorism, but at the same time recognizes that that struggle is, in the nature of the case, probabilistic, contingent, long term, and never fool-proof; and (2) the term is a comprehensive one, implying a multiplicity of adaptive strategies. The analyses in chapters 2 through 4 revealed that the conditions and causes of terrorism are themselves comprehensive and differ in generality and significance in the value-added process that determines terrorist activity. It follows that our consideration of adaptive strategies against terrorism ought to correspond in complexity to the range of conditions and causes behind it. Not all of these strategies can be regarded as equally realistic or effective. After evaluating a more or less complete repertoire of strategies of discouragement, I develop a critical analysis of the contemporary American approach and sketch a more positive statement of discouragement to which I give the name "death by strangulation."

A Schematic Representation of Strategies
of Discouragement

Following the principle that the catalogue of strategies of discouragement of terrorism parallels the catalogue of the conditions and causes of terrorism, I list the following strategies:

- To take initiatives to modify the political, economic, demographic, and cultural conditions that constitute the broadest background for the rise of terrorism, as well as for generating and sustaining audiences supportive of it. This range of conditions has come to be referred to as "root causes." Focusing on these causes aims to influence the impulses and motives of terrorism by modifying their most general determinants.
- To attack terrorist activity at its source. This strategy includes assembling reliable intelligence; infiltrating and disrupting terrorist operations; choking off their access to financial resources and weapons; engaging in military operations (including war) against terrorist organizations and governments that harbor, support, encourage, or permit them; and applying sanctions against and using persuasion to influence host societies to cooperate in repressing, disrupting, or neutralizing terrorist activities.
- To discredit or undermine ideologies that constitute a core element of the motivation of terrorist groups. This strategy includes both propaganda and shaping policies and actions in a way that minimizes confirming evidence for those ideologies.
- Closely related, to attempt to diminish support and sympathy for terrorism from its various audiences.
- To monitor and control movements of both people and weapons at the nation's borders and other entry points. This is one of the most salient ingredients of homeland security.
- To "harden" potential targets of terrorism (airplanes, buildings, electrical systems, dams, and the like) in such a way that makes them more inaccessible to attack and susceptible to less damage if attacked. The "discouraging" aspect of this strategy is to make attacks less attractive by increasing their risks and reducing their

payoffs. Hardening is in part a matter of applied technologies of detection but inevitably it involves human dimensions as well— in administering the technology, guarding, and identifying and apprehending suspects.

Getting at the Root Causes

In principle, this strategy has appeal because it rests on the assumption that if the basic causes of a phenomenon are eradicated, then the phenomenon itself will wither, if not disappear. An example of this line of reasoning is found in a recent book entitled *Nonviolent Response to Terrorism* (Hastings, 2004). The blurb listing of the long-term structural causes that are to be addressed includes "halting the arms trade and militarism, stopping arms flow to terrorists, 'defunding' the military, building sustainable and just economies, aid to the poor, reducing privileged over-consumption, peace and conflict education, using the media, refugee repatriation, and helping indigenous struggles." In a more focused analysis, Cragin and Chalk (2003) argue for a strategy of economic and social development as an approach to inhibiting terrorism. In practice, this line of analysis is fraught with a number of complexities and questionable assumptions that do not destroy its value but do limit it as a strategy of discouragement.

The discussion of root causes has become inextricably involved in bitter partisan divisions in this country. Its advocates often (but not always) frame their recommendations in the context of a worldview that encompasses (variably) elements of pacifism, sympathy with the less privileged, social justice, concern for environment, and a wholesale indictment of America's economic, political, and military role in the world—a worldview associated with the longstanding efforts of Noam Chomsky (1999, 2003) and others. (Chomsky wrote a favorable blurb message for the Hastings book.) Predictably, this context feeds into the deep and overlapping partisan divisions between dove and hawk, left and right. Critics from the latter charge "America hating" and covert sympathy with terrorists, and regard the whole notion of root causes as an unacceptable deviation from the "real" moral and criminal "causes" (for a firsthand account of this division, see the box entitled "Politicizing the Causes of Terrorism"). The resulting division is as unproductive as it is absolute and seemingly irreconcilable.

Politicizing the Causes of Terrorism

The Committee on Science and Technology for Countering Terrorism was convened by the National Academies within a matter of months after the attacks on New York and Washington on September 11, 2001. This group was composed of two dozen eminent scientists, engineers, public health experts, and a few persons who had held positions in the federal government or had undertaken activities related to terrorism for it. The group proceeded very expeditiously, and within a year the influential report, *Making the Nation Safer* (Committee on Science and Technology for Countering Terrorism, 2002), made its appearance.

The greatest part of the report was understandably dedicated to the role that scientific knowledge might play in defending against and responding to terrorism. The co-chairs and members of the committee felt, however, that a few pages ought to be devoted to the origins, causes, and significance of terrorism in our time, intended as orienting material for readers.

The first attempt to prepare these pages was undertaken by a few members of the committee, but the product of their work raised significant controversy in the committee. Their draft pages had a high moral tone, using the term "evil" freely (the phrase "axis of evil" had recently been introduced into the political dialogue by President George W. Bush). The pages described contemporary terrorism as primarily the work of fanatics, and made wholesale comparisons with the fascist movement in Nazi Germany and other reprehensible historical episodes. The explicit "causal" framework was that the causes of terrorism were its agents themselves, and, by implication, to understand where they came from and why was of little or no interest.

A number of us—I suppose I was the ringleader—took objection to this language, not because we had any positive disposition toward terrorism, but on the grounds that the message was too ideological in character and that such language had no place in a science-based report. In response to the controversy the co-chairs asked me—as one of the two social scientists on the committee and as chair of its subpanel on social and behavioral aspects—to write some alternative pages. I did so, being careful to use the most neutral language I could. My draft, however, did emphasize the current international power situation, economic penetration of non-Western societies, and demographic imbalances in the (mainly Middle Eastern) societies from which international terrorism was emanating—factors that fall under the heading of "root causes." My draft also represented the ongoing thinking of the subpanel I chaired.

Far from clarifying or settling the situation, my draft created another tempest. It raised strong objections on the part of the small group that had drafted the initial language, who labeled my prose "ideological" and to be dismissed as unacceptable social science thinking. In the face of this kind of polarization, the co-chairs did the only thing that was possible. They deemed both versions unusable. As a result, the report says very little about the background material we thought would be useful in the first place. I considered this paralysis to be a bittersweet victory in that our own sub-panel, given complete freedom by the parent committee, was able to proceed with its own line of analysis and incorporate it in its own independent report, *Terrorism: Perspectives from the Behavioral and Social Sciences* (Smelser and Mitchell, 2002a).

The political issues involved in this skirmish were, of course, much larger than the particular language to be incorporated in a particular report. One line of response to the terrifying aspects of terrorism is a primarily moral one: to think in terms that match, sometimes point for point, the kind of moral justification that terrorists themselves live by (I discuss this tendency in chapter 3). This response often involves the idea that terrorists (or terrorism) are our known and detested enemy, and that the main job is to repress or destroy them and protect our nation. This is an understandable and perhaps predictable response. It is certainly the response that dominated the thinking of the incumbent administration of President Bush, and it is reasonable to suspect that a similar ideological response would have developed if the other national party and another president had been in power. The further implication of this kind of response is that there is neither need nor place for understanding contemporary terrorism, because we already know what we have to know about it. A further twist to this is a certain antagonistic belief: that to understand the economic, political, and demographic conditions that give rise to terrorism in the world—in some of which the policies and practices of the United States are surely implicated—lies on the road to forgiving or, worse yet, sympathizing with the terrorist forces. In this process a dispassionate understanding of causes and conditions—to which the social sciences can contribute—becomes politically suspect, as do the scientists who strive for this understanding.

I found an extreme rendition of this political opposition to understanding voiced by Gill (2002), a former police officer and member of the National Security Advisory Board in India. He described terrorism as "the gravest threat, not only to individual nations, not, indeed, just to the entire civilized world, . . . but possibly, even to the long-term survival of the human race" (ibid., p. 1). In the context of this reasoning, he attacked a mentality of "unyielding moral ambivalence" toward terrorism, which has "insidious expressions." Under this heading of dangerous thinking, he includes the search for causes of terrorism:

> The most powerful and tenacious line of intellectual reasoning . . . is the "root causes" [poverty, unemployment, illiteracy, historical wrongs] that has embedded itself in the liberal-democratic and "human rights" discourse on terrorism. Much of this discourse is, of course, motivated—orchestrated by front organizations of terrorist groups who seek to exploit the instrumentalities of democracy to destroy democracy . . . it has progressively been translated into a justification and an alibi for terrorism. (ibid., p. 3)

In the same spirit, Maley argued "[if] a mad dog invades one's house, it is rarely an adequate response to write out a cheque for rabies research" (2002, p. 83).

While these are extreme formulations, they underscore the ready possibility of converting the effort to understand into a political threat. The unfortunate consequence of this polarization is that it tends to encourage blindness with respect to understanding and rules out the reasonable possibility that one can be simultaneously horrified by and antagonistic toward terrorism but at the same time make an effort to understand its origins. Such understanding, indeed, widens the possibility of knowing how to contend with it.

This polarization over causes may not be limited to scholarly debates, but may spread more widely into politics. It is likely to become assimilated to wider political divisions between hawks and doves, even conservatives and liberals. It is likely to affect decisions on the part of agencies about what they want to know about terrorism in their efforts to confront and defend against it. And it may spread into research-funding agencies (including the Homeland Security Department) and affect their priorities for distributing research grants concerning terrorism.

In the few comments that follow, I attempt to distance myself from this polarization and assess the validity of the proposition that an attack on structural conditions is an effective way to discourage terrorism. The following observations are in order:

- As indicated in the language of Entrapment 1, many of the evident causes of terrorism trace to centuries of history that are effectively beyond policy intervention. I refer, for example, to the world constellation of nation-states and the lack of correspondence between these units and the subnational identities and loyalties of ethnic, racial, linguistic, and religious groups. Other factors, such as world birth rates, are certainly beyond unilateral efforts on one nation's part, though cooperative efforts and assistance provided to willing countries may have a long-term effect. Still other measures, such as "helping indigenous movements" and the economic efforts of rich countries to equalize world income, are politically fraught and uncertain in their consequences (including the possibility that relative deprivation may increase as real deprivation is alleviated).
- To focus on the general structural conditions of terrorism as their effective cause is to ignore the principle that terrorism is the result of a complex combination and accumulation of conditions and causes and that, by the time actual terrorist activity crystallizes, it is not only remote from general influences but also develops an internal momentum largely independent of those causes (see chapter 4). Whatever influence that dealing with general economic and political conditions might have is more likely to be in the

realm of long-term effects on various audiences that are actual or potential supporters of the terrorism that they regard as protest against the United States and its policies.

- To make these points is not to denigrate the pursuit of enlightened, responsible, and humanitarian policies on the part of the United States and other wealthy and powerful countries. They are morally defensible and should be pursued in their own right. Furthermore, such policies and actions promise reap a range of beneficial long-term consequences for stability and peace in the world. They cannot accurately be extended to read, however, as a direct or effective defense against or "cure" for terrorism itself. It is difficult for one of generally liberal persuasion to come to these conclusions, and difficult to venture them without being drawn into the deep partisan divisions kindled by the "war on terrorism," but the conclusions seem to be consistent with what we know about the causes of terrorism.

Attacking Terrorism at Its Source

This range of discouragements is indifferent to its conditions and causes. It takes terrorism as a given reality and involves the proactive destruction or debilitation of terrorist countries, groups, and individuals, wherever they may be. It includes a range of options, from preemptive strikes to foiling attacks as they are about to occur. I begin with some critical observations on waging war on the phenomenon, and then turn to a more positive line of analysis.

The Attractions and Limitations of Dramatic and Massive Responses to Contemporary Terrorism

Two orienting observations are in order:

(1) It has been pointed out repeatedly by economists and political scientists interested in long-term planning and environmentalists that democratic systems based on relatively short-term electoral cycles are not conducive to long-term planning in these areas. The reason is that those aspiring to remain or accede to political office are well advised to

appeal to the perceived interests of significant constituencies, which are most often read as attending to bread-and-butter issues, maintaining law and order, and protecting the nation—all in their short-term significance. An extension of this reasoning is that with respect to terrorism, the interest of most is in their immediate safety and security. Politicians do best, it is perceived, when they score victories. There are compelling reasons to believe, however, that contemporary terrorism is a long-term phenomenon, ineradicable in the immediate term by either military action or hardening, and best discouraged by patient, coordinated, multilateral, and diversified approaches, including the method of "death by strangulation," to be discussed at the end of the chapter.

(2) When international threats of terrorism appear, or, even more, when a terrorist attack occurs, there arises an immediate public demand for retribution (see chapter 5). Writing two decades ago, Martha Crenshaw put the point forcefully:

> A vehement public reaction to terrorism may force the government to adopt policies that independent decision-makers would consider unwise. Public pressure increases governments' propensity to act, a tendency already encouraged by the apparent simplicity of the immediate response. . . . Terrorism frequently involves dramatic and emotional confrontations that attract publicity. The manner of the communication of the terrorist message in part determines perceptions of the content and influences the nature of public reaction. Because the suspense and horror of terrorism make it instantly newsworthy, its importance as a threat to stability may be exaggerated. (1983, p. 16)

Even if not in open evidence, the perceptions of such demands feed political leaders' assumptions that to do nothing or to respond clumsily and inadequately constitutes a political liability. Historical examples provide evidence for this principle. When the administration of Jimmy Carter, after long delays, bungled the dramatic rescue attempt of American hostages in Iran in April 1980, it was widely perceived to have hurt his political standing decisively. The nonresponse of the Clinton administration to the bombing of the Khobar Towers and the U.S.S. *Cole* also drew criticism. On the other side, President Reagan's aerial assault on the Qadaffi compound following the killing of American soldiers in a West Berlin nightclub in 1986 boosted his approval ratings.

President Putin's immediate and forceful response to the hostage taking at a Moscow theater in October 2002 drew strong public approval. Finally, the combative and unilateralist line voiced and acted upon by President George W. Bush in the years since September 11, 2001, has proved generally appealing to the American electorate, though support for this activist stance has waned as criticisms of the Iraq War have weakened public support for the administration.

As a general rule, then, the pressures generated by terrorist threats push toward immediate and dramatic responses by political authorities—to take a tough line. In the past several decades, the responses to major threats to the United States have been met by high-tech military actions, which have an immediate appeal because of their swiftness and their presumed efficiency. It is the kind of action at which the United States is best and strongest. Yet the effectiveness of this mode has proved equivocal, possibly counterproductive, as a review of the results of this mode in the wars of the last half-century reveals. Most of that period was dominated by the cold war, in which both superpower adversaries were paralyzed and prevented from attacking one another by the threat of retaliatory nuclear strikes. The United States engaged in four wars in that period—the Vietnam War, the Gulf War, the Afghan War following September 11, 2001, and the invasion of Iraq. All were high-tech wars from the American side. In the Vietnam War, this strategy proved highly destructive but ultimately futile against the guerrilla-like war of the enemy, and our military action resulted in heavy civilian casualties in Vietnam. Both factors—the stagnation of the war and the killing of civilians—provided the fodder for the domestic backlash against that war, which ultimately proved a major factor in the defeat of Hubert Humphrey, closely associated with the war as vice president in the administration of Lyndon Johnson, in the 1968 election.

The Gulf War was precipitated by Iraq's invasion of Kuwait, but antiterrorism was an overtone in the campaign against Saddam Hussein. The war was a dramatic success from an immediate military point of view, but the subsequent consequences attendant upon occupying the enemy's territory were not realized, for the simple reason that the first President Bush stopped short of invading and occupying the country and toppling the regime of Saddam Hussein. The Afghan War was explicitly an antiterrorist campaign against the Taliban government and the Al-Qaeda terrorist organization headed by Osama bin Laden. It was an immediate military success, but the continued presence of American forces in Afghanistan has been accompanied by periodic insurgent activity, mainly from surviving Taliban elements. The Iraq War, legitimized by assertions of Saddam Hussein's possession of weapons of mass destruction and by enveloping it in the rhetoric of a "war on terrorism," was also a stunning military success. Yet that war alienated many of America's closest allies, and its aftermath has been much more troubled than the Afghan situation, with widespread resentment of the presence of American forces and a situation of insurgency that, despite counterclaims about its success or failure, threatens to persist.

The apparent lesson from these wars brings to mind Caleb Carr's (2002) historical study of the counterproductive effects of the warfare against civilian populations, encompassing the military strategies in the Roman Empire, the Crusades, the Napoleonic Wars, and the American Civil War, among others. Though scarcely producing a universal historical law, Carr argued that the military killing of civilian populations has historically been unsuccessful in that it generates an irreducible alienation and motive for revenge in the decimated population. He went so far as to argue that "terror must never be answered with terror" (ibid., p. 13), even though he was careful not to argue for pacifism but, rather, for other means of counterterrorism. Counterexamples to his principle can be cited, particularly from World War II, in which both the Axis Powers and the Allies engaged in massive killings of civilian populations without creating the precise effects Carr posited. Nevertheless, it is worth entertaining the ideas that waging destructive military wars in the name of attacking terrorism—except in cases of direct involvement or sponsorship—carries with it prospect of endless counter productive effects. This applies even to the United States' contemporary aims of warfare: no American casualties, maximum enemy combatant casualties, minimum enemy civilian casualties. In the nature of the case, high-tech, target-specific operations have produced a great deal of collateral damage and a politically significant number of civilian casualties. Political reactions to these, furthermore, are by now international in character and not limited to the directly affected populations alone. To press this line of reasoning to its end, it can be argued that of the three American wars in which counterterrorism was in the mix of motives, the only apparent success in defeating international terrorism was the Afghan War, and that one has been sullied by the resurgence of Taliban forces.

Considerations such as these lead to the conclusion that dramatic military assaults on nations in the name of winning a war on terrorism are to be relied on sparingly, both because of their questionable effectiveness and because of their unwanted counterproductive effects. To advance this conclusion is to ask that political authorities in threatened or attacked countries act against their perceived short-term political interests, so the idea is advanced with limited hope of its consideration, despite its merit.

Intelligence

The gathering of intelligence on the nature of the enemy and the enemy's intentions, resources, plans, and intended activities is a central need in any form of conflict, and terrorism is no exception. There is something of a consensus in the literature on terrorism, moreover, that intelligence should be given the highest priority (for example, Simon, 1990).

Terrorism in its current international manifestations poses a number of special difficulties with respect to gathering intelligence:

- The contemporary terrorist situation of fluid, elusive, and mobile cells of potential imposes a new level of difficulty of tracking and infiltration, because the units are forever appearing and disappearing in different places and different forms.
- By their very nature, terrorist organizations must rely on secrecy, stealth, and surprise, and this places the highest priority on protecting information and leaving no records of it.
- Most cells and networks in the current situation are presumably composed of radical Muslims and share a culture that is distinctively geographic, linguistic, and religious; this is true whether they are located in the Middle East or drawn from Arab or Muslim

immigrants to other countries. It is extremely difficult for "foreigners" to penetrate these organizations.

- This difficulty is compounded by the additional fact that the cells
  are often recruited along kinship, friendship, neighborhood, and
  religious lines (see chapter 4). This means that internal knowledge,
  trust, loyalty, and suspicion of insiders are high, and skepticism
  of and antagonism toward strangers are extreme.

- Pooling of information regarding terrorist activities among different intelligence and security agencies is a longstanding and well-
  understood vulnerability of intelligence operations (National
  Commission on Terrorist Attacks Upon the United States, 2004).
  Most of the difficulties arise from the dynamics of jurisdictional
  jealousies and turf control. The problem is multiplied at the international level as national sensitivities are added to bureaucratic
  ones, despite the known usefulness of sharing intelligence on suspects, movements of persons, and organizations' activities. Infor-
  mation-sharing arrangements are typically stimulated by a major
  episode (September 11, the London Underground attacks of
  2005), when nations recognize, if only temporarily, their common
  interests. This underlies a maxim generally applicable to counterterrorist activities: things have to get worse before counterterrorism gets better.

Attacking Terrorist Organizations

Authorities' responses to domestic terrorist episodes have
been facilitated because they *are* domestic and can be dealt with by
single states and their authority and police systems, despite chronic
difficulties of coordination among agencies. The short lives of domestic
terrorist movements can be attributed in large part to the arrest of
leaders and political repression by the state (Ross and Gurr, 1989). Such
coordination of political response, however imperfect, can rarely be
realized at the international level. The police, military, and security
forces of nations that have been attacked or that face the threat of attack
cannot simply move into another country without authorization unless

the nation that has been attacked goes to war with the attacker or otherwise violates its sovereignty. Any intrusion on the activities of terrorist cells abroad, therefore, almost necessarily dictates a level of international cooperation. The impulse to cooperate, moreover, like the impulse to share, is dependent mainly on the realization on the part of cooperating nations that they have counterterrorist interests in common; that realization in turn typically becomes salient when an attack potentially threatening to all occurs. An example of acting out of common interest is the considerable success on the part of the Summit Seven (Canada, Great Britain, France, West Germany, and the United States) in the late 1970s and 1980s in containing hijacking and hostage taking (Levitt, 1988). The longstanding failure of the United Nations to reach either consensus or common action on terrorism reflects a corresponding lack of common interest (see chapter 2). Backsliding appears when the threat diminishes or when a controversial action is undertaken, such as the bombing of Libyan targets in 1987, which precipitated "sharp divisions between the United States and its European allies on how to deal with state-supported terrorism in general and Libya in particular" (ibid., p. 76). The sources of difficulty in cooperation include the following:

- Different national traditions and understandings of conflict. The permissive themes in France, Sweden, and Holland contrast with the more activist mode of Germany and the United States.
- Different population compositions and internal political geographies, to which political leaders are sensitive.
- Considerations of self-interest. For a nation to take a hard line out of deference to another country when it does not regard itself as immediately threatened may be seen domestically as way of increasing the threat of attack against itself. Such sentiments were a part of the politics of Britain, Spain, and Italy when these countries opted to cooperate with the United States in the Iraq war. Terrorists are aware of the political divisions that result, and the attacks on these countries were interpreted in many quarters as punishment that would not have been forthcoming had these countries not allied themselves with the American invasion.

What Kind of Force to Use and When to Use It

The framing rationale for this question is provided by an assessment of the structure of terrorism by Simmons and Tucker (2003). At the innermost layer is the terrorist organization itself, comprised of strategists and operatives firmly committed to the cause. In the layer immediately surrounding the terrorists are their supporters, who provide them logistical assistance and intelligence. The supporters in turn are protected by a layer of less active sympathizers. Then there are the neutrals. Finally, in the outer rings are individuals who oppose the terrorists, their methods, and their aims (see also Century Foundation Task Force Report, 2004, pp. 16–18).

This characterization, consistent with that of relevant audiences (see chapter 4), provides the basis for appreciating precisely how limited the arena for the deployment of force is and what kind of force that should be. Put simply, the only feasible locus for the employment of force is the innermost layer, because that is the locus of the exercise of force by terrorists. Efforts to use military force on supporters, sympathizers, and neutrals will be regarded by many (including citizens of the country applying that force) as misdirected and politically counterproductive, largely because such efforts are perceived as misdirected and inhumane violations of the sovereignty of other nations. The exception to this rule is the use of military force against nation-states that are themselves engaging in terrorist activities or are abetting or encouraging it. (The military attacks on Libya in 1987 and Afghanistan in 2001 would qualify on this count.) Other sanctions, mainly economic measures and diplomatic pressures, are the principal and appropriate means to be employed at the outer layers.

Because of the limited range of the appropriate use of force and the fleeting and elusive character of contemporary international terrorist cells, the evidently recommended modes of attack are strategic and surgical. Large-scale military operations and even strategic military strikes appear to be too grand, too blunt, and frequently unable to hit the mark. Nye (2004) put the issue in the following way:

[M]ilitary force is not the major source of the solution. Afghanistan provides a good example. The United States' skilful use of force was necessary and effective in defeating the Taliban government which had provided a safe haven for terrorists, but the war destroyed only a quarter or so of Al-Qaeda, which is a network organization with cells in sixty countries. Precision bombing is not an option for countering cells in Hamburg, Singapor [sic], or Detroit. (p. 210)

The logic of the structure of terrorism points toward alternative, more precisely directed uses of force. From the United States' point of view, the most effective approach would be to secure the cooperation and support of the police authorities of allied nations and neutrals with suspected terrorist networks and cells with them. This cooperation and support can take the form of supplying antiterrorist expertise, sharing intelligence, offering economic assistance, and working to improve extradition arrangements. The advantage of this form of cooperation has already been noted: internal police authorities have both better access to and greater legitimacy in controlling and disrupting the activities of domestic insurgents (including terrorist cells) than do outside intelligence, police, and military interventions.

Given the existing array of national antagonisms in the world, however, the United States is faced with the reality that it cannot secure cooperative relations with all other states. Even in these cases, directed and multilaterally exercised economic and diplomatic sanctions may have some effect in inducing inimical states to diminish their support or tolerance of terrorist activities. In the last analysis, however, since terrorism in its essence is violent, counterviolence (including unilateral forms) cannot be ruled out. The question is, what form should that take?

Many who write on terrorism point to the use of "special forces" in this regard—highly trained, small military units that engage in targeted, limited, and focused missions (Combs, 2003; Simmons and Tucker, 2003). Many nations facing terrorism have generated such units; some examples are the Egyptian Force 777, Israel's Sayeret Mat'Kal, Mista'Aravim, and Ya'Ma'M, France's Groupement d'Intervention de la Gendarmerie Nationale (GIGN), Germany's Grenzschutzgruppe 9 (GSG9) and the Kommando Speziallkraefte (KSK), and Russia's Alpha Units (Davies, 2003). American units in this genre are the Green Berets, the U.S. Army Rangers, and the U.S.

Navy's SEALs. These forms have advantage over larger-scale military and air operations because they are better tailored to the kinds of targets that international terrorism offers, because their intrusion is a lesser assault on the nation in which these targets are located, because they are not as likely to inflict civilian casualties, and because they are not likely to generate as much international political opposition as invading armies and devastating air attacks. The logic that calls for tailoring any war on terrorism to the nature of terrorism's war dictates that high priority be given to some, perhaps newly invented special strike forces, including international ones if that option ever becomes a realistic one for agencies such as NATO and the United Nations.

Stopping the Flow of Resources to Terrorists

Three kinds of resources were discussed in chapter 2—finances, weapons, and the media. I will make only brief supplementary comments about each, since the issue of effectiveness of efforts to control them was included in those discussions.

Finances. Choking off financial support for terrorist activities is clearly an effective mode of discouragement, and efforts to achieve this, mainly through international banking practices, have been attempted periodically, usually in response to major attacks. These efforts are constrained, however, by the countertendency of banks to serve whatever customers appear without clearing them in some way, and by the less than complete compliance in the world banking system. These efforts are also undermined by the adaptive capacities of terrorist organizations, which have shown ingenuity in turning to other sources, such as gems and drug dealing, and reliance on more informal and less detectable modes of transferring financial assets.

To point to these obstacles is not to recommend against efforts to make transparent the information on depositors and to freeze known and suspected accounts. In carrying out these efforts, two cautions appear essential. The first is that the effort to control finances is best understood within the frame of discouraging, not preventing; prevention will never be attained, and the maximum effect that can be hoped for is crippling, not fully starving. Second, the only realistic logic of pursuing financial constriction is a cooperative one, involving as it necessarily does the efforts of many governments and many banks and banking systems whose efforts must be courted, not dictated.

Weapons. The weapons for terrorists include those that have been and continue to be actually used—mainly guns and bombs—and that vast array of more destructive biological, chemical, and nuclear weapons of mass destruction. Several givens must be noted about the former: the omnipresence of small arms throughout the world and the willingness of suppliers to supply them, the simple and easily teachable technology of making and using conventional explosives, and the relative ease of smuggling arms. Systematic attempts to eliminate such weapons—beyond discouraging their possession and use through national criminal laws—involve such a comprehensive effort and such great expense that it appears inadvisable to place such attempts very high on the priority list of discouraging strategies.

Weapons of mass destruction are another matter. Though radioactive weapons have been used only once in history and chemical and biological agents on a mass basis have been used only once or twice, these constitute the most menacing specter. So unsettling is their spread to the security of the world and so destructive if ever deployed by terrorists that prevention of their availability and use has the highest priority in counterterrorist policy. The most immediate threat is the availability of unknown stocks of nuclear weapons in the former Soviet Union, but the acquisition of nuclear power and nuclear weapons by nations that do not now have them is also a clear and growing danger. Current modes of dealing with the issue of spread, however, appear to be carried out in an inherently unstable setting. Aspiring nations believe, realistically or not, that the possession and capacity to use weapons of mass destruction enhances their international clout and their defense against attack. The policies of the United States and its weapons-equipped allies simply to prevent the spread while maintaining gigantic destructive stockpiles themselves are realistic goals for those countries but are regarded as a source of continued domination by those who do not possess these weapons. The nub of the instability is that the status quo is unacceptable to the have-nots in both the short and the long run. The

possibilities for controlling chemical and biological weapons are perhaps more favorable. The world is not in the same stalemate of imbalance as it is with respect to nuclear weapons, and models based on
international agreements forged out of the common interests of most
nations—for example, the prohibition on the use of poison gas worked
out after World War I—constitute a more realistic path.

Media. The entire discussion of media as resource see (chapters 2 and
4) pointed to the conclusion that while the media are a clear resource
for terrorists, direct attempts to control the media by interested governments represent such a compromise of democratic principles and
such a source of internal division that this policy of discouragement
is not a feasible one. Self-developed codes for media with self-admin-
istered systems of monitoring and conduct are feasible, however, as
part of the institutionalization of professional responsibility on the
part of the media.

Influencing Audiences for Terrorism

Throughout the analysis I have stressed that terrorism is inevitably a political phenomenon from the standpoint of its course of
development, its aims, and the reactions it incites in nations that regard
themselves as its real or potential targets. Like political activities in general, the success of terrorism depends in great measure on the support,
indifference, or enmity of its audiences. Correspondingly, one of the
main ways to discourage terrorism is to delegitimize it and limit its
support from its main audiences.

This being acknowledged, it also has to be said that the pursuit of
this form of discouragement is among the most uncertain and is
fraught with possibilities of failure. These include the following:

- Some of terrorism's audiences are virtually inaccessible by influence, propaganda, or deed. In particular, these are the hard-core
  terrorists themselves and those groups that support their activities
  on ideological grounds. The dynamics of ideology are such that
  almost any word, message, or deed can be interpreted in ways to

be made consistent with the internal logic of that ideology. This suggests that efforts along public relations lines to influence these two audiences are likely to backfire.

- Other audiences—international friends, international neutrals, international critics, and less committed political groups in nations in which terrorism is bred—are more likely targets for influence. As I suggest in the next chapter, however, these groups tend to be influenced more by international policies and actions than by international words and media blitzes. In the end, however, these audiences are inevitably so diverse in orientation that any given posture will be regarded as positive by some, negative by others. The strategies in dealing with potential audiences almost always have to be calculated in relative gain-loss probabilities rather than as successful or unsuccessful in some absolute sense.

- The audience of world opinion, whether this is the United Nations, the international media, or a vaguely imagined world entity, is an especially elusive one, in large part because it is not an entity, and because one cannot have reliable knowledge about what it listens to or how it reacts. But world opinion cannot be ignored altogether, because, largely out of pluralistic ignorance, it is believed in by interested parties and continuously referred to as if it were real.

- Influencing international audiences on the issue of terrorism is invariably constrained by the necessity of dealing with internal audiences, whose responses may take the form of threats of partisan opposition by critics and desertion by friends on account of unpopular policies. In most democratic societies, courting domestic support trumps the interest in influencing international audiences, given the fundamental fact that the political survival of the party in power depends on the first but not the second.

The unsatisfactory conclusion emerging from these points is that attending to the diverse audiences of terrorism is an essential ingredient in discouraging it and must be taken into account in calculating strategies of counterterrorism, but at the same time it is the slipperiest and most uncertain of all means of discouragement.

Controlling the Movement of People

and Weapons

This strategy is carried out under the dual logic of prevention and deterrence: on the one hand, terrorist attacks requiring the
domestic presence and activity of agents will not occur if they can be
kept out of the country, and on the other hand, if barriers to entry and
the risk of apprehension are sufficiently raised, this will deter terrorists
from even trying to enter and may turn their efforts toward attacking
other relevant targets abroad.

With respect to the movement of people across domestic borders
and other points of entry, the problem is formidable, because the sheer
number of persons passing and entering for legitimate reasons (business, visiting, tourism) is so enormous as to sap the time, energy, and
resources of the agencies controlling this movement. Furthermore, if
wholesale restrictions were placed on the movement of people in and
out of the country, the economic costs would be significant and adverse
for our globally involved nation (and the economies of other nations).
The same principle applies to the movement of goods. It is virtually
impossible to track and check all cargo carried by airplanes, ships, and
motorized vehicles, and wholesale measures to restrict these transports
would be very damaging economically. Efforts to identify persons and
activities selectively are also an uncertain matter, given the current extent and ingeniousness of document forging. Finally, and with special
relevance to Mexico, systematic efforts to control the movement of potential terrorists across the Mexican-American border is inextricable
from the thorny problems of the legal importation of Mexican labors
as well as their illegal entry.

One special feature of the contemporary scene is that visas for
persons seeking to enter the United States for any purpose must be
approved by several agencies (namely, the Department of State, the
Department of Homeland Security, and the Federal Bureau of
Investigation). One would expect that, in enforced cooperative relations
such as these, a normal amount of jurisdictional competition would
develop. A special circumstance has arisen on top of this, however, in
the aftermath of the September 11 attacks. It is well known (National

Commission on Terrorist Attacks Upon the United States, 2004) that especially the FBI and CIA operated in many cases with laxness and inefficiency prior to those attacks. Their reputations were severely damaged, they have been the objects of various reforms, and as a result they are beleaguered. The State Department, while not so tarnished, is still aware that if it is found responsible for errors, it, too, is vulnerable.

These conditions are especially conducive to risk-aversive behavior on the part of the responsible agencies. The stakes are such that they do not pay a price if they refuse entry to any foreign national who appears at all suspicious, and they may be expected to pay a terrible price if they approve and let in someone who turns out to be an agent of terrorism. All agencies are intrinsically motivated to stay out of trouble, and especially so under these circumstances. The working motto becomes "when in doubt, keep them out," and not very much doubt is required because the stakes are so high. The results of an accumulation of these protective practices may be both economic and political. Economically, the resulting discouragement of talented scientists and students (many of whom are of value for our continuing scientific leadership and economic productivity) tends to send them elsewhere, and thereby has the effect of giving an edge to competitive scientific and business activities abroad. Politically, insofar as our tradition of civil liberties may extend to the treatment of internationals (as part of the definition of human rights), they may be seen to be unjustly treated if they are denied entry wrongly or without good cause. Furthermore, perceived hassling or mistreatment of foreign nationals often raises sensitive diplomatic issues with the governments of their home countries.

Hardening Targets of Terrorism

This strategy, located at the "end of the line" of the terrorist process, has two facets. The first is to put security arrangements in place so that terrorists cannot gain access to the targets. The most conspicuous example is the protection of aircraft through processing passengers and their belongings, using detection devices, locking pilots' cabin doors on aircraft, and other discouraging measures. Similar

security precautions can be observed in buildings of national significance (the White House, the Library of Congress, state capitols) and
at public gatherings of people at significant events (political conventions, the Super Bowl, the Olympic games). The second is to contain
the effects of attacks once they occur. Under this heading fall the engineering soundness of buildings, the use of backup electric generators,
preventing the spread of computer damage, and backing up information. Also included is the readying of human populations with knowledge of how to prepare for and respond to attacks in ways that will
limit death and injury. Both types of hardening have their "discouraging" aspect, which is to convey to potential terrorists that their aims
of destruction and the terror derived from it are difficult and less likely
to be successful.

Really Local Preparedness

It is generally agreed that the English model of preparation for heavy
bombings in London during 1940–41 had many strong points. There
was a formal, top-down warning system in place that involved siren
soundings and supply of information about where to go before and
during raids (underground stations, other shelters). In addition, however, there was a system of local air raid wardens who patrolled the
neighborhoods and personally directed and shepherded people during
times of danger. This local supplement made preparedness and reaction
a face-to-face community matter. In a completely different setting, the
Israeli government established a Civil Guard shortly after the 1967 war.
Directed by police, part of the operation consisted of "residents of vil-
lages, suburbs, or town quarters [who volunteered] for patrolling . . .
and [committed] themselves to regular guard duties in their neighborhood"(Gal-Or, 1994, p. 154). These neighborhood groups knew their
areas and could often discern aliens and suspects better than the police
and other authorities.

I live in Berkeley, where the principle of localism has been built into
earthquake warnings and response. The city is divided into neighborhoods, and once or twice a year there is a neighborhood gathering,
which a police officer or earthquake safety official also attends. Most of

the meeting is not about earthquake safety at all. Some people bring food or drinks, and most of the conversation is inquiring and comparing notes about children, talking about neighborhood affairs, or simply gossiping. It is a social affair, not exactly replicated by any other such occasion in the neighborhood. At a given point the attending official reviews basic facts about earthquakes and reviews the most adaptive kinds of behaviors with respect to setting food and water aside, turning off gas, taking cover, responding to fires, and possibly evacuating. There is also some mutual exchange of information; it has been said of one neighborhood that every resident knows where and how to turn off his or her neighbors' gas lines. The Berkeley community arrangements are related to a larger California effort called Community Emergence Response Training, which has been adopted as a national model by the Federal Emergency Management Agency (Simpson, 2001). The U.S. Department of Homeland Security (2004) dedicated a half-page of its National Response Plan to describing, in very general terms, a U.S. Citizen Corps, which "works through a regional network of state, local, and tribal Citizen Corps Councils that bring together leaders from law enforcement, fire, emergency medical and other emergency management volunteer organizations, local elected officials, the private sector, and other community stakeholders" (p. 14). The mechanism involved in all these efforts is geared specifically to responding to threats, but bears no resemblance to the suggestion to create a "civilian militia" or "home guard," which has been suggested as a civilian supplement to the National Guard (Cottrol, 2005), a scheme fraught with many more ambiguities and difficulties.

The main point about essentially local preparation arrangements is that they become built into the meaningful social fabric of people's lives. This gives the information they require more indelible meaning than top-down communications from authorities via newspaper, radio, television, mail, or even local posters. Moreover, they are more likely to hear and pay heed if the message is local rather than coming from regional authorities whom they do not otherwise know (Dow and Cutter, 2000). The local embeddedness also adds an ingredient of trust, which is, for better or worse, often weaker when information comes from authorities with whom one is not acquainted personally. It stands to reason that as a result of personal and neighborhood involvement, responses on the part of citizens are more likely to be informed and systematic. Disaster research shows some consensus on the principle that "emergent human resources" (that is, local) responses to disaster tend to be more effective than "command and control" arrangements (Drabek and McEntire, 2002; Dynes, 1994). To put the issue another way, since it has been demonstrated how omnipresent kinship and other close social ties are in responses to emergency situations (see chapter 5), does it not make sense to attempt to harness this fundamental dimension of social life in the phases of preparation, training, and warning as well?

It would be idle to suggest that the model I have described could be generalized to all communities. Berkeley citizens typically have a high level of education and social self-consciousness, the community is moderately affluent, and residential continuity is relatively high. In some urban centers and other places where these conditions are not met—that is, in places where neighborhood ties are weak—attempts to mobilize the neighborhoods for responding is correspondingly more difficult. Also, earthquakes are discrete types of events, whereas terrorist threats involve many different kinds of threats—bombings, disruption of events, radiological attacks, and chemical and biological poisoning. Nevertheless, the principle of the potency of localism should not be forgotten. If people are able to organize themselves intelligibly for one kind of threat, it is plausible to imagine that they can be similarly organized for the four or five most likely kinds of terrorist attacks. The costs of localizing preparation, warning, and response are not low, but the likely payoff is high in terms of protecting life and health and preventing chaotic social responses and political backlash against bad planning for disasters.

The most comprehensive treatment of targets is found in the report of the Committee on Science and Technology for Countering Terrorism (2002), a group consisting mainly of scientist, engineers, health experts, and a few social scientists (see the box, "Really Local Preparedness"). This group moved systematically through the special problems of nuclear and radiological threats, human and agricultural health systems, toxic chemicals and explosive materials, information technology, energy systems, transportation systems, cities and fixed infrastructure, and human populations. Systematic interrelations among these sources of vulnerability were also identified.

In some cases the committee made a judgment that a given system (for example, information systems) was not highly vulnerable to catastrophic attacks, whereas other areas (such as the national system of electrical power) were highly vulnerable. One avenue the committee did not pursue systematically was the cost of achieving adequate hardening. In a way this was unfortunate, because in this area the costs are especially salient as a limiting condition. Several principles should be kept in mind.

- *Total cost.* Even without careful calculation, it is apparent that to implement fully all the measures explicitly and implicitly called for by the committee would threaten to bankrupt the nation. Furthermore, the task is endless because of the possible efforts of determined terrorists to get around protective arrangements and forever to seek new, as yet unprotected areas of destruction and disruption. The inescapable conclusion is that not everything can be done.
- *Cost-effectiveness.* The cost of hardening cannot be calculated in absolute terms, but systematic estimates should be made, to include the level of risk, the likelihood of damage in the event of attack, and the actual protection gained by investment of resources. Full protection of the nation's dams, for example, is an enormously costly enterprise. The amount of explosives required to destroy a reservoir and the difficulties of delivering these to the site raise questions about the advisability of this line of investment. The same kind of question could be raised and systematic estimates could be made for every kind of vulnerability as a way of setting priorities, making investments more efficient, and limiting the total cost of hardening.
- *Source of funding.* The division of responsibility for preparedness is a chronic source of difficulty at the federal, state, and local levels, with each level striving to justify off-loading costs on the others. This is as much a political as an economic problem, and often results in the application of politically derived formulas for distribution (United States House of Representatives, 2004). The same

contest appears in determining the relative responsibilities of the government and the private (often corporate) sector, for example in the protection of chemical processing plants.

These questions of political economy appear to dictate the need for reliance on systematic planning and priority setting. Under present arrangements, protection agencies tend to concentrate sequentially on areas of recent attack or those given high priority on account of the relative political clout or resistance of one interested party or another. This issue is only one of the many adverse consequences of the politicization of counterterrorism, a topic discussed more fully in chapter 7.

A Partially Self-Imposed American Dilemma:

Chronic Anxiety and Political Conflict

over Terrorism

After the attack on the World Trade Center and the Pentagon in 2001, an unequivocal cultural trauma for the country, the American government and the American public are still in a high state of fever about international terrorism against the American homeland. A very strong pattern of reactions developed shortly after 9/11, and the country has been living with them ever since. In this section I identify the distinctive confluence of cultural and situational factors that has gone into making this pattern and suggest some dysfunctional aspects of it.

The initial given is the nature of the terrorist threat itself. It is correctly regarded as omnipresent, uncertain as to time and place of occurrence, and potentially profoundly lethal (if nuclear, biological, and chemical attacks are taken into account). The number and types of targets are multiple: electrical installations, transport systems, dams, public buildings, urban centers, public gatherings at sporting and ceremonial events, churches, hospitals, schools, child-care centers. The list goes on and on; because of the extreme uncertainty, imagination, exercised through "if I were a terrorist" mental experiments, suggests that the list of potential vulnerabilities can be expanded almost indefinitely. Two further consequences follow from this realistic situation:

- It is impossible to defend all targets completely and effectively.
- There is every reason to believe that if some targets are protected effectively, terrorists have sufficient ingenuity to switch to other ones.

These conditions apply with varying force to all societies that are targets of terrorism. However, in the American case this realistic situation has become embedded in a number of distinctive social-psychological, cultural, and political contexts.

In consequence, an early result has been to define the post-9/11 terrorist threat in mainly moralistic terms, treating the fundamentalist Muslim-inspired attacks as evil and their perpetrators as murderers, criminals, and mortal enemies. This dualistic tendency runs deep in American cultural history and finds religious roots throughout the Judeo-Christian tradition. This militant crusading impulse reached full flower in the rhetoric of the Bush administration in the months after 9/11. The characterization unquestionably resonated with most of the America public, though some Americans and most Europeans expressed distaste for if not outright disgust with the righteous "cowboy talk." Be that as it may, the moral dimension has been especially salient. It has been reinforced by the country's impulse to export democracy, American style, to Middle Eastern and other countries.

The second contextual factor has been the instrumental-technological approach to the terrorist issue. Derived from a longstanding American faith in science and technology generally, this mentality was solidified by twentieth-century American wartime experiences. It is generally accepted that in World War II, our technological superiority in firepower, weaponry, detection (such as radar), and above all nuclear power contributed to our ultimate victory. In the cold war similarly our technological superiority prevailed over the numerical weapons superiority of the Soviet bloc. Vietnam was a highly technological war, though the technology did not exactly mesh with the conditions of warfare there. But the great technological triumphs were the brief Gulf War, the Afghan War, and the Iraq War, all of which were "won" from the standpoint of achieving military objectives through the most highly sophisticated technological weaponry ever developed.

This technical-instrumental mentality continues to dominate thinking about attacking, detecting, and defending against terrorism, even though many features of contemporary terrorism—its elusiveness if not invisibility, its reliance on guerrilla-like tactics, and its tendency to reappear even if "defeated" in a given episode or setting—strongly suggest that warlike "victories" through technologically sophisticate military action are not achievable. This fact has been appreciated in high places. In 1986, Ambassador-at-Large for Counterterrorism Robert B. Oakley declared that terrorism did not lend itself to quick solutions, that dealing with it is a "long-term effort," and that "there are no simple knockout punches [or] . . . quick fixes in this business" (quoted in Wilson, 1994, p. 202). Others have sounded the same notes of patience, long-term persistence, and the unwinability of a war on terrorism.

The combination of uncertainty, dread, moralism, and technological instrumentalism yield a number of corollaries that work themselves into the body politic, as follows:

- The assumption (and expectation) that a successful international terrorist attack on United States territory is politically unacceptable, because it will mean loss of lives in a society committed to the sanctity of human life (Gearty, 1991, p. 11), and because in the moralistic and instrumental contexts described, any attack would represent a moral wound and a technical and organizational failure. This assumption reigns despite almost ritual periodic admonitions that terrorist attacks will happen again and that it is a matter of "when, not if."

- The derived assumption is that if a successful terrorist attack occurs, someone or some agency will be deemed responsible for that failure. This dread keeps government, its security apparatus, and first response agencies in constant uneasiness and in a mode of always looking over their shoulder for criticism. It also serves these agencies to claim credit if attacks do not occur.

- Because of these two assumptions, a third arises—the ever-present tendency to criticize government for not doing enough. This tendency is derived from the bottomless nature of the terrorist threat (it can happen anywhere and at any time) and the expectation that terrorist events are intolerable and should not happen. Derived from this line of criticism, the corresponding tendency on the part of government is to be constantly either on the defensive or in a mode of attack against its critics as unsympathetic to its heroic efforts in the moral crusade.

• The end result is a more or less chronic situation of political division, which, in a competitive political democracy, inevitably spills over into partisanship and party conflict, especially in moments of crisis and in election campaigns, when the holding of power is at stake.

The reason why I call this convergence of tendencies a "partially self-enforced entrapment" is because it is a combination of the objective realities and the distinctive psychological and cultural principles that we as a nation have brought to the terrorist situation.

Nowhere were all the elements of this situational-cultural complex expressed better than in two editorials in the *New York Times* early in 2005. The first, published on February 20, 2005, was entitled "Our Unnecessary Insecurity." It was a savage criticism of the Bush administration's inaction in defending against terrorism. The editorial was both a statement of and a symptom of the social-psychological complex I have just described. The editorial assaulted the administration for inadequate protection of chemical plants, nuclear power plants, ports, and hazardous waste materials, and for its non-response to the threat of bioterrorism. It also criticized the administration for neglecting critical priorities (giving more domestic security funds per capita to Wyoming than New Jersey) and for spending too much on preventing the hijacking of commercial aircraft. The administration, the *Times* complained, "does too little on one hand [and] overreacts on the other, and seems oblivious to how its excesses are actually making America less safe." On March 21, a second editorial, "Our Terrorist-Friendly Borders," appeared, complaining "how little progress has been made in securing our borders" and making a number of recommendations, all involving significant costs, to protect the Mexican and Canadian borders, to track stolen and lost visas, to shorten lengths of visits, and to introduce tougher requirements for issuing driver's licenses and other forms of identification.

An irony emerges from the editorials. Even if one deems the criticisms justified, a reallocation of government expenses on defense would not satisfy matters, because the security would never be made foolproof, and interested groups and interests would always charge "too much" or "too little." The preparedness issue makes life difficult if not impossible for any political administration, because of the bottomless nature of the problem and the high expectations regarding its solution. This sets the country up for chronic political dissatisfaction and partisan conflict. And it does not bode well for what reactions might be like in the event of a successful attack. The *Times* concluded its first editorial by saying, "If the United States is hit by another attack at one of these [unprotected] points, we will have only ourselves to blame." It would have been more nearly correct to say that we will blame one another in a vigorous season of accusation and scapegoating.

A Social Scientist in the National Academies

As described in the box titled "Politicizing the Causes of Terrorism," the National Academies (National Academy of Science, Institute of Medicine, National Academy of Engineering) undertook a major assignment after the 9/11 attacks: to ask how science, as represented by the Academies, could be of help in understanding and confronting terrorism. This question was tangibly implemented in the formation of the Committee on Science and Technology for Countering Terrorism, constituted late in 2001. It issued a major, influential report, *Making the Nation Safer*, in 2002.

The committee focused mainly on defensive measures—protecting borders, hardening targets, and homeland security. As might be expected, it was composed mainly of natural scientists, engineers, and medical and public health experts, along with a few with government experience in security matters. There were two social scientists on the committee. One was Tom Schelling of the University of Maryland, an economist and long-reigning authority on deterrence theory and strategies. I was the second, a sociologist with broad interdisciplinary interests and a longstanding interest in collective behavior and social movements.

Speaking for myself—and no doubt for all others on the committee—I had no ambivalence about undertaking this important assignment. It was a moment of evident national crisis in which no one knew exactly how to be helpful, and to join the work of this committee was surely a positive and productive step.

At the same time, I had very modest expectations about how meaningful the voice of a social scientist could be. I had been in the National Academy of Sciences long enough to appreciate fully the marginality of the behavioral and social sciences in that establishment. They were historical latecomers to the Academy, compared with mathematics, the natural sciences, and the life sciences. The number of behavioral and social science members elected each year is low in relation to the number elected in the other fields. Furthermore, the members elected from these fields tend to concentrate in the "hard"—quantitative and empirical—sciences, as the large numbers of members who are physical and biological anthropologists, demographers, and experimental psychologist indicate. Interestingly, however, the National Research Council (the wing of the Academies that establishes panels and synthesizes knowledge on a wide range of policy-relevant issues) takes on many issues that have organizational, social, political, and psychological dimensions. As a result, the behavioral and social science members tend to be overworked on the NRC panels.

On the more informal side, I was also aware that the behavioral and social sciences experience second-class citizenship in the Academies. Scientists and engineers have long regarded those fields as "soft" sciences, if sciences at all. Their research is frequently—not always—more controversial politically than work in the "hard" sciences, and as a result there is the vague feeling that they give science a bad name while contributing little to it. There is also a general assumption that behavioral and social scientists are politically left—justified for some disciplines, not at all for others. One incident captured all of this for me. Another member of the committee, a physical scientist, remarked to me, "I used to think all sociologists were worthless, but now that I've got to know you, it's all but one." He extended this comment as a genuine compliment instead of the insult it was.

All this lay behind my low expectations about any effectiveness we might have had in the committee. I could not have been more mistaken. From the beginning, the committee assumed that the human dimensions of all aspects of terrorism were paramount. There was an early commitment to a chapter on populations' response to terrorist attacks. Other chapters, for example the one on the protection of cities, had significant sections focusing on the human side of things. Also to my surprise, Schelling's and my interventions, with a few exceptions, were received respectfully and taken seriously. As the committee's work came to a close, I could feel honestly that I had contributed to its work, and that I hadn't had to fight to do so.

In the context of this generally positive experience, one more observation must be made. That has to do with the expectations of the scientists and engineers and to some degree the others had of us and the sciences we represented. Those expectations concerned the kind or quality of contribution we were expected to make. One incident captures this. During the course of one of our conversations, the subject of civilian morale under the long-term threat of terrorism arose, and some discussion ensued. At a given moment, one of the committee members responsible for drafting turned to me and said, "You handle morale, Neil, write us a paragraph." The message was clearly one of "fix it," as if morale might fall into the same category as protecting a dam site or using sensors to detect weapons and explosive devices by airport security.

That incident was a small and extreme one, but it revealed a very widespread mentality—among many scientists to be sure, but also government officials, security personnel, and funding agencies—that the problems of defending against terrorism are in large part technical and that solutions are in large part instrumental. (In another discussion at an Academy meeting, one of the participants said, "What we need to whip terrorism is another Manhattan Project.") In a confirmatory episode late in 2004, I learned, in discussion following a presentation I made at the Lawrence Livermore Laboratory, that the Department of Homeland Security was supporting research in excess of $100 million at the Lab, all for defensive gadgetry and none for research on the organizational and psychological aspects of defense. In reality, many of the human problems in confronting terrorism do not lend themselves well to this instrumental approach—sometimes called "the American way of thinking." Human reactions and purposive efforts are characterized by individual and group variation, incomplete information, adaptability in the face of new information, unanticipated conflicts, unfounded predictions, unanticipated consequences, and above all reactions to efforts to monitor and control their behavior. Behavioral and social scientists have produced definite and valuable knowledge about all these human contingencies. For planners, policy makers, and security personnel to take these into account, they must resort to more complex and contingent models than currently dominate our thinking about defending against terrorism.

An Alternative: Patience and
Death by Strangulation

The review of strategies of discouragement has yielded mixed results that can be summarized in the following way:

- Terrorist attacks are not preventable in an absolute sense, even if all avenues of discouragement are pursued aggressively; "put simply, stopping terrorist attacks is impossible" (Davies, 2003, p. 242).
- Some forms of discouragement are not feasible because they involve such high political costs (for example, government regulation of the media, compromising Bill of Rights guarantees).
- Some forms of discouragement are so costly economically that they cannot be carried out as fully as, in principle, desired (for example, controlling the borders, hardening all targets).
- Some forms of discouragement are likely to be relatively ineffective as immediate discouragements of terrorism (for example, the control of international movements of money, attempts to reduce firearms and explosives as weapons, the waging of international [including preventive] military wars, and attempts to ameliorate long-term structural conditions that operate as remote causes of

terrorism). The word "relatively" is the operative word; none is irrelevant to the control of terrorism, and some might be addressed in the longer run, but they appear to be limited as direct strategies of discouragement.

The reasons for ineffectiveness vary: the limitations of controlling international movements of money rest on the constant adaptations of terrorist organizations; the limitations of controlling conventional weapons are, first, it is a seemingly endless and futile strategy, given the widespread dispersion, availability, and reproducibility of these weapons, and second, there are constitutional and political obstacles to limiting weapons domestically; and the limitations of military incursions are, first, that they are instruments that are too blunt because they are not directed at the precise locus of terrorism (unless this is state-conducted or state-sponsored terrorism), and second, they appear to generate multiple counterproductive effects, namely, strengthening anti-American sympathies among sentiment pools that may support terrorism and alienating friends and neutrals, who are likely to regard them as unilateral overreactions and bullying by the world's most powerful nation.

The last set of observations suggests that both of the main ideological ends of the American counterterrorist dialogue are misplaced as strategies for discouraging contemporary terrorism, given *what we know about the nature of the phenomenon itself*. With regard to the ideology of the hawkish right, preventive military action in most cases misses the target of terrorist activity itself and generates counterproductive effects (in terms of international support and internal political unity). On the dovish left, strategies such as reducing military expenditures, and building just and sustainable economies can legitimately be put forward as justifiable policies in the long-term pursuit of international justice and peace, but as shorter-term strategies for discouraging terrorism they also miss the mark by unduly concentrating on the remote causes of terrorism and ignoring the proximate ones, which are the proper targets of discouragement. As I argue in the final chapter, the debate over whether the United States should aggressively pursue its interests (including by military means) in maintaining and solidifying its dominant world status or whether it should exercise a more muted, incorporative, beneficent form of leadership is perhaps the most critical long-term dialogue facing the nation and the world. However, to regard either side of this debate as a strategy for discouraging or defeating terrorism, or to use the defense against terrorism as a justification for the pursuit of either, reflects a misunderstanding of terrorism itself.

This line of reasoning suggests a different package of strategies to discourage terrorism that is more knowledge-based and does not rest on expectations of either delivering a knockout blow to terrorism or eradicating it by curing its root causes. What comes to mind is a policy of hounding terrorists and of selective, targeted concentration on those aspects of their activities that are essential for their effectiveness. To put this case the other way around, the most productive strategy would be to concentrate on those lines of discouragement that would increase the probability that the impulse to pursue terrorism would wither as a force. This is what is meant by the phrase "death by strangulation," which is a strategy different from either destruction or cure. This approach is more consistent with the idea of a war of attrition than with the idea of a war to be won—a process, it has been argued persuasively, that was most decisive in grinding down two of the most persistent terrorist movements, the Basque ETA and the Irish Republican Army (Sanchez-Cuenca, 2004). It is perhaps too much to hope that political leaders will pursue such a strategy, which demands a longer-term, more patient outlook and clearly is not as politically electric or compelling a posture in an ideologically polarized nation as are fantasies of destruction or permanent cure.

The package of strategies that is implied by the notion of strangulation includes the following (for a similar package, see the Century Foundation Task Force Report, 2004):

- A *selective* hardening of domestic targets, based on the best scientific knowledge of their relative vulnerability to attack, the best analysis of the likelihood that terrorists would choose them as targets, the extent of damage that might be result from attacks, and a calculation of the costs involved in hardening. Part of this strategy would be to insulate the process of making decisions to harden from politically derived formulas and from the day-to-day struggle of groups interested in hardening or not hardening *their* specific targets, which results in a scattered and ad hoc accumulation of protective activities.

- A more *selective* and *cooperative* approach to the process of monitoring the international movement of persons and potential weapons. This would involve a higher level of exchange among nations' security agencies regarding international movement of suspected persons, and preclearing of passenger lists and cargo manifests at their source.

- More generally, a greater insistence on *sharing* intelligence information, both internally and internationally. This is simultaneously one of the most difficult and most important areas of concern, given the growth of different bureaucratic cultures and jurisdictional jealousies, which defy efforts to reduce obstacles by creating umbrella agencies such as the Department of Homeland Security (see Kettl, 2004). Sharing would also include assistance in developing counterterrorist machinery in other countries and supporting that activity logistically and financially.

- Encouraging all countries in which terrorist activity is suspected to repress *illegal* activities of protest groups in their midst, but making efforts to engage them in appropriate ways in the domestic political process. Most terrorist groups, we discovered, have domestic as well as international agendas, and increasing political responsiveness rather than inflicting wholesale repression would work toward diminishing the effectiveness of their efforts domestically. Special attention should be given to actual and potential audiences of support for terrorist groups; militant terrorist groups themselves are less likely to be affected by strategies of political co-optation.

- To rely first on *economic, diplomatic and political sanctions* against nations suspected of harboring or supporting terrorism, and to reserve military intervention as a final resort. This also implies turning first to international bodies such as the United Nations and to international coalitions among nations, reserving unilateral action as an option when those others fail.

- When targeted *force* against terrorist groups is employed, this should be internationally supported to the greatest degree possible, and full justification of its specific purpose as a direct attack on terrorism— and not something more general—should be undertaken.
- To *prosecute* apprehended terrorists and terrorist suspects within the context of criminal law.
- To stress taking *measured* rather than *wholesale* action against terrorist groups and activities, on the grounds that the latter are much more likely to be regarded as overreactions, the perception of which is a principal source of domestic and international opposition to counterterrorist policies.
- To appreciate the limits of *ideological war making* against the ideological beliefs of terrorist groups that justify their activities, on the grounds that these strategies are most likely to polarize.

It would be presumptuous to claim that this package of strategies is either complete or definitive, because our knowledge is not adequate enough to make that claim. We do know, however, that terrorist organizations and individuals are vulnerable to sustained periods of inaction, boredom, flagging commitment, and internal dissention, that support among sentiment pools can stagnate if not fed by "evidence" of injustice and atrocity, and that highly targeted deterrence makes attacks more difficult to execute. The counsel of patience—the persistent but undramatic pursuit of the package of policies indicated—is a mix of containment and deterrence theory. Unlike its classic cold war formulations, however, which stressed the fear of nuclear destruction as the principal deterrent, this strategy aims at deterring by instilling a combination of fear, failure, boredom, and desperation. As such, the package is ventured as the most likely to be successful in promoting death by strangulation.

CHAPTER 7

The Long-Term International

Context of Terrorism

THE LONG-TERM significance of international terrorism for the United States and other countries cannot be treated in isolation from the broadest social, economic, political, and cultural situation of the world as it presents itself. Terrorism as a specific form of conflict is simultaneously an expression and a microcosm of that situation, and its likely future cannot be estimated without reference to the larger scene. Accordingly, this chapter offers several broad lines of diagnosis of the recent past, present, and likely future world situation, and extracts several conclusions from that diagnosis. Most of the analysis concerns the context for international terrorism rather than terrorism in general. This contextual assessment begins with the issue of international power and proceeds from there, because terrorism is above all else a political force, deriving from the political configuration of the contemporary world. The assessment, however, must also respect the historical dimension and include reference to economic and cultural factors.

The Shape of the World After the End

of the Cold War

A Sample of Interpretations

As the cold war came to an end, an apparently unprecedented era of international history emerged. Much of the novelty of the international situation derives from the particular international supremacy of the United States. As one might expect, the years since 1990 have produced a veritable spate of diagnoses, evaluations, and predictions about the future in light of these novel circumstances. Writing such books has become something of a competition, with an author usually selecting a dominant theme of analysis and telegraphing it in a striking title or subtitle of the book. The author runs with the theme, often denigrating competitive interpretations along the way. The style of the books ranges all the way from serious scholarship to journalistic foray. Most are highly selective with regard to evidence and are laden with evaluative judgments. Most are written by American authors, and for that reason they focus on the role of the United States in the world order. The books range over the ideological map, but the most prominent motif is one of criticism of America's world role, stressing the country's unilateralism, its bullying foreign policies, its imperialism, and its hypocrisy. In the end, however, they provide a jumble of assessments and fail to add up to the kind of contingent and synthetic thinking that is most appropriate for understanding an uncertain, evolving world and the role of violence in it.

To begin, I present the skeletal arguments of a limited sample of these interpretations. At the optimistic end of the spectrum is the "end-of-history" interpretation ventured by Francis Fukuyama (1992) shortly after the fall of communism. He advances the argument that all principal competitors to the legitimating principles of market capitalism and democracy have failed: "we have trouble imagining a world that is radically better than our own, or a future that is not essentially democratic and capitalist" (p. 46). He mentions Islam as the sole competitor. Fukuyama posits a kind of Hegelian unidirectionality, universality, and inevitability of the conquest of capitalism and democracy—thus the end of history. If to this argument is added the view of some political scientists that democracies tend not to go to war against one another (Doyle, 1983), the picture becomes even rosier.

In polar opposition lies the argument of Robert Kaplan (2000), who presents the view that the forces of scarcity, crime, overpopulation, tribalism, and disease are destroying the social fabric of the planet. Not only is the United States unable to export democracy, it finds democracy eroding at home. Kaplan invokes a number of analogies to Gibbon's account of the decline of the Roman Empire (pp. 113–14). Along the same lines. Henry Giroux (2004) writes about the "demise of democracy" that will be the result of new fascist tendencies in the United States.

Several works predict the decline of American power in the world, basing this analysis alternatively on broad historical analogies with hegemonic powers that engaged in "imperial overstretch" (Kennedy, 1987), on the decline of America's share in the world economy and its economic dominance (Gilpin, 2001), and on a neo-Marxist diagnosis of the dynamics of the world system of economies and nations (Wallerstein, 2003). A political version of the decline thesis is found in Robert Cooper's *The Breaking of Nations* (2003), in which he argues that the world order has broken down into anarchy in the twenty-first century, threatening an international chaos that "may be worse" than the Hundred Years War, the Thirty Years War, and the first half of the twentieth century (p. vii). Much of this traces to the weakening of the territorial, military, and economic capacities of nation-states through globalization. States, however "remain stubbornly national" in their identities and democratic institutions.

One of the most influential diagnoses is Samuel Huntington's (1996) thesis that the ideological-political divisions of the cold war period have given way to cultural-political ones, and that the resulting clash of civilizations (principally but not exclusively between Islam and the Christian West) will continue to dominate the shape of world conflict.

Benjamin Barber provides a not dissimilar cosmic-cultural diagnosis in the volume entitled, dramatically, *Jihad versus McWorld* (1995). McWorld is the multifaceted behemoth of American-dominated world globalization, involving the world penetration of capitalism and markets, the export of democracy, and the spread of global culture through products and the media. The reaction is not only Islamic traditionalism, as the term jihad suggests, but would include it; it is the more general reassertion of localism, tribalism, balkanization, and religion. Nor is the anti-McWorld impulse limited to less developed regions; it manifests itself in the developed West as well. Like Huntington's view of the clash, Barber's thesis reads contemporary times and future history as a dualistic antagonism between diffuse cultural principles.

A compelling power-based analysis is provided by Robert Kagan (2003), who posits an American political, economic, and military domination that permits and encourages this country to pursue unilateral political, economic and political strategies, "exercising power in an anarchic Hobbesian world." Europe, by contrast, is moving "beyond power into a self-contained world of laws and rules and transnational negotiation and cooperation" (p. 3), in large part because it has lived under the protective cloak of American power since World War II. Kagan argues that America can "go it alone" (p. 39), though he hopes that the country will realize the weight of this overwhelming power superiority and show "more understanding for the sensibilities of others, a little more of the generosity of spirit that characterized American foreign military policy during the cold war" (p. 102). Joseph Nye (2003), by contrast, points to the counterproductivity of relying on political, economic, and military muscle and stresses America's success with and need to rely on "soft power," the power of diplomacy, ideas, and culture.

Two other books take more continuous views of the shape of the world. Jim Hanson (1996) downplays the emerging ideological conflicts and argues that "the cold war of the twenty-first century will begin as economic battles occur over markets as battlegrounds" (p. 114), though ideological conflicts will be mobilized in these struggles. The world's chief problems are economic, demographic, and environmental, and these "may not be solvable by the next generation" (p. 158). Likewise, C. G. Jacobsen (1996) dismisses ideological and cultural analysis and predicts the continuation of self-interested behavior on the part of nations. "Today's defining parameters remain, essentially, those of the past" (p. 11).

Finally, a number of other works, shorter-term in perspective, more or less explicitly hold the United States—and the George W. Bush administration in particular—responsible for contemporary world problems and evils. Claes Ryn (2003), in a book entitled *America the Virtuous*, develops the theme of the "new Jacobism" that is coming to dominate Western societies, especially the United States. This involves aggressively exporting the ideology of freedom, equality, and democracy, backed by a righteous attitude that brooks no opposition and justifies reckless military adventures. The Bush administration has carried this new Jacobinism to an extreme, despite its early protestations against engaging in "nation-building." Barber's recent critique (2003) is in the same genre but not the same language. Emmanuel Todd (2003) goes so far as to say that "[only] one threat to global stability hangs over the world today—the United States itself, which was once a protector and is now a predator." Both Douglas Kellner (2003) and Alex Callinicos (2003) develop a savage attack on the imperialism and foreign aggression of the Bush administration and the Republican right. Other titles weigh down the shelf of call number 902 in the University of California, Berkeley, library: *Imperial Overstretch: George W. Bush and the Hubris of Empire* (Burbach and Tarbell, 2004), *Bush League Diplomacy: How the Neoconservatives Are Putting the World at Risk* (Eisendrath and Goodman, 2004), *Losing America: Confronting a Reckless Presidency* (Byrd, 2004), *Imperial America: The Bush Assault on the World Order* (Newhouse, 2003), and *The Bush Betrayal* (Bovard, 2004).

In light of this admittedly superficial but not inaccurate survey, the reader can appreciate the appropriateness of applying the word "jumble" to the literature. It is apparent that not all, and perhaps not any, of these analyses can be right. Each one begins with a different set of orienting assumptions—and sometimes ideological positions—and moves forward from there to develop its respective thesis to its limits, paying little heed to the enormous range of contingencies that the economic, political, and cultural future that the twenty-first century holds out. The end result is a jumble, pointing in numerous directions and dictating or suggesting different solutions. Rather than retreat from the literature in desperation, however, I will attempt to undertake a more modest characterization of major world forces as they present themselves at present and into the coming decades, stressing contingencies more than absolutes and framing the characterization selectively so that it points toward a broad and long-term contextual assessment of terrorism and its likely fate.

A Synthetic Assessment of the Origins, Nature, and Dilemmas of American Power

I will first outline a number of historical origins of the growth of American power, and then consider various accelerating factors and events in the twentieth century.

Historical origins. Among those historical factors that have been identified by foreign commentators and American historians, the following are the most salient in contributing to American economic, political, and military power in the world:

- Favorable geographic circumstances, which include a large land mass, ample raw materials and other natural resources, a temperate climate, rich soil, and the transfer of European flora, fauna, and agricultural know-how.
- A situation of oceanic protection that has virtually safeguarded the nation from foreign military intrusion and exploitation of its peoples and resources by others. The historical exception was the War of 1812; fears of Japanese invasion appeared in World War II, especially in the western states, but these did not materialize.
- The religious-economic factor, stressed by Max Weber, which included the absence of ecclesiastical domination by a single church (Catholicism, Anglicanism). The early separation of religion from the polity partially insulated religious conflict from the political arena. In addition, the vigor of ascetic Protestantism, particularly in New England, appeared to encourage both a sense of independence and an entrepreneurial spirit. This "Weber thesis" has been relativized since its initial conceptualization, as many other ideologies, particularly nationalistic ones, have proved to be potent sources of economic development, but its historical significance in Northern European and American history still stands.
- A fortuitous political heritage that included the adoption of some elements of the British tradition: an impulse to representative democracy (only partly developed in Britain in the eighteenth century), a common law tradition, and a number of legal precedents guaranteeing personal liberty, freedoms, and legal protection of citizens. But it also rejected the monarchical, clerical, and aristocratic impulses, mainly in the name of Enlightenment rationalism. In this connection, the early republic institutionalized a distrust of centralized authority, manifested mainly in the constitutional separation of powers, states rights, and the Bill of Rights, combined, however, with an exuberant patriotism (it has been said of Americans that they hate their state but love their nation). All these factors contributed to the relative political stability—the Civil War excepted—and openness of the society.
- As the new republic developed, its religious and civic leaders expressed a profound faith in mass education, initially to promote citizenship and "republican virtue," but at the same time this

made for widespread literacy, itself a significant asset for a labor force in an economy moving toward commercial and industrial development.

- A constitutional provision for internal commerce free from tariffs, customs barriers, and other restrictions on the movement of goods and services across state lines. Ultimately these provisions established the legal framework for a massive free market that expanded as new states were added and as population increased.

- A prolonged situation of expensive labor (relative to capital) that contrasted with many European countries. This contributed not only to technological innovation but also to the impulse to bring cheaper labor to the country via immigration (Habbakuk, 1967).

To these factors should be added that the nation avoided a number of roads taken by others abroad. Because the nation's "imperialism" was largely carried out on its own continent, it avoided in large part the complications of Spanish, British, and French colonialism and grand military adventures.

Accelerating factors in the twentieth century. Among the most salient of contributing factors to the more recent expansion of American economic, political, economic, and cultural power are the following:

- The continued economic growth of the country, aided by ongoing foreign immigration; of particular significance was the brain drain of highly skilled talent mainly from Europe before and after World War II.

- America's escape from the ravages of totalitarianism in the interwar period, despite national destabilization during the Great Depression.

- The weakening of Germany by the two world wars and Japan by World War II; the withdrawal of the European powers from their colonies after the war.

- The revitalization of Europe through the Marshall Plan and military alliances. This also added to the solidification of American power, mainly via the expansion of its own markets, its continued military domination of Europe through NATO, and the containment of communism and Soviet influence. Despite the remarkable successes of the Common Market and the European Union, the continent's political unity and effectiveness continue to be restricted.

- Continued American economic predominance, despite a lessening of its share of world income occasioned by the recovery of nations after World War II and by the worldwide spread of economic development.

- The implosion of the Soviet Empire in 1989–90 and Russia's relative economic impoverishment and political weakness since 1990. The end of the cold war effectively eliminated conventional military threats against the United States and marked the effective demise of world's major ideological alternative to capitalism.

- The rise and consolidation of English as the commercial, political, and media lingua franca.

The nature of American dominance. Like most historically distinct outcomes, the United States' rise to world dominance has thus been overdetermined by the confluence of many positive factors and few negative ones. By now, that dominance has been clearly established in the realm of conventional military (including naval and air) power, nuclear capability, technology and communications, popular culture as spread through the media, and the nation's centrality in international trade (despite dependencies and trade deficits), multinationalism, and international finance (including its predominance in international organizations such as the World Bank).

The fact of American dominance is almost incontrovertible, but its precise extent, nature, and usefulness or harmfulness to the nation and the rest of the world are in perpetual dispute (as our sample of contemporary interpretations revealed). The dispute is in part a matter of empirical assessment but also in part a semantic (and ultimately ideological) contest over words such as imperialism, hegemony, domination, and dominance. After identifying the major features of American dominance, I will give reasons for preferring the latter term.

We begin with what we regard as the essence of the American place in the world. The contemporary pattern is an economic dominance, realized through greater economic productivity (and its concomitant, wealth) based on a superior, science-based technology. This dominance is realized and exercised through the mechanisms of trade among nations, capital and financial investment, influence in an international monetary system, and the periodic exercise of economic sanctions. There is also an aspect of military domination, though this is not realized primarily through military conquest and administration of occupied territory but through a technologically superior arsenal of weaponry, occasional wars and peacekeeping interventions, and, above all, military intimidation. American dominance also has a less tangible ideological ingredient, namely, a conviction of the moral superiority of a particular (American) version of democracy and its accompanying characteristics of personal liberty, the constitutional rights of citizens, mass political participation, and to some degree its understanding of human rights. This ideological dimension affects—without too much consistency—American foreign policies toward other nations, generally favoring nations like itself politically and distancing itself from or applying pressures on nations unlike itself.

Those defining characteristics point toward the contrasts between the contemporary American form of world domination and the two contrasting cases of imperialism and colonialism. Imperialism is above all a system based on military conquest, territorial occupation, and direct governmental/military control by the dominant imperial power. This characterization clearly applies to the Classical Roman and Ottoman empires and is also evident in other cases, such as the Austro-Hungarian and Soviet empires. The political sovereignty of occupied regions is not an issue; the notion simply does not apply to militarily occupied and controlled territories. Imperial powers are also dominant economically, but the mechanisms are extraction and exploitation of resources through the mechanisms of expropriation, direct control of economic activities, and coercion (including slavery in some cases).

If we regard the eighteenth-, nineteenth-, and twentieth-century European cases as the major referents, colonialism overlaps with but is distinguishable in important ways from imperialism. Military conquest, territorial opposition, and administrative rule—sometimes military, sometimes civil—are the essence, but in practice the administrative rule varied from direct rule resembling imperialism to indirect rule involving a symbiotic relationship between colonial rulers and indigenous authorities. Nineteenth- and twentieth-century colonialism also involved striking economic contrasts between the technological and industrial superiority of the developed colonial powers and the undeveloped colonial countries. The resultant pattern was the extraction of primary products as the necessary resources for industrial production (such as cotton from Egypt) or for consumption in the colonial countries (such as tea, sugar, coffee, spices).

Such are the bare essentials. We now mention some additional, more nearly ancillary characteristics of American dominance, accompanied by other observations on the imperialist and colonial modes. Under the heading of ideology we mentioned the American predilection to export its political arrangements, including democratic ideals. In imperial regimes, this seems to be weaker. Imperialism is certainly accompanied by an imperialist ideology (the glory of the empire), but this culture is not conspicuously imposed on the "natives," over whom direct military control is more important. Accordingly, imperially controlled territories tended to manifest a duality of culture—that of the ruler and that of the ruled. Colonialism was mixed in this regard, with cultural dominance one model (notably French colonialism), cultural distance another (British indirect rule), and a mixture of political control supplemented by religious proselytization still another.

Another dimension of cultural domination should be mentioned. One aspect of the American model of the world is its popular culture, realized through the longstanding and remarkable presence of Hollywood, American television, the technological capacity to spread American culture, and the receptiveness to many consumer goods abroad. Such is not the case with "elite culture" (with the exception of scientific culture, in which America predominates), which is maintained intact and well in many other nations and is by no means believed be inferior to or overwhelmed by American culture. Indeed, sometimes the opposite is the case.

Qualifications to the dominance theme. The first qualification to the essentials just outlined is that despite its overwhelming power, the United States remains a nation in the world environment. Although the European continent is a lesser presence as an international military force, it remains a focus of international alliances, commitments, and involvements built up after World War II. The positions and policies of European nations and the European Union are a significant force in the foreign activities of the United States. The relationship is asymmetrical, however, and is threatened with instability because of the ultimate power of the United States to disappoint by ignoring the strength of these ties, usually accompanied by European opposition and resentment. To maintain the role of Japan as a largely subordinated political ally but at the same time a major economic competitor is also a source of constraints. American dependence on Middle Eastern oil supplies and its derived interest in subduing those it regards as antagonists who might threaten political stability in the region are still another conditioning parameter of its role. More generally, America's trade interdependencies with all regions of the world stand as limits on its capacity simply to call the tune. Chronic trouble spots in the world—North Korea, the India-Pakistan standoff, the Israel-Palestine conflict—are situations that the United States cannot simply set right by its own actions. Finally, the United States cannot have its own way in the United Nations. The balance between the capacity to dominate by the exercise of power and the operation of external constraints on that domination cannot be precisely specified, because it is in flux from time to time as the international situation changes. But it must be acknowledged as a balance.

A second qualification to the assertion of American dominance is the fact that the country itself has displayed a historical ambivalence toward international involvement and aggression throughout its history. This factor also must be raised as a critical qualification of the simplified "America as bully" theme repeated in the sample of diagnoses cited earlier. Clever phrases meant to capture this quality, such as "reluctant sheriff," "empire lite," and "imperial understretch," have appeared in the literature (see Tetrais, 2004). This ambivalence has manifested itself in a variety of ways:

First, U.S. history has been characterized by a motif of isolationism, always latent and sometimes salient. Activation of this impulse has been a recurrent factor in the country's foreign policies and, in its most notable manifestation, retarded American entry into World War II.

Second, the country's colonial history has been of a qualified character. Its anticolonial heritage was established in consequence of its own experience as a colony successfully breaking away and its resistance to European colonization in Latin America through the Monroe Doctrine. It has a colonial history of acquiring territories by purchase or force (notably in Mexico, the Philippines, and various island territories), but that history is modest by comparison with the history of the major European powers. On the contemporary scene, its imperialism "is also anti-imperial: on the one hand it [America] tells countries how they should be run; on the other it tells them they should do the running themselves" (Cooper, 2003, p. 49).

Third, the country's history of wars illustrates the ambivalence. The United States has been involved in many wars and other episodes of international meddling, and these have varied greatly with respect to popular support. The underlying theme is high moral justification if the country has been attacked but guilt and self-criticism if it is suspected that "we started it," a theme developed by Mead (1965 [1942]), who elaborated on the theme of "the chip on the shoulder." This echoed historical notes of "don't tread on me" and "trailing one's coat," that is, dragging one's coattails along the ground, thus inviting another to step on them, which would be a provocation to fight (Lieven, 2004, p. 3). A brief scan of the level of popularity of American wars, both at the time and in the writing of historians, illustrates this ambivalence.

World War II was started by what was almost universally perceived by the American population as an unprovoked and perfidious attack on the country (no matter how complex its background). As such it was a "natural" war for the United States. The "culture" created by the attack—as well as the venom felt toward Hitler's Germany—facilitated one of the great wartime mobilizations in history. Yet ambivalence showed up in two contexts during World War II, and left the country with two corresponding national traumas for which it now carries burdens of guilt. The first was the incarceration of Japanese-Americans in camps in the context of a national (especially West Coast) hysteria about a Japanese invasion and the loyalty of Japanese-Americans. The second was the dropping of atomic bombs on the cities of Hiroshima and Nagasaki in 1945. Both these lines of action were generally felt to be fully justified at the time, in the context of a fully justified war. Yet over time, the United States has paid a great price, in compensation, regret, and guilt over the former and deep ambivalence and political division over the latter. Both sets of events stand out as national scars incurred in the context of an otherwise heroic and blameless national mission.

Other wars have not been regarded as so glorious. World War I was generally perceived as one the nation was dragged into, but as it moved along it gained a crusade-like status of a war to make the world safe for democracy, a status much compromised by the United States' failure to follow through in the establishment of a postwar peace. The Korean War was from the beginning a thoroughly ambivalent one, thought to be justified by many in light of suspected aggression by mainland Chinese and Soviet communism but criticized as a reckless adventure in a remote part of the world by others, despite the involvement of the United Nations. Only in the decades following the Korean War has its heroic status in the context of the cold war come to be established.

The Vietnam War is a very different story. Legitimized by its advocates and perpetrators as necessary to stem the tide of international communism (the domino theory), that justification never really stuck, even in the partial way it did for the Korean War. That fact, accompanied by stalemates and failures in the war itself and by revelations of Americans' cruelties to the civilian population, established that war as one in which the country was illegitimately involved and therefore blameworthy. For that reason, Vietnam has been something of a national shame ever since. In the Gulf War of 1992, the United States experienced an extraordinary burst of patriotism against Iraq and Saddam Hussein, labeled as an unprovoked aggressor against Kuwait and our Middle Eastern interests and regarded as an evil personage. At the time of that war I observed that the mighty if temporary surge of patriotic enthusiasm had to be explained in part by reference to the dark shadow of Vietnam: the Gulf War was a welcome, "clean" war, provoked from outside, about which it was possible to experience both relief and fervor.

Other wars and warlike adventures have left the country with a sense of national shame as well. The partial eradication of the American Indian population during the westward expansion has come to be widely regarded as a history of genocide, and the territorial wars against Mexico do not stand as episodes of particular national pride, symbols such as the Alamo notwithstanding. The American Civil War is an anomaly among these comparisons. It was the country's war against itself. It was a different kind of moral crusade for each side—it still is, to some historically muted extent today—that was divisive rather than uniting (despite its political outcome) and that has come to be set aside from all other wars because of its irrevocable entwining with the greatest of the country's internal traumas, the institution of slavery.

The common threads that run through all these comparisons are those of responsibility and blame for national aggression. It is remarkable, moreover, how closely the past few years have conformed to this script of ambivalence. The attacks on September 11 constituted, as far as national perception was concerned, the "purest" of attacks from outside: an unprovoked assault on the historically inviolable mainland and a slaughter of innocents. The event generated a panoply of emotional reactions, but the nearly universal experience was a combination of shock and righteous rage. The sentiment of sympathy and support for a wronged nation spread immediately to many other nations of the world, which temporarily pulled together in response to the monumental attack. This unity provided the basis for the widespread international support of the American attack on Afghanistan, which was interpreted as a direct and justified attack on the perpetrators of the attack and the regime that supported them.

When, however, the Bush administration planned and executed the invasion of Iraq, the positive sense of unity and support at home and abroad began to erode, out of suspicion that this was not so much the pursuit of terrorists guilty of the aggression as it was an occasion for settling an unfinished score with an unpopular dictator. Some European allies assented and lent military support, but others balked and opposed. As revelations about the lack of Iraq's possession of weapons of mass destruction accumulated, the opposition increased, and the Bush administration found itself in a bogged-down international situation that opponents claimed was of its own making. The legitimating force of 9/11 and the "war on terrorism" has continued to carry weight, but the 2004 presidential election was an especially bitter one, dividing the nation deeply on many issues, including the legitimacy of the Iraq

War. Despite the administration's victory in that election, popular support of the war continued to dwindle, and some tangible signs suggested the crystallization of a more activist antiwar movement. Regarded in light of these themes, the Iraq War has been a replay of past themes of ambivalence and guilt, and will probably find a place in history closer to Vietnam than to the country's glory wars.

By now my reasons for preferring the term dominance over its competitors of imperialism, hegemony, and domination should be clear. American superordination in the world is real, but is hedged in by the admittedly lesser influence and power wielded by other nations, by a range of dependencies and sticky involvements around the world, and by the United States' own ambivalence over how it conducts itself internationally. The word dominance is the better than the more absolute ones for keeping those qualifications in mind while at the same time recognizing the country's might.

A further consequence of dominance: Heightening international ambivalence toward America. As a nation, the United States enjoys a kind of self-satisfied patriotism that includes an abiding pride in its democratic institutions, freedoms, opportunities, and prosperity. Despite the presence of contrary evidence in our own history, American patriotism also carries with it the belief that we are a peace-loving nation. This general sense of purity and innocence was never more salient than in the aftermath of September 11, 2001, when the question, "Why do they hate us?" was repeatedly and naively asked. An informal party-line answer dominated the words of political spokespersons: "They" resent those very qualities that make us proud and which "they" do not have.

There is no doubt some truth in this assertion, but it is only the tiniest part of the general picture. A much more realistic assumption is that anti-Americanism is endemic, to be regarded as the normal state of affairs. Moreover, it is highly variable, as the following partial listing of its bases indicate:

- The United States is resented as the most powerful nation in the world—unprecedentedly so—and correspondingly resented both by those nations that were once more powerful (mainly European) and those that have never been so.

- As a corollary, the United States is perceived as an economically, politically and militarily bullying nation, a perception readily reinforced by any evidence or suspicion of U.S. unilateralism.
- Americans and American institutions are regarded as uncultured. This is an out-of-date perception but one still strongly held, especially among European cultural elites.
- The United States is regarded as hypocritical in its pronouncements of high democratic ideas and its history of support of some brutal and totalitarian regimes.
- The United States' wealth and prosperity are both resented and envied by most of the rest of the world.
- For many religious fundamentalists at home and abroad, the United States is the haven of materialism, corruption, godlessness, and sin.

All these themes are voiced by some Americans themselves. Moreover, most of them are not about to go away, even in the face of contravening evidence. Finally, and paradoxically, they all exist side by side with feelings of admiration and support for the American way and America's role in the world, as well as the continuing desire of many to emigrate to the United States.

A social-psychological principle underlies this complex of attitudes. That principle is that when any relationship is asymmetrical in such a way that one party becomes dependent on the other, that party will develop a relationship of ambivalence toward the stronger one (Smelser, 1998). That relationship develops whether the dependence is political, ideological, or emotional. It manifests itself in evidently unlikely situations, such as identifying with the aggressor in prison-camp situations (Bettelheim, 1943) and the Stockholm syndrome, in which hostages and captives become emotionally involved with their captors (Ochberg, 1979). The ambivalent response is based on the fact that the dependent party is not free to escape the relationship of subordination. In the case of the contemporary international situation, the degree and type of dominance on the part of the United States are less important than the fact that this asymmetry is consistently perceived by those subordinated to. It appears, moreover, that that perception is more or less universal, and promises to remain so for an indefinite period.

It is difficult for Americans to accept this complexity and ambivalence of attitudes around the world—in contrast to being naively surprised all the time by antagonism from abroad—but a realistic grasp of its existence, importance, and normalcy would constitute a valuable ingredient in our international conduct.

The Persistent Dilemmas and Some Constructive Suggestions

Taking the Long Perspective

On the basis of the foregoing analysis, it is reasonable to expect that the world will continue for an indefinite stretch into the future to see (1) an imbalance of world power resulting from American economic, political, and military domination, (2) a tempering of that domination by the continued interplay of international competition of interests and alignments, and (3) persistent deep ambivalence about American society, polity, and policy, both at home and abroad. On the basis of these expectations, it is also reasonable to assume that the impulse to international terrorism will continue as well, if for no other reason than that this set of continuities constitutes the broadest set of determining conditions for terrorism as a form of conflict, and terrorism remains one of the few options for the weak in their political struggles. Despite these continuities, it is essential to leave room for contingency and change in the conditions that foster international terrorism and in our broad responses to it. This contingency applies to both the international and the domestic scenes.

Terrorism is a phenomenon of the highest salience at this moment in history but of unknown salience in the longer sweep. From the vantage point of the Western world, international political terrorism is a fairly recent phenomenon (to say this is not to deny terrorism's long and sporadic history, documented by its historians). Selecting beginning points for modern terrorism is an arbitrary game, but certainly a new era of salience was begun after World War II in the period of anticolonialism and the dismantling of the West's colonial empires.

Since that time it has been episodic but has generated accelerating concern (for a sketch of the historical contours, see chapter 2).

In the period leading up to the beginning of the twenty-first century, a typical sequence emerged. One or more dramatic manifestations of terrorism (both domestic and international) would capture the attention of citizenry and government alike. A season of rhetoric and language of resolve would follow, and for more serious episodes (such as the Oklahoma City bombing), new antiterrorism legislation was passed, budgets were increased for intelligence agencies, and sometimes new, special military units were created. By and large, however, both public and governmental memory of these periodic incidents or seasons of incidents (including the domestic terrorism from the far right and the far left in the 1960s and early 1970s) was short, and the general tendency was to relegate the issue of terrorism to secondary status in relation to the cold war or to politically significant domestic issues.

Then came September 11, 2001, a qualitative escalation in international terrorism. The short-term impact and the vivid memory of these events since they occurred have occasioned the permanent loss of innocence about terrorism in the United States, and the events remain a major cultural trauma. From periodically noticed but quickly forgotten events, terrorism emerged as the defining international issue for the country. International terrorism has become the signature concern for the administration of George W. Bush and has served as justification for many of that administration's foreign policies, which have strained relations with many allies and indubitably increased anti-Americanism in the Arab Muslim world, and probably in other countries as well. The preoccupation with terrorism has spawned new organizations, such as the Department of Homeland Security, and initiatives to restructure and improve the nation's main security agencies.

One of the by-products of the cultural trauma is to fix our thinking on the "era of terrorism," and the "war on terrorism" which, it is thought, will extend as defining motifs indefinitely into the future. In addition to noting the seriousness and the drama of contemporary terrorism, however, we also must ask how long the salience of terrorism as well as our preoccupation with it will last, and what its ultimate significance in history will be.

Many world developments suggest that the specific conditions that spawn contemporary terrorism will not endure in their present form. In chapter 6 we examined the real possibilities for the withering of contemporary terrorism. Furthermore, it cannot be assumed that current economic social, economic, and political conditions in the Muslim countries—which now hold center-stage in international terrorism—will persist. The improvement in literacy in these countries in the recent past has been striking, and many Muslim countries show a marked downward trend in fertility rates (Roudi, 2002). There is also the possibility that democratic arrangements and social reforms, for example in the arena of women's rights and participations, will also move forward, however haltingly, and that the current flood of fundamentalism will subside. Although these kinds of changes do not guarantee the diminution, much less the end, of terrorism in the region, it is probably safer to predict continuous change rather than fixity.

Equally if not more important are likely changes in international terrorism occasioned by shifting international economic and political realities. The United States emerged as economically, politically and militarily dominant after World War II, though this was tempered by decades of cold war. Since that time its economic dominance—measured in terms of share of world production and wealth—has receded, despite its central role in the globalization process. This trend is likely to continue. China is most likely to emerge as the major world competitor, and the future international significance of India and Russia is likely to grow. The economic role of the European community is also in question. Changes in economic strength in all these regions will occasion shifts in political and military power. It is not guaranteed that the United States, with or without the help of its allies, can stem the spread of weapons of mass destruction, and if not, the military balance of the world will also be altered.

To point out these different directions of change is neither to predict nor to vote for a specific one but to underscore that changes in these international balances carry direct implications for the level and kind of terrorist activities. It has been argued plausibly that American dominance as a superpower is a major factor in the appearance of terrorism and that it, rather than other forms of conflict, violence, and war, is now salient. Insofar as this dominance is muted, terrorism may change in its significance. It may also turn out that with new alignments of nations (for example, China with oil-producing Middle Eastern nations (see Tetrais, 2004), foreign policies will return to competitive state-sponsored terrorism, reminiscent of the cold war, prolonging if not intensifying this form of international combat. Or it may be that a coalition of the mighty nations will conclude that international terrorism is a danger to all, and these nations might turn to a more cooperative mode in delegitimizing, discouraging, or suppressing it. A systematic global response of this sort might go so far as to end the "era of terrorism" as we understand it. In the end, variation and fluidity seem a safer bet than continuation of the status quo. To recognize these long-term contingencies might well mute our current, myopic view that terrorism is the new way of the world and is here to stay in the form in which we now know and fear it.

Along with these kinds of international contingencies, uncertainties about the domestic politics of the United States must also be taken into account. I have noted from time to time how deeply divided the country has become over the issues of terrorism and the postures of defense and offense that the country should assume. The responses of the administration of George W. Bush have been at the hawkish end of the spectrum. The aggressive response toward terrorism has drawn general political support in the population but widespread opposition to the Iraq War, justified by the Bush administration as an integral part of the war on terrorism but regarded by the opposition as a misguided adventure in international aggression. The 2004 presidential election apparently reflected how nearly equal sentiment was on the matter, and presidential popularity in regard to the war continued to decline into 2005 and 2006 as new revelations accumulated. The administration was also shaken by unrelated events, notably its response to Hurricane Katrina, political scandals, and the bogging down of major presidential initiatives to change the social security system.

Given this train of events, and given the general tendency for the American system to experience political cycles, it is reasonable to believe that in the coming decade, a change in the balance of domestic political control will occur, and with it a modification of the militancy toward terrorism that the country has witnessed for several years after 9/11. Such changes would have different impacts on terrorist impulses and the audiences that support it. To point out these possibilities is to assert the reasonable but not to issue predictions; too many unknown forces, such as the recurrence of major terrorist attacks or sharp changes in the country's economic fortunes, will operate in its domestic political environment. But domestically as well as internationally, it seems safest to leave room for contingency and change.

A Major Dilemma: Reaction to Future Domestic and International Attacks

It is the consensus among political leaders and scholars that terrorist attacks will recur, and that has been the operative assumption in my analysis as well. It is also safe to bet that included among those attacks will be some that approach the catastrophic—dirty bombs, chemical contamination, efforts to poison or infect sizable populations. Traditions of terrorist activity, the cost of mounting major attacks, and other obstacles make these less likely, but it would be surprising if some terrorists in the proliferation of international organizations and networks did not turn their attention to these kinds of attacks.

How the nation responds to such attacks poses a crucial dilemma, with huge stakes involved. The dilemma plays out differently with respect to attacks on the American mainland and attacks elsewhere in the world. I will consider each in turn.

If attacks on the American mainland are small—for example, of the dimensions of the attacks on the London Underground in July, 2005—it is plausible to assume that our own response would be not unlike that of the British, namely, to undertake a major but controlled and systematic effort to identify and apprehend the perpetrators and proceed against them within the confines of the criminal law, and to shore up defensive preparations, at least for a time.

In the case of really major attacks, however, such as the simultaneous detonation of dirty bombs in several urban centers or a major contamination of the nation's food supply, the likelihood of a more blanket aggressive response is much greater. As was the case in the aftermath of 9/11, everything points toward lashing out with an immediate, passionate, and massive response. The forces driving this response are the enormous wave of shock and rage that is immediately created, the demand for revenge against the perpetrators, and the full appreciation on the part of political authorities that passivity under these circumstances is a sure route to political suicide.

Such a response has its problems. If the enemy can be identified with some certainty, as was the case with Al-Qaeda after September 11, the response it triggered will appear to be on target and legitimate. Such is the nature of many terrorist attacks, however—including some catastrophic ones—that the consequences may unfold gradually, their perpetrators may not be known, and intelligence failures may be involved in predicting or understanding the event. All these consequences increase the likelihood that a quick, massive response against a suspected but not known enemy may be misdirected or excessive. If so, then the more remote consequences are internal and external political criticism.

In an otherwise abstract and unhelpful essay on terrorism, Baudrillard (2002) made the provocative observation that "when [events] speed up you have to move more slowly—though without allowing yourself to buried beneath a welter of words, or the gathering clouds of war" (p. 4). In one respect such advice is hopelessly unrealistic, given the overwhelming tendencies that militate against measured responses and for quick, decisive ones. At the same time, it is important for the nation to get it right in its response, both to make its response more effective and to cultivate the sympathy and support of friends and neutrals at a time when they are sympathetically disposed. To argue thus is not to argue against retribution, punishment, or even revenge; it is, however, to point out the advantages that accrue if these results are properly directed and disadvantageous if they are not.

Finally, it should be pointed out that a terrorist attack on one's own land provides an opportunity to cultivate and capitalize on the considerable international support that wells up. Important steps toward international cooperation and several significant actions by the United Nations—all directed toward the terrorist threat—were taken after 9/11. It may appear—but is not—a sacrilege to point out that one of the self-destructive tendencies of terrorism is that inflicting attacks on and slaughtering the innocent is to hasten terrorism's demise via the effective cooperation among nations to bring collective pressure to bear on its sponsors, to defend against it, and to delegitimize it as an international phenomenon.

If an attack is made on a country other than the United States, a different but equally daunting number of consequences may be envisioned. As a general principle, it would be both prudent and positive for the United States to respond by offering assistance for recovery, by helping to track down perpetrators, and, when appropriate and welcome, by cooperating with the attacked country in developing intelligence and defense arrangements. These responses constitute a convergence of humanitarian impulses and national self-interest in maintaining the best diplomatic and political relations with other societies.

If an attack abroad is a catastrophic one, more complicated and delicate issues arise. I recently participated in a working group, made up mainly of Berkeley faculty, known as the "big bang" group. Its purpose is largely scenario building, and the scenario that commands its attention is the hypothetical detonation of a nuclear device in central Moscow. In contemplating such an event, it does not appear to be all that remote or unrealistic. In any case, the group has made a systematic attempt to trace out the ramifications of such a catastrophe. These are multiple. Some domestic responses, such as movements to evacuate American urban centers, might be expected. A major ambiguity would probably be the identification of the perpetrator; Chechnya would emerge as an immediate prime suspect, though the United States would also have to deal with the fact that some groups— many Russians, many in the less developed world, some Europeans on the anti-American left, and a minority of Americans—would believe that the United States was the perpetrator, and this suspicion would have to be dealt with directly by American authorities. Perhaps most important, the ensuing international chaos that would probably result from such a catastrophe might be taken as an opportunity for countries so inclined—Pakistan, China, Iran, South Korea, and many others—to use the occasion for undertaking bold adventures to advance their own interests, perhaps by military means. If this were to happen, the peace- and stability-keeping activities of the United States would be taxed to the limit. To the best of my knowledge, very little thought has been given to preparing for catastrophic terrorist events abroad, largely because of our preoccupation with the possibility of domestic ones, but the work of this group has established a convincing case for the importance of the issue.

America's International Leadership Style

If there is a single most salient preoccupation that runs through the sample of international commentaries summarized at the beginning of the chapter, it is the way in which the United States exercises its strength in the world. Not all dwell on this, but most do. Within that general topic, moreover, the most important recurrent issue has to do with the tension between the reliance on direct and forceful wielding of economic, political, ideological and political power, on the one hand, and relying on gentler economic sanctions, persuasion through diplomatic pressure, a show of respect for other nations, and scrupulousness in the observance of international law on the other. This tension is partially captured by the unilateral-multilateral distinction; it is close to Nye's distinction between hard and soft power; it is also evident in Kagan's distinction between the direct exercise of power and the reliance on rules and laws and international negotiation and cooperation. The distinction was also personified historically by the struggle between the Bush-Cheney-Rumsfeld-Wolfowitz approach to international style and that of Colin Powell during the first term of the George W. Bush administration (see Woodward, 2004).

The tension is of general significance in relation to America's general role in the realm of international politics, especially in light of this country's overwhelming power. In my estimation it constitutes the single most important political variable with respect to the country's long-term policies relating to the threat of international terrorism. Terrorism is a world phenomenon in that its contemporary manifestation is the presence of cells in dozens of different countries, and its strikes occur and threaten to occur in many different countries, depending on terrorists' perceived significance of targets in those countries and their calculation of opportunities. The issue of key significance for the United States, as the prime target nation of international terrorism, is, in addition to defending itself and dealing directly with terrorists by force, to enlist willing nations in a coordinated worldwide campaign against terrorism and to influence less willing nations—through persuasion, sanctions, and isolation—to forgo whatever kinds of support they are extending to terrorist activities.

So deep is the tension between assertiveness and a softer style that it continuously pervades our national political debates as a constant reminder of our perpetual national love-hate affair with international aggression. In consequence, there is a plethora of rhetoric on both sides of the tension—that terrorism is a threat that knows no rules and we must accept it for that, that the only way to respond to an evil enemy is by decisive force, that terrorists and their supporters have grievances and they should be the focus of our attention, that bullying only serves to alienate the world, and on and on. Furthermore, it would be mischievous to argue that some direct application of dispassionate, scientific knowledge could cut through the ideological rhetoric and provide an acceptable, definitive preference for either style. There is no single formula. We cannot predict what the precise consequences of strategies at either end of the spectrum will be, and, in line with the analysis of international relations given earlier, there is reason to believe that a large residue of resentment and suspicion toward the United States will persist independently of its policies, because of the sheer facts of its power and the relative dependence of others on the United States.

In light of this indeterminacy, the best that can be done is to make a loose calculation of relative costs and benefits that each line of leadership might entail with respect to long-term efforts to deal with terrorism. In this connection, several observations, consistent with the analysis that has informed this book, can be made:

- Neither side of the tough-gentle dimension should be made the exclusive basis for policy. It can be argued that war or other major military action ought to be used sparingly—on humanitarian grounds, on the grounds of its limited effectiveness, on the grounds of its cost, and on the grounds of inability to control its negative ramifications. Furthermore, it is a lasting lesson from the Iraq War that interventions not informed by proper intelligence are especially counterproductive. Yet these considerations cannot be justifications to rule out military actions altogether.
- The costs of unilateral military action appear to be to fortify the ideological predispositions of terrorists and their supporters and to create resentments among friends and neutrals. The cost of gentler means of persuasion is how often they fail because they

are not in the national interest of others to go along with American initiatives, whether out of a sense of risk to themselves or out of considerations of national independence, pride, and interests. In line with the analysis of the previous section, the opportunities for cooperative and coordinated action are greatest at times of an evident increase on danger or after a significant terrorist action. To capitalize on those opportunities, however, requires a special effort, because the most likely response to threat or attack is to strike back immediately and forcefully. Domestically, the cost of aggressive action on the part of a political administration is to polarize the nation along hawk-dove lines. The cost of proceeding cautiously and gently is to excite the same polarization, which takes the form of accusation of softness. To appreciate these costs cannot be the only basis for action, but it is more advisable to know them than to deny or ignore them.

The second point leads to the issue of unified or divided action against terrorist threats, and raises the question of the role of partisanship in our own polity.

The Issue of Domestic Political Polarization

One of the hallmarks of a functioning democracy is the presence of a responsible political opposition, one that honors the constitutional rules of the game (for example, due process of law) and is loyal to the nation at the most general level but at the same time has the opportunity—through the media, through legislatures and other institutionalized forums, and through periodic elections—to call political authorities to account and replace them. In the American system of democracy, this process works itself out in practice through the major political parties, the influence of pressure groups and lobbies, and the rise and activities of social movements of all sorts, along with constant reporting and commenting by the mass media.

Over the past several decades, two different and in some respects contradictory tendencies have altered partisan politics greatly. The first is the weakening of power of political parties in the political process, occasioned by the institutionalization of direct and often binding primary elections, the decline of the political significance of the national convention as a decisive political process, the conquest of television, and the correspondingly increased salience of the individual candidate. These tendencies point toward the decline of party control over politicians and a strengthening of the direct relationship between candidates and their constituencies. The second tendency, observable over approximately the past thirty years, has been an increasing polarization of parties and party votes in Congress (Poole and Rosenthal, 1997; Hetherington, 2001), which has been gradual but with visible moments of punctuation, such as the "Gingrich revolution" of the early 1990s and the attempted impeachment of President Bill Clinton in his second term. This development has heightened the significance of holding a majority position in Congress (because crossing over is rarer), an increasing enmity between the two parties, and the tendency for everything to take on partisan significance—or given a spin to achieve that aim. The result is a push to politicize everything. The media augment this tendency with their ongoing and visible public commentaries on who has apparently gained and lost advantage in a given political situation.

The tendency to politicize has infused the nation's response to terrorism. It can be argued that this should not have happened, because terrorism resembles wartime in the sense that it is a threat to the whole nation and all are imperiled, and for that reason partisan differences should be set aside in a solidified effort to contend with it. This response was in full evidence after the 9/11 attacks, but partisan wrangling soon became the rule of the day: who was or is being negligent in defending the nation, whose policies are the right or wrong ones, who is spending money in misdirected ways, who is being tough and who is being soft on terrorism. The result is that both the party in power and the opposition party are pushed toward regarding partisan advantage or disadvantage as more important than collective assessment of the appropriateness of policies. Ullman put the matter most starkly:

With an excessive fixation on campaigning for, winning, and keeping office rather than providing good governance as its sad outcome and with the profoundly partisan nature of politics today, we will fail in the task of keeping America safe, secure and prosperous, unless our government radically changes its priorities, policies, and organization. (2004, p. ix)

This tendency revealed itself in the aftermath of Hurricane Katrina—not a case of terrorism but a kindred disaster. While there was a national outpouring of sympathy, support, and aid, the process also revealed an overlay of not only jurisdictional (federal, state, local) struggle but also a drama of partisan desperation and partisan glee at the embarrassment of the Bush administration for an apparently mismanaged response and the presumably derived advantage for the Democratic Party, with the media commenting and keeping score on the political implications in the ongoing drama. At the very least, this tendency to politicize constitutes a diversion from intelligent and effective response in the face of crisis and its aftermath.

Conclusion

From time to time in this book I have identified several factors in the terrorism complex that are double-edged swords:

- The considerable potency of an extreme antiterrorist ideology to mobilize public support to attack and defend versus the limited world view that such an ideology offers, the narrowing of options it entails, and the possibly counterproductive domestic and international political effects arising when aggressive actions are taken in its name.
- The advantage the United States enjoys from its overwhelming economic, technological, political, and cultural position in the world versus the counterproductive effects of exploiting that advantage in intemperate ways.
- The country's accumulated technological superiority in waging military attack on enemies versus the evident limitations of this technology in relation to extremely decentralized and elusive terrorist organizations.
- The advantages of the country's technological know-how in detecting and thwarting terrorists' activities at all stages of their op-

erations versus combining these capabilities with knowledge of the human and organizational aspects of defending against terrorism.

- The advantages of periodic elections and partisan and political divisions along party lines for ensuring the accountability of political leaders versus the subordination of informed, consensual counterterrorist strategies to ploys calculated to gain political advantage.
- The evident importance of the play of public opinion and the media in a democratic society versus the role that they play in a sensationalist, win-or-lose approach to terrorism.

In recording these tensions, I acknowledge that versus is not the most exact term, because they do not represent mutually exclusive, right-or-wrong approaches but rather the dimensions that appear to be most important in shaping our outlooks and policies. Nor do they present definitive or foolproof directions for policy. They are the broader conflicts of principles that frame the dilemmas and struggles over policies. Absent definitive solutions, the most salutary effects of recognizing these tensions may be those of enlightenment. To identify and take into account the general bases of conflict and confusion may increase the probability that debates may develop not as unconscious repetitions of unenlightened struggles but proceed with the most important underlying dilemmas consciously in mind.

Appendix

The Infernal Problems of Definition

and Designation

A READING of the scholarly and journalistic literature on terrorism, particularly from the 1970s to the present, leads to a curious conclusion: an analytically precise, empirically sound, and consensual definition apparently cannot be generated. Even as early as 1977, Walter Laqueur, who was to become a doyen of terrorism studies, announced that "a comprehensive definition of terrorism ... does not exist nor will it be found in the foreseeable future" (1977, p. 5; see also Laqueur, 1999, p. 5). Richard Baxter, a judge of the International Court of Justice, complained in 1974 that "We have cause to regret that a legal concept of 'terrorism' was ever inflicted upon us. The term is imprecise; it is ambiguous; and above all, it serves no legal purpose" (quoted in Murphy, 1989, p. 3). A decade later, Clifford-Vaughan (1987) observed that "studies of terrorism commence with difficulties over nomenclature" (p. 170). Long (1990) complained that "[t]here is virtually no unanimity in defining terrorism, either among scholars or among those operationally involved with terrorist threats" (p. ix), and Arnold wrote about a "war of definitions" over the term (1988, chap. 1). Very recently Nye proclaimed that terrorism is not "an entity" (2004, p. 206).

Such gloomy indictments, however, have not deterred those who write about and deal with terrorism from trying. There is scarcely a writer who does not feel the need to put forward a definition. In fact, the search for a definition brings to mind all the classical characteristics of a clinical neurosis: a compulsion to gratify a need, correspondingly compulsive but unsuccessful efforts to gratify it, but in the end, a failure to learn from the disappointments and an endless repetition of the effort. In this chapter I attempt to unscramble the resulting analytical mess and come up with a generally workable solution.

What Is the Problem of Definition, and What Are Its Origins?

From a scientific point of view, a definition must specify the *essentials* of the defined concept: the features an event or situation must possess in order to qualify as an instance of it. At the same, a definition proclaims that all instances included are *identical* to one another with respect to the central defining characteristics. It must also specify the basis for *not* including other events or situations under the definitional rubric. Put most succinctly, a definition must specify a conceptual and empirical set, and this involves both rules for inclusion and exclusion (Smelser, 1976, pp. 75–77).

Applying this criterion for definition, it is possible to see immediately why the attempt to define terrorism inductively—that is, to identify systematically the common characteristics of historical events and situations that have been called terrorism—is bound to fail. That historical accumulation has not yielded a workable consistency. A number of features associated with use of the term guarantee this result:

- Definitions of the term manifest the principles of recency and myopia—that is, focus on aspects that are particularly dramatic at a given time. Early meanings, put forward in the long shadow of the French Revolution and its Reign of Terror, emphasized state terrorism. In the late nineteenth century, anarchism and assassination were at the core of concerns. The use of terror associated with guerrilla activity was salient in post–World War II anticolonial uprisings and the era of the ideas of Mao Tse-tung and Che Guevara (Chaplin, 2003). The 1960s and 1970s focused both on left-wing terrorism in Western democracies and on the emergence of serious international terrorism in the form of skyjackings, hostage taking, and assassinations, perpetrated mainly by Palestinian groups. State-sponsored international terrorism became salient in the 1980s, and attention focused on the activities of countries such as Iran and Libya and on the sometimes clandestine, sometimes open terror-sponsoring activities of the superpowers (Cline and Alexander, 1984; Piszkiewicz, 2004). Ethnic, nationalist, and secessionist ingredients have been a regular feature of definitions of terrorism for decades, but more recently, with the salience of terrorism emanating from fundamentalist Islamic movements, the religious and international dimensions have become more prominent. These changing emphases over time show up sequentially in generic definitions, which reflect the unending effort to catch up with history.

• Almost all discourse that invokes the term "terrorism" is normative, that is, condemnatory of the actions of an individual, group, or nation inimical to one's own interests The stigma of terrorism, moreover, is "applied in a thoroughly selective and partial way" (Jenkins, 2003, p. ix). Very few terrorists, with the notable exception of Carlos Marighella, the Brazilian urban guerrilla theorist, have proudly used the word for themselves. Radical Islamic fundamentalists have labeled the centuries of Crusader and Jewish intrusions into the Middle East as terrorism and their mission as a heroic struggle against it. Osama bin Laden, generally regarded in American eyes as the quintessential terrorist, said in 1998, "the worst terrorists are the Americans" (quoted in National Commission on Terrorist Attacks Upon the United States, 2004, p. 72). In the West we do not hesitate to characterize the attacks by Muslim fundamentalists as terrorism. Such an array of uses brings to mind Bertrand Russell's idea of emotive conjugations—"I am firm, you are stubborn, he is pigheaded" (cited in Goldstick, 2002, p. 17). The logic seems clear and inescapable: if the term is used mainly in a negatively evaluative way and the resulting game is a contest over pinning and avoiding the label, what other result is possible than shifting definitions and elusive and inconsistent empirical references?

Some writers argue that it is acceptable to be normative if terrorists are fighting undemocratic regimes or combating demonstrable injustices (Crenshaw, 1983), and others argue that definitions of terrorism ought not to be jettisoned merely because they involve evaluative judgments of legitimacy (Wilkinson, 1987, p. xi). The main social scientific impulse, however, has been to look for analytical or value-neutral and inclusive typologies that avoid selective judgments (Hocking, 1992). In all events, the history of the term is a history of condemnations, and the dynamic involved is that the term chases many events and situations that have little else in common other than the fact that they are perceived by some party as threatening and offensive. In the last analysis, it becomes clear that "the very process of definition is in itself part of the wider conflict between ideologies or political objectives" (Thackrah, 1987a, p. 25). As a general rule, partisans forever attempt to load words—"liberal," "conservative," "right," and "left" are but a few examples—with primarily emotive or evaluative responses, and the word "terrorism" appears to be an extreme example of this practice. Gearty observed in 1991 that "the words 'terror' and 'terrorism' have come to be regarded as such powerful condemnations that all those looking for a suitable insult have wanted to appropriate them" (p. 5). If one attempts to find commonalities in the kaleidoscope of events and situations that have been labeled terrorist, one soon becomes hopelessly mired in contradictory results.

• It is to the credit of Alex Schmid, a Dutch scholar of terrorism, and his colleagues to have specified the relevant *structural* bases for the proliferation and divergence of meanings of terrorism. In an edited volume they laid out the different perspectives of researchers, terrorists, governments, broadcasting organizations, editors, reporters, victims, and "the public" (Paletz and Schmid, 1992), all of which pull the concept of terrorism in different directions. Each of these groups gravitates toward a systematic bias. Government and security agencies, for example, are inclined to tilt their definitions of terrorist acts in the direction of inclusiveness, as an expression of their positional interest in gaining maximum flexibility in monitoring, pursuing, apprehending, and prosecuting individuals and groups. Victims tend to focus on those types of events that have affected them directly. Terrorists, as indicated, almost never identify their own actions as terrorist, but readily describe their enemies as dangerous terrorists. Journalists live by the imperative of striving for authenticity in making terminological judgments, but they are also driven by the continuous pressures to scoop, to dramatize, and to excite public attention and readership by highlighting that which is conflictful and violent. To discover or assert that something is "terrorist" surely meets those requirements. Scholars normally live in universities, which constitute "an intellectual forum where [they] can discuss terrorism without being suspected of sympathizing with terrorists" (Schmid, 1993a, p. 7), but they often cannot resist being drawn into the evaluative game. And finally, the most elusive group, "the public," will experience shifting perceptions that are influenced by all the sources mentioned. It should be added, however, that the public is not a homogeneous entity but always reflects partisan differences and debates. Because all these interested constituencies are more or less permanent parts of the social landscape of societies, their own divergent views about what terrorism is may be expected to assert themselves periodically in the flow of historical events.

Enough has been said to establish the hopeless side of the enterprise of attempting to arrive at a definition of an essentially contested term—one that invites advocating its contradictory versions. The issue of definition can thus be identified as Entrapment 5 in our attempt to fathom the phenomenon of terrorism:

Entrapment 5. The fruitlessness of attempting to arrive, inductively or deductively, at a scientifically precise definition of a term that, in its historical evolution, has shown no consistency in denotation, connotation, emotional loading, or operational indices.

To identify such an entrapment should be the beginning point of analysis. It is appropriate, then, to turn now in a more positive direction.

A Sample of Definitions

In 1988, Schmid and colleagues, surveying a large number of sources for definitions of terrorism, came up with a discouragingly long list of 109 distinguishable though overlapping ones (Schmid et al., 1988). It would serve little purpose to conduct another such survey today, other than to document further the accumulating confusion. Instead, I offer a handful of seriously proposed definitions illustrative of the dilemmas I have just laid out:

> A *normative definition*: "Terrorism [is] any type of political violence that lacks an adequate moral or legal justification, regardless of whether the actor is a revolutionary group or government" (Falk, cited in Davies, 2003).
>
> *Comment*: The definition, like few others, aims to include both terrorism from above (state terrorism) and non-state terrorism (but only revolutionary violence); it ignores, however, that with few exceptions, behavior described as terrorist is embedded in a moral or political ideology that represents the acts of the perpetrators as legitimate.
>
> A *manifestly historically specific definition*: "Terrorism is a clandestine and undeclared warfare against the West and therefore must be recognized as a clear and present danger both to the individual and collective security of the United States" (Livingstone, 1982, p. 40).
>
> *Comment*: While not factually wrong, the definition excludes most of the separatist, nationalist, ethnic, and internally revolutionary uses of terror, to say nothing of the United States' involvement in terrorist activities, in evidence even at the time the definition was put forth.
>
> *Two inclusive, spare definitions*: (1) "Terrorism is a violent act aimed at influencing the political process" (Taylor, 1988, p. 3). (2) "Terrorism is the intentional generation of massive fear by human beings for the purpose of securing or maintaining control over other human beings" (Cooper, 2002, p. 3).
>
> *Comment*: Taylor's definition is hopelessly overextended, since it appears to include war generally as well as political demonstrations that employ violence. Cooper's definition includes the vague and probably inaccurate "massive" to describe the effects of all terrorism; his phrase "securing or maintaining control over other human beings" seems accurate enough for state terrorism but is very vague with respect to the diverse political aims of different non-state terrorist organizations.
>
> *Two agency definitions*: U.S. Department of State: "Terrorism [is] premeditated, politically motivated violence perpetrated against noncombatant targets by subnational groups or clandestine state agents, usually intended to influence an audience" (U.S. Department of State,

1988). The state of California: "Any person who willfully threatens to commit a crime which will result in death or great bodily injury to another person, with intent to terrorize another or with reckless disregard of the risk of terrorizing another, and who thereby either (a) Causes another person reasonably to be sustained fear for his or her or their immediate family's safety; (b) Causes the evacuation of a building, place of assembly, or facility used in public transportation; (c) Interferes with essential public services; or (d) Otherwise causes serious disruption of public activities, is guilty of a felony and shall be punished by imprisonment in the state prison. . . . As used in this title, "terrorize" means to create a climate of fear and intimidation by means of threats or violent action causing sustained fear for personal safety in order to achieve social or political goals" (California Penal Code, Code 11.5, 422, quoted in Murphy, 1989, p 14).

Comment: Framed in generic terms, the State Department's definition nonetheless has a flavor that skews it toward the agency's own interests as perceived at the time (a concern with international state and non-state violence). It includes neither states' terrorism against their own peoples nor revolutionary terrorism directed against what are perceived to be oppressive governments nor much guerrilla terrorism directed against government forces, not noncombatants. The phrase "usually intended to influence an audience" is open-ended and vague with respect to inclusion and exclusion of cases. The California code, drafted in the language of criminal law, is something of a rambling essay. It gives vague reference to "social or political goals," but the remainder of the language appears to include acts beyond that scope. More generally, the statute assembles a grab bag of behaviors that are of interest to law enforcement officials and does not specify—as the State Department language does—the political status (state or non-state) of the perpetrators.

An inductive listing of frequently present characteristics: A RAND corporation definition:

Terrorism . . . is defined by the nature of the act, not by the identity of the perpetrators or by the nature of their cause. All terrorist acts are crimes—murder, kidnapping, and arson. Many would also be violations of the rules of war, if a state of war existed. All involve violence or the threat of violence coupled with specific demands.

The violence is directed mainly against civilian targets. The motives are political. The actions generally are carried out in a way that will achieve maximum publicity. The perpetrators are usually members of an organized group, and unlike other criminals, they often claim credit for the act. And finally, the act is intended to produce effects beyond the immediate physical damage. (Jenkins, 1980, pp. 2–3)

Comment: The definition has the benefit of being inclusive. It is certainly on target when it calls for a definition based on concrete acts, not motives. Yet in the middle of the definition, motives appear as part of it. The assertion that some acts, such as arson, are violations of the rules of war is debatable. The assertion regarding "specific demands" is consistent with the political character of terrorism, but demands certainly vary in their level of specificity (for example, "Remove U.S. troops from Saudi Arabia" versus "Exact revenge for centuries of abuse at the hands of Crusaders and Jews"). Finally, the appearance of words such as "mainly," "often," and "generally" indicates that the definition not only looks for essentials but also includes commonly though not universally present characteristics (for further criticism, see Thackrah, 1987a, p. 27).

A definition based on scholarly consensus: In connection with a 1992 conference on Western responses to terrorism, Schmid sent out a definition of terrorism to some fifty scholars. He secured an agreement on his definition from a large majority of them, but some proposed additions and qualifications. After taking these into account, he came up with the following, quite inclusive definition:

Terrorism is an anxiety inspiring method of repeated violent action, employed by (semi-) clandestine individual, group, or state actors, for idiosyncratic, criminal or political reasons whereby—in contrast to assassination—the direct targets of violence are not the main targets. The immediate human victims of violence are generally chosen randomly (targets of opportunity) or selectively (representative or symbolic targets) from a target population, and serve as message generators. Threat- and violence-based communication processes between terrorist (organization[s]), (imperiled) victims, and main targets are used to manipulate the main target (audience[s]), turning it into a target of terror, or a target of demands, or a target of attention, depending on whether intimidation, coercion, or propaganda is primarily sought. (Schmid, 1993a, p. 8)

Comment: The definition, helpful in many respects, also has the markings of a consensual product that tries to incorporate all suggestions. (It brings to mind the cynical quip that "a camel is a horse drawn by a committee.") The effort is to be as inclusive as possible and to take into account historical contingencies (even though assassination seems to be explicitly excluded). There is an effort to encompass all potential types of actors, targets, meanings of targets, reasons, and intentions. The emergent difficulty is that if all of these ingredients are presented as essential, the definition becomes replete with possibilities and hedged with qualifications. In the process, it becomes as unhelpful as the spare definitions that are couched in language meant to include all things without specifying what those things are.

Definitional Problems

It would be helpful to illustrate the nettlesome problem of defining terrorism with an account of how I experienced it in the trenches. This calls for telling the story of how the sub-panel on Behavioral, Social and Institutional Issues in Terrorism (National Research Council), which I chaired, confronted the problem.

Assembled in late 2001 and on a very fast track to prepare a report, our panel was aware of the necessity to define terrorism from both scientific and policy standpoints, or, in the words of Crelinsten and Schmid,

> Before you start combating a monster you have to understand its nature and *modus operandi*. For this you need a good description of its characteristics—a workable definition. A wrong definition—like the Ptolemaic definition of the earth as a flat disk—makes solutions impossible because they are not thinkable in that particular framework. (1993, p. 315)

We were therefore prepared to craft a definition and go about our work.

At that early stage, none of us was deeply acquainted with the literature on terrorism from the past twenty-five years, nor with the extent of the conceptual confusion involved in defining it. (As it turned out, that was just as well; we could have spent our entire panel effort in trying to sort out the issue.) We did know, however, that Schmid and colleagues (1988) had identified more than one hundred separate, overlapping, and competing definitions in the terrorist literature, and we could only imagine how many more had accumulated since their effort. We also were aware that terrorism is a term of opprobrium, seldom applied by its perpetrators to describe their own actions but typically applied to them by their target populations and their enemies. As a result of this, we knew that the same event or situation could be defined either as terrorism or as something else by contending parties. To underscore this point, we compiled a list of such events that could be thus ambiguously regarded:

· British and American firebombing of Dresden in World War II
· Dropping atomic bombs on Hiroshima and Nagasaki in World War II
· Sherman's march through Georgia during the American Civil War
· Palestinian suicide bombing
· Israeli punitive strikes on Palestinians
· Lebanese Phalangist militia attacks on Muslims
· The Bay of Pigs
· Project Camelot
· Hagannah and Irgun attacks on the British in Palestine
· The original Sicilian Mafia as an organization to protect the peasants
· Organized crime, especially protection rackets
· Lynching, church bombings, and Ku Klux Klan activities generally
· International drug trade and the financing of guerrillas
· The "reign of terror" in postrevolutionary France
· Stalin's purges of the 1930s
· Ruby Ridge
· Waco
· Frank and Jesse James

In recompiling that list now we could have included the attacks of September 11, 2001 (almost universally regarded as a quintessential act of terrorism in the United States, but described as justifiable retribution for injustices in radical Islamic statements), as well as the "shock and awe" tactics of the American military in the Afghan and Iraq wars (words used to described effective military tactics by American commanders, but at the same time directly implying the effect of creating terror in the enemy).

We thus faced a dilemma of needing a definition and not being able to come up with a consistent or consensus-based one. In the end, we were forced to conclude that terrorism—like other concepts such as art, democracy, and poverty—falls into the category of an "essentially contested concept," a term invented in the field of linguistics fifty years ago (Gallie, 1956). This term refers to a concept that is not totally incoherent or without meaning but whose essential features are literally contested. Such terms are used differently by parties of different persuasions for the same events and situations according to their political predilections.

After confronting this dilemma, the panel decided not to try to generate a universally valid definition of terrorism. We would not treat the diverse empirical phenomena associated with it as evidence of the "thing" of terrorism with known essential characteristics. Rather, we placed it in a family of behaviors that differ along a number of dimensions—for example, who are the actors, who are the victims, what means are used, in the name of what political orientation and ideology is it executed, what are the ultimate targets, and what are the intended and actual consequences? A typology of violent actions and episodes could thus be identified without reducing all of them to a blanket category, "terrorism." We believed this strategy of identifying salient dimensions would be most satisfactory in specifying the characteristics of "terroristic" events and providing a corresponding level of precision in identifying the variable nature of the specific "monster" in question.

The panel believed that this strategy was a sensible and productive approach to the definitional conundrums that pervade the literature on terrorism. We were shaken from this comfortable belief, however, by three comments that appeared in the scientific review of the panel draft (a mandatory process for all National Research Council reports). The first comment, stated most forcefully and as a condition for even considering the document for approval, was that we must come up with *single* definition of terrorism, even though we had developed a case that our dimensional-typological approach was the only sensible one. Faced with this coercive demand, the panel caved and put forth a "working defini-tion" that we thought incorporated the most commonly described characteristics:

> [Terrorism involves the] illegal use or threatened use of force or vio-lence; an intent to coerce societies or governments by inducing fear in their populations; typically with ideological and political motives and justifications; an "extrasocietal" element, either "outside" society in the case of domestic terrorism or "foreign" in the case of interna-tional terrorism. (Smelser and Mitchell, 2002a, p. 15)

We knew this definition to be limited and thus wrong according to our reasoning—because such a single inclusive definition could not be pro-duced in principle, and because it omitted some events and situations, such as state terrorism, that have been put under that label—but we produced one anyway, in deference to the almost universally experienced compulsion to produce a single definition of the phenomenon.

The second and third objections confirmed the sensibility of our origi-nal approach. The second, coming from a positivistically minded scientific reviewer, said that our solution was all wrong, and that the proper ap-proach was an inductive one, that is, identifying all terrorist episodes that have occurred and locating their common characteristics (for an articula-tion of this inductive approach, see Levitt, 1988). This was a demand that flew in the face of what we knew to be impossible, given terrorism's essen-tially contested status, and given the methodological truth that at least an implicit definition must already be in mind even to classify and count events. The third objection was to our "catholicity" and implied moral relativism for including so many diverse events as possible cases of terror-ism on our illustrative list. This reviewer argued that we all know for certain what terrorism is: it is what the Palestinian terrorists were currently perpetrating against Israel. The reviewer went so far as to suggest that the panel's approach concealed a possible anti-Israeli or anti-Semitic bias, a suggestion absurd on its face.

As a panel we rejected both criticisms, which we regarded as coming from opposite extremes—one as a theoretically and methodologically naïve and impossible "know-nothing" mentality, and the other as an a priori "know-everything" mentality. Taken together, the two objections revealed many of the scientific and ideological confusions that reign in the ongoing debates about the nature of terrorism.

A Pragmatic Definition and Its Defense

Sufficient effort has gone into demonstrating the difficulties of attempting a satisfactory definition of the word terrorism so as to include every kind of violence that has been labeled terrorism by its victims, by political actors, by the media, and by scholars seeking general characterizations. At the same time, it is essential to know what we are talking about when we use the term. This suggests a pragmatic approach—admittedly incomplete, but at the same time aiming toward specification of most salient elements for purposes of describing and understanding. In attempting to generate such a definition, I have relied on the following guidelines:

- The elements included in the definition must be regarded as *essential* rather than merely associated or accidental; they must be present if an event or situation to qualify as an instance.
- It seems advisable to stress that terrorism is an empirically identifiable, generic kind of *act* or *behavior*, and not attempt to include the panoply of perpetrators, causes, reasons, intentions, types of targets, and political consequences (see Hoffman, 1998, p. 34). Some of these elements, particularly reasons and intentions, often defy precise identification. All of them are variable historically. Choosing one makes for excessive narrowness of reference and sacrifices generality; specifying all contexts makes for an undesirable sprawl. Reasons and intentions can be addressed only when different historical contexts frame specific occurrences of the generic phenomenon.
- It is necessary to include the kinds of terrorism that have become salient in the last three or four decades and that may overshadow

conventional war as the dominant mode of belligerence for some time to come. At the same, time it is necessary to avoid regarding recent manifestations of terrorism as the generic form.

- It is essential to give salience to the *political* dimension of terrorism if for no other reason than that seems to be its most common and consequential form. Furthermore, the fact that violence or the threat of it is almost always an element guarantees that terrorist actions constitute a threat to the long-established principle that the state claims a legitimate monopoly on violence, however tenuous its ability to enforce that monopoly. This explicitly political reference excludes certain types of violence that do not have primarily political aims (for example, extortion rackets with threats of violence, some narcoterrorism, "pathological" violence such as the school shootings perpetrated by psychologically disturbed adolescents, and "private" violence such as stalking and sadistic mind games)—all of which, however, may generate terror.
- I will add an explanatory word about terror carried out by states after laying out a definition.

With these criteria in mind, I propose the following formal definition:

Terrorism: *intended, irregular acts of violence or disruption (or the threat of them) carried out in secret with the effect of generating anxiety in a group, and with the further aim, via that effect, of exciting political response or political change.*

I now offer an explication of the reasons for including each of the main ingredients:

- "Intended" specifies the obvious fact that acts of terrorism involve human agency and so are to be distinguished from natural disasters and accidents.
- "Irregular" seems a better word than "random"—used in some definitions—because terrorist actions frequently display patterns in the selection of targets according to their importance, accessibility, and symbolic significance. "Irregular" seems an essential feature, because the notion of terrorist-induced anxiety involves both threat and the uncertainty of occurrence.

- "In secret" also seems essential, because that characteristic is so intimately linked with the idea of irregularity and the component of uncertainty in generating anxiety. "In secret" refers to the perpetration of acts themselves (which is almost always done clandestinely), but there is variation in the way that threats and warnings are issued and in the extent to which perpetrators or other parties admit or take credit for terrorist acts after the fact.

- "Violence" alone does not seem broad enough to cover many terrorist activities, even if the term is extended to include property as well as persons. Many current forms of terrorism, such as fouling economic institutions, disabling electronic systems, or creating mayhem, are systemic efforts to destabilize or cripple society's infrastructure but are not violent unless one stretches that concept. The term violence does not extend comfortably to them. This observation modifies the dictum that "all terror is necessarily violent, but violence is not necessarily terrorism" (Quinton, 1990, p. 35).

- "Anxiety" is a better term than "fear" or "apprehension" because it connotes uncertainty about when, where, and how terrorism endangers. Anxiety is closer to terror in connotation than the other two terms; fear is an affect typically attached to a specific threat or object, whereas anxiety is more diffuse; apprehension is close to anxiety but is milder in connotation and less descriptive of reactions to acts and threats of terrorism.

- Specific target groups are not included as part of the definition. They must be understood to include not only noncombatants (a defining word that appears frequently) but also governmental and military targets and personnel (such as the attack on the destroyer U.S.S. *Cole*, presumably by the Al-Qaeda group, in October 2000) as well as property and institutions.

- It seems essential to include both "political response" and "political change," because while many terrorist actions are accompanied by specific demands for political change, many are nonspecific in this regard. All such actions, however, are politically provocative because they involve violence that threatens the monopoly of the state over police and military force, and so threatens the role of the state as the ultimate mediator of conflict through institutionalized political processes (see Addison, 2002, p. 73; Crenshaw, 1983, p. 25).

- It is possible to specify the relations between terrorism and several kindred phenomena, namely, war, crime, and political protest. Terrorism has been described in the literature as an instance of all of these. Such assignments are both correct and incorrect. War, crime, and political protest are three overlapping sets. The area common to all three is terrorism, because it shares some of the characteristics of each. In that sense it is a subtype of each. However, terrorism does not share all the characteristics of each.

- The definition I propose shares many characteristics with it but is not coterminous with conventional war. Terrorism is not normally state versus state (though state-sponsored terrorism against another state comes close), terrorism does not pit armies against armies, and the pattern of weapons use typically differs between terrorism and war. However, some acts of war can properly be regarded as acts of terror, for example, *blitzkrieg*, the use of shock troops, fire-bombing and round-the-clock aerial attacks on cities, and "shock-and-awe" battlefield tactics. The definition is also meant to include many tactics of modern guerrilla warfare, though many authors have attempted to distinguish between guerrilla war and terrorism (Clutterbuck, 1977). Terrorism involves criminal assaults on people and property, but its terror-inducing intent sets it off from many other forms of criminal activity. And while usually expressing political discontent, terrorism is only one type of political protest. The definition thus shares some characteristics with known, similar, and overlapping phenomena, but it is a conceptual and empirical error to identify it solely with any one of the three.

- The definition comfortably includes the major forms of terrorism that have dominated the scene in the past half-century and commanded most attention from scholars: ethnonationalist-separatist terrorism such as that in Northern Ireland, in the Basque area, and in many other multiethnic societies; domestic ideological terrorism such as perpetrated by the Red Army Faction (Germany), the Red Brigades (Italy), and the Weatherman faction (United States); "single-issue" terrorism, such as that associated with the antiabortion movement, the animal rights movement, and the environmental movement; some of the terrorist attacks by "loners," such as Timothy McVeigh (the Oklahoma City bomber) and Theodore Kaczynski (the Unabomber), because of the political context and justification of their actions by the perpetrators; and international violence, typified by many activities of groups associated with the Palestine Liberation Organization, the Japanese Red Army, and more recently Al-Qaeda and its associated networks. The definition is not intended to include historically remote incidents that bear some resemblance to the definition (for example, the *sicari* of ancient Roman Palestine and the Order of the Assassins in the eleventh century, which some scholars include) (Laqueur, 1999, p. 11). The definition also discriminates terrorism from much criminal violence that occurs in "issueless riots" (Marx, 1970), violence institutionalized in sports, and the violent behavior of fans and youths associated with sports partisanship (such as the soccer riots). All of these may incite terror in people, but they do not encompass the other ingredients of the definition. Finally, despite the inclusion of assassination in many treatments of terrorism, the proposed definition cannot comfortably include it. Assassinations have certainly been in the repertoire of both historical and contemporary terrorism in Europe, but often they are acts of attack or revenge in internecine struggles, and often they are vague in their intent, including the intent to spread terror. Many assassinations, moreover, especially in the United States, have been individual attacks by psychologically marginal loners, not groups (Crotty, 1971).

- In principle, the proposed definition could include "state terrorism," including state-organized genocide, both of which seek political consequences. The literature, however, shows a distinct ambivalence about grouping the two under the same definition. After sustained efforts to come up with a comfortably inclusive definition, I decided not to try to force state terror under the heading, and in this book I do not consider it in the same analytical camp as insurgent terrorism. The reason is that it defies or stretches too many of the ingredients of the definition proposed. For example, state terrorism is likely to be more systematic and "regular"; it is not aimed so much at disruption as to enforce state domination and social order by systematically killing and intimidating a designated group; it strikes a delicate balance between being secret and being known, in that it is often though not always concealed from outsiders' view, though to have its intended effect it must in some sense be known by the home population; and it is not meant to excite political responses but rather to repress them. Finally, turning to determinants, state terrorism is not the activity of those who feel themselves to be dispossessed and weak but rather violence carried out by the very group that claims a legitimate monopoly over force and violence in society. Thus, while state terrorism, genocide, and ethnic cleansing constitute clear areas for study and explanation (see, for example, Naimark, 2001), it seems inadvisable analytically to force them into a marriage of definitional and conceptual identity with "terrorism from below."

Before identifying lines of variability of terrorist activities, I confess to at least one ambiguity in my own definition that I have not been able to overcome. That ambiguity is found in the words "effect of generating anxiety" and the words "further aim." The ambiguity is whether the term "effect" refers primarily to the intentions of the perpetrators or to the experience of target populations. Both are often in evidence. However, with respect to *intent*, actions that disrupt electronic communications or stock market operations or that generally create mayhem are aimed mainly at creating disarray, with causing anxiety a more remote intent. Furthermore, many perpetrators of terror do not openly admit that their purpose is to create terror but rather see themselves as setting the world right according to their own diagnosis of things. With respect to *consequence*, some events, such as random bombings of subways, hostage taking, and the killing of schoolchildren, appear to have the uniform consequence of generating anxiety, but for different kinds of events other consequences may be more salient. For example, although anxiety was clearly one of the immediate consequences of the September 11, 2001, attacks ("Will they attack again?"), the affects of shock and collective outrage seemed more salient. I do not know how to handle this difficulty from a definitional standpoint, but in the end regard it as an inevitable residue of the historical vicissitudes of the use of the word "terrorism," with all its ambiguities and inaccuracies.

Variants of Terrorism

Having made a pragmatic attempt to identify the essentials of terrorism as accurately as possible, I now turn to a discussion of those characteristics that are sometimes present but vary in time and place and give different historical meanings to the phenomena designated as terrorism. At the same time I will attempt to pinpoint the particular aspects of those lines of variation that are especially salient on the contemporary scene, hoping thereby to throw initial light on why current terrorism is a more formidable threat to organized political and social life than it has ever been. Many of these threads of variability have been analyzed in more detail in the chapters of this book.

Who Are the Actors?

The historical panoply of terrorism has yield a vast array of individual and group perpetrators of intended and irregular acts of violence: individuals or "loners"; clubs and societies (such as anarchists); splinter groups within larger political parties and social movements; revolutionary movements; guerrilla movements; states; state-sponsored or state-supported organizations; "stateless" groups; cells and shifting networks of cells. These perpetrators also vary in the degree to which they identify themselves publicly through writing, propaganda, and taking credit for violent actions.

How Do the Actors Justify Their Actions?

This is the ideological question, and a similarly great range of variation can be observed. Some of the ideologies justifying violence appear on the surface to be without substantial reasons, such as that propounded for its own sake or as an aesthetic experience (as in some anarchist and existentialist worldviews). However, close examination of these "negativist" beliefs usually reveal more positive ideological elements—a hidden, implicit, utopian conception of community or society. Some ideologies are more or less private syncretisms in the mind of a single actor, even though ingredients of more public political ideologies may be found (see the box, "The Professor and the Unabomber," in chapter 3). Other ideologies are highly explicit and include frequent references to historical events (especially atrocities) and elements from contemporary social movements and cultural drifts. Examples are the primordially based ideologies of nationalist, separatist, and minority ethnic groups, appealing to blood ties, assertions of "rightful" territorial claims, a distinctive cultural heritage, a language, and sometimes a religious heritage. Examples are found in the Tamil separatist movement in Sri Lanka, the Basque separatist movement, and some of the radical black protest in the United States in the 1960s. Others appeal to more frankly political ideologies, as in the radical leftist-based Red Brigades in Italy and the Red Army Faction in West Germany in the 1960s and 1970s, as well as the radical right ideologies of the Ku Klux Klan and neo-Nazism in Germany and the United States (these "political" movements often have quasi-religious ingredients), and some single-issue political ideologies such as environmentalist protest. Still other ideologies are frankly religious in character; most of these are rooted in fundamentalist revivals, particularly in Protestantism and Islam. The main point to be underscored is that very little terrorism occurs in the absence of some kind of ideological justification, but very different ideologies can serve the purpose. Chapter 3 focuses on ideologies in detail.

What Do Terrorists Demand?

Very little terrorism is completely pointless, and that is why the words "the aim . . . of exciting political response or political change" appears in the generic definition. Yet variation is apparent here as well. Terrorist activities such as hostage taking have been closely tied to very specific demands for release of imprisoned comrades of the terrorists. Closely related were the evident political demands of terrorists who bombed Spanish trains on March 11, 2004: to influence the upcoming Spanish election and to coerce Spain to end its military support of the United States in Iraq. Other actions are couched in the context of demands for specific political changes, such as the Palestinians' demands for abolishing the state of Israel and expelling the Jews from that land. At one stage the demands of Osama bin Laden were for ending policies supporting Israel and removing American troops from Saudi Arabia, the land of Muslim holy places. On the more diffuse end of the continuum, revolutionary ideologies that have spawned terrorism have called for the overthrow of governments and the obliteration of capitalist society. Perhaps the most diffuse demands come when terrorist aims are couched in the context of an absolute war. For example, a former leader of the Hezbollah organization (out of Lebanon) stated, "We are not fighting so that the enemy recognizes us and offers us something. We are fighting to wipe out the enemy" (quoted in Hoffman, 1998, p. 96).

The history of terrorism displays variation among types of perpetrators, their ideologies, and their demands. Where does the terrorism of 9/11 stand with respect to these variations? The targets were a mix of civilian noncombatants and military personnel (the military in the Pentagon), but above all the targets were symbolic, the World Trade Center being the most visible symbol of American-dominated global capitalism and finance and the Pentagon the most visible symbol of American military domination. With respect to actors, these were Middle Eastern terrorist groups that had engaged in international terrorism directed toward the United States and its allies for a number of years. Its organizational form was the dispersed, mobile, evasive, ever-fluctuating networks of cells, not known to one another, that are variably not known about, ignored, tolerated, or supported by the states out of which they operate. These characteristics were "personified" in the Al-Qaeda organization, whose associated cells have since become more numerous, more dispersed, and less centrally directed since the damaging assault on its center in the Afghan War. The inspiring ideology of this dominant form is a mélange of Islamic fundamentalist, anti-Israeli and anti-American beliefs. And finally, the demands of this group of (largely) Middle Eastern terrorists have evolved from more specific political demands and conditions into a more generalized jihad with the more remote but more general aim of bringing down the West (and all the cultural and international evils assigned to it) and establishing a community, society, and political-legal order consistent with the principles of traditional Islam. From the standpoint of defining essentials, 9/11 was unequivocally an act of terrorism, but it was a unique act because of its special combination of variable characteristics.

A Concluding Remark

The purpose of this appendix has been one of conceptual house cleaning, an activity that is normally not as exciting intellectually as identifying and explaining the causal dynamics of what one is studying. It a necessary ingredient of analysis, however, negatively because of the confusion that has surrounded the study and understanding of terrorism, and positively because of the need for precision and clarity in defining the object of study.

Acknowledgments

WORKING on this book has been largely a solo operation, but I have received some help along the way. Michelle Williams provided valuable research assistance. Arlie Hochschild and Victoria Bonnell read and commented incisively on chapter 3. Discussions with many colleagues at the National Academies of Sciences found their way into my thinking, as did questions and criticisms from audiences at presentations I made at Northern Illinois University, Illinois State University, the University of Illinois (Champaign-Urbana), the University of California, Berkeley, the University of Trento, the American Sociological Association, the Pacific Sociological Association, the National Academy of Sciences, the California Council for Science and Technology, and the Livermore National Laboratory. Jeff Robbins of the National Academies Press and Tim Sullivan of Princeton University Press saw the manuscript through various stages of preparation and production. I am also grateful to four anonymous readers for Princeton University Press, all of whom liked the book but also had many helpful things to say. I wish I could thank other assistants, administrative staff, and secretaries, but, being retired, I no longer enjoy such infrastructure. I can only congratulate myself and my computer for getting the work done.

References

Abrams, Courtney, Karen Albright, and Aaron Panofsky. 2004. Contesting the New York community: From liminality to the "new normal" in the wake of September 11. *City and Community* 3(3):189–220.

Adams, James. 1986. *The Financing of Terror: How the Groups That Are Terrorizing the World Get the Money to Do It.* New York: Simon and Schuster, 1986.

———. 1987. The financing of terror. In *Contemporary Research on Terrorism*, ed. Paul Wilkinson and Alasdair M. Stewart, 393–405. Aberdeen: Aberdeen University Press.

Addison, Michael. 2002. *Violent Politics: Strategies of Internal Conflict.* New York: Palgrave.

Addison, Tony, and S. Mansoob Murshed. 2002. *Transnational Terrorism as a Spillover of Domestic Disputes in Other Countries.* The Hague: Institute of Social Studies.

Aguirre, B. E. 2004. Homeland security warnings: Lessons learned and unlearned. University of Delaware Disaster Research Center Paper 342. Newark, DE.

Âhmad, Rif'at Sayyid. 2002. Is Usama bin Ladin the culprit? Has World War III started? In *Anti-American Terrorism and the Middle East: A Documentary Reader*, ed. Barry Rubin and Judith Colp Rubin, 291–92. New York: Oxford University Press.

Akhtar, Salman. 2002. The psychodynamic dimension of terrorism. In *Terrorism and War: The Unconscious Dynamics of Political Violence*, ed. Coline Covington, Paul Williams, Jean Arundel, and Jean Knox, 87–96. London: Karnac.

Alexander, Dean C. 2004. *Business Confronts Terrorism: Risks and Responses.* Madison: University of Wisconsin Press.

Alexander, Dean C., and Yonah Alexander. 2002. *Terrorism and Business: The Impact of September 11, 2001.* Ardsley, NY: Transnational Publishers.

Alexander, Jeffrey, Ron Eyerman, Bernard Giesen, Neil J. Smelser, and Piotr Sztompka. 2004. *Cultural Trauma and Collective Identity.* Berkeley and Los Angeles: University of California Press.

Alexander, Yonah. 1990. Terrorism: The nuclear threat. In *International Responses to Terrorism: New Initiatives*, ed. Richard H. Ward and Ahmed Galal Ezeldin, 41–50. Chicago: University of Illinois at Chicago, Office of International Criminal Justice.

Alexander, Yonah, and Richard Latter. 1990. The U.S. perspective. In *Terrorism and the Media: Dilemmas for Government, Journalists and the Public*, ed. Yonah Alexander and Richard Latter, 43–46. Washington, DC: Brassey's (US).

Alexander, Yonah, and Kenneth Myers, eds. 1982. *Terrorism in Europe.* London: Croom Helm.

Alexander, Yonah, and Dennis A. Pluchinsky, eds. 1992. *Europe's Red Terrorists: The Fighting Communist Organizations.* London; Frank Cass.

Anderson, Benedict. 1991. *Imagined Communities*. London: Verso.

Appadurai, A. 2001. Globalization, anthropology of. In *International Encyclopedia of the Social and Behavioral Sciences*, ed. Neil J. Smelser and Paul B. Baltes, 9:6287–92. Oxford: Elsevier.

Arnold, Terrell E. 1988. *The Violence Formula: Why People Lend Sympathy and Support to Terrorism*. Lexington, MA: Lexington Books.

Arora, Subhash Chander. 1999. *Strategies to Combat Terrorism: A Study of Punjab*. New Delhi: Har-Anand Publications.

Avrich, Paul. 1967. *The Russian Anarchists*. Princeton, NJ: Princeton University Press.

Bandura, Albert. 1990. Mechanisms of moral disengagement. In *Origins of Terrorism: Psychologies, Ideologies, Theologies, States of Mind*, ed. Walter Reich, 161–91. Cambridge: Cambridge University Press.

Barber, Benjamin R. 1995. *Jihad vs. McWorld: How Globalism and Tribalism Are Reshaping the World*. New York: Times Books.

———. 2003. *Fear's Empire: War, Terrorism, and Democracy*. New York: W. W. Norton.

Baudrillard, Jean. 2002. *The Spirit of Terrorism and Requiem for the Twin Towers*. London: Verso.

Berry, Nicolas O. 1987. Theories on the efficacy of terrorism. In *Contemporary Research on Terrorism*, ed. Paul Wilkinson and Alasdair M. Stewart, 293–306. Aberdeen: Aberdeen University Press.

Bettelheim, Bruno. 1943. Individual and mass behavior in extreme situations. *Journal of Abnormal and Social Psychology* 38:417–52.

Beyer, P. 1970. Globalization, subsuming pluralism, transnational organizations, diaspora, and postmodernity. In *International Encyclopedia of the Social and Behavioral Sciences*, ed. Neil J. Smelser and Paul B. Baltes, 9:6287–82. Oxford: Elsevier.

Biersteker, Thomas J. 2004. Counter-terrorism measures undertaken under UN Security Council auspices. In *Business and Security: Public-Private Relationships in a New Security Environment*, ed. Ayson J. K. Bailes and Isabel Frommelt, 59–75. Oxford: Oxford University Press.

Bjørgo, Tore. 1995. Introduction. In *Terror from the Extreme Right*, ed. Tore Bjørgo, 1–16. London: Frank Cass.

Bolin, Robert. 1994. Postdisaster sheltering and housing: Social processes in response and recovery. In *Disasters, Collective Behavior, and Social Organization*, ed. Russell R. Dynes and Kathleen J. Tierney, 115–27. Newark: University of Delaware Press.

Borowitz, Albert. 2005. *Terrorism for Self-Glorification: The Herostratos Syndrome*. Kent, OH: Kent State University Press.

Bovard, James. 2004. *The Bush Betrayal*. New York: Macmillan Palgrave.

Bresser-Pereira, Luiz Carlos. 2002. After balance-of-powers diplomacy, globalization's politics. In *Critical Views of September 11: Analyses from Around the World*, ed. Eric Hershberg and Kevin W. Moore, 109–30. New York: New Press.

Brill, Stephen. 2003. *After: The Rebuilding and Defending of America in the September 12 Era*. New York: Simon and Schuster.

Buechler, Steven N. 2004. The strange career of strain and breakdown theories. In *The Blackwell Companion to Social Movements*, ed. David A. Snow, Sarah A. Soule, and Hanspeter Kriesi, 47–66. Oxford: Blackwell.

Burbach, Roger. 2002. Globalization's war. In *September 11 and the U.S. War: Beyond the Curtain of Smoke*, ed. Roger Burbach and Ben Clarke, 12–17. San Francisco: City Lights Books and Freedom Voices Press.

Burbach, Roger, and Jim Tarbell. 2004. *Imperial Overstretch: George W. Bush and the Hubris of Empire*. New York: Zed Books.

Byrd, Robert C. 2004. *Losing America: Confronting a Reckless Presidency*. New York: W. W. Norton.

Callinicos, Alex. 2003. *The New Mandarins of American Power: The Bush Administration's Plans for the World*. Cambridge: Polity Press.

Carr, Caleb. 2002. *The Lessons of Terror: A History of Warfare Against Civilians: Why It Has Always Failed, and Why It Will Fail Again*. New York: Random House.

Castles, S. 2001. Migration: Sociological aspects. In *International Encyclopedia of the Social and Behavioral Sciences*, ed. Neil J. Smelser and Paul B. Baltes, 14:9824–28. Oxford: Elsevier, 2001.

Central Intelligence Agency. 2002. Global trends 2015. In *America Confronts Terrorism: Understanding the Danger and How to Think About It: A Documentary Record*, ed. John Prados, 13–24. Chicago: Ivan R Dee.

Century Foundation Task Force Report. 2004. *Defeating the Jihadists: A Blueprint for Action*. New York: Century Foundation Press.

Chaplin, A. 2003. *Terror: The New Theater of War: Mao's Legacy: Selected Cases of Terrorism in the 20th and 21st Centuries*. Lanham, MD: University Press of America.

Charters, David A. 1994a. Conclusions: Security and liberty in balance--Countering terrorism in the democratic context. In *The Deadly Sin of Terrorism: Its Effect on Democracy and Civil Liberty in Six Countries*, ed. David A. Charters, 211–29. Westport, CT: Greenwood Press.

Charters, David A., ed. 1994b. *The Deadly Sin of Terrorism: Its Effect on Democracy and Civil Liberty in Six Countries*. Westport, CT: Greenwood Press.

Chinoy, Ely. 1955. *Automobile Workers and the American Dream*. Garden City, NY: Doubleday.

Chomsky, Noam. 1999. *Profit over People: Neoliberalism and Global Order*. New York: Seven Stories Press.

———. 2003. *Hegemony or Survival: America's Quest for Global Dominance*. New York: Metropolitan Books.

Chopra, V. D. 2001. Introduction. In *Rise of Terrorism and Secessionism in Eurasia*, ed. V. D. Chopra, 15–26. New Delhi: Gyan Publishing House.

Clark, John, Michael D. Langone, Robert E. Schachter, and Roger C. G. Daly. 1981. *Destructive Cult Conversion: Theory, Research, and Treatment*. Weston, MA: American Family Foundation, 1981.

Clarke, L. 1999. *Mission Improbable: Using Fantasy Documents to Tame Disaster*. Chicago: University of Chicago Press.

Clifford-Vaughan, Frederic Macadie. 1987. Terrorism and insurgency in South Africa. In *Contemporary Research on Terrorism*, ed. Paul Wilkinson and Alasdair M. Stewart, 270–89. Aberdeen: Aberdeen University Press.

Cline, Ray S., and Yonah Alexander. 1984. *Terrorism: The Soviet Connection*. New York: Crane Russak.

Clutterbuck, Richard. 1977. *Guerrillas and Terrorists*. London: Faber and Faber.

Cohen, Eliot A. 2005. Obligations of leadership: The Khobar Towers bombing and its aftermath. In *Terrorism and Peacekeeping: New Security Challenges*, ed. Volker Franke, 99–123. Westport, CT: Praeger.

Cohn, Norman. 1951. *The Pursuit of the Millennium*. New York: Harper and Brothers.

Cole, David, and James X. Dempsey. 2002. *Terrorism and the Constitution: Sacrificing Civil Liberties in the Name of National Security*. New York: New Press.

Combs, Cindy C. 2003. *Terrorism in the Twenty-First Century*, 3rd ed. Upper Saddle River, NJ: Prentice-Hall.

Committee on Science and Technology for Countering Terrorism. 2002. *Making the Nation Safer: The Role of Science and Technology in Countering Terrorism*. Washington, DC: National Academies Press.

Cooper, H.H.A. 2002. Terrorism: The problem of definition revisited. In *Essential Readings on Political Terrorism: Analyses of Problems and Prospects of the 21st Century*, ed. Harvey W. Kushner, 1–15. Lincoln, NB: Gordian Knot Books.

Cooper, Robert. 2003. *The Breaking of Nations: Order and Chaos in the Twenty-First Century*. London: Atlantic Books.

Cordes, B. 1987. Euroterrorists talk about themselves: A look at the literature. In *Contemporary Research on Terrorism*, ed. Paul Wilkinson and Alasdair M. Stewart, 318–36. Aberdeen: Aberdeen University Press.

Cottrol, Robert. 2005. A home guard should be created to increase homeland security. In *Homeland Security*, ed. Andrea C. Nakaya, 117–20. Farmington Hills, MI: Greenhaven Press.

Cragin, Kim, and Peter Chalk. 2003. *Terrorism and Development: Using Social and Economic Development to Inhibit a Surge of Terrorism*. Santa Monica, CA: RAND Corp.

Crelinson, Ronald D. 1987. Terrorism as political communication: The relationship between the controller and the controlled. In *Contemporary Research on Terrorism*, ed. Paul Wilkinson and Alasdair M. Stewart, 3–23. Aberdeen: Aberdeen University Press.

Crelinson, Ronald D., and Alex P. Schmid. 1993. Western responses to terrorism: A twenty-five-year balance sheet. In *Western Responses to Terrorism*, ed. Alex P. Schmid and Ronald D. Crelinson, 315–40. London: Frank Cass.

Crenshaw, Martha. 1983. Introduction: Reflections on the effects of terrorism. In *Terrorism, Legitimacy and Power: The Consequences of Political Violence*, ed. Martha Crenshaw, 1–37. Middletown, CT: Wesleyan University Press.

———. 1988. The subjective reality of the terrorist: Ideological and psychological factors in terrorism. In *Current Perspectives on International Terrorism*, ed. Robert O. Slater and Michael Stohl, 12–46. New York: St. Martin's Press.

———. 1990. The logic of terrorism: Terrorist behavior as a product of strategic choice. In *Origins of Terrorism: Psychologies, Ideologies, Theologies, States of Mind*, ed. Walter Reich, 7–24. Cambridge: Cambridge University Press.

———. 1991. How terrorism declines. In *Terrorism Research and Public Policy*, ed. Clark McCauley, 69–87. London: Frank Cass.

———. 1995a. Thoughts on relating terrorism to historical contexts. In *Terrorism in Context*, ed. Martha Crenshaw, 3–24. University Park: Pennsylvania State University Press.

————. 1995b. The effectiveness of terrorism in the Algerian war. In *Terrorism in Context*, ed. Martha Crenshaw, 473–512. University Park: Pennsylvania State University Press.

Cronin, Isaac, ed. 2002. *Confronting Fear: A History of Terrorism*. New York: Thunder's Mouth Press.

Crotty, William J. 1971. Assassinations and their interpretation within the American context. In *Assassinations and the Political Order*, ed. William J. Crotty, 3–53. New York: Harper & Row.

Cutter, S. L., and K. Barnes. 1982. Evacuation behavior and Three Mile Island. *Disasters* 6(2):116–24.

Cutter, Susan L. 1995. The forgotten casualties: Women, children, and environmental change. *Global Environmental Change* 5(3):181–94

Dacy, Douglas C., and Howard Kunreuther. 1969. *The Economics of Natural Disasters: Implications for Federal Policy*. New York: Free Press.

Dadge, David. 2004. *Casualty of War: The Bush Administration's Assault on a Free Press*. Amherst, NY: Prometheus Press.

Daly, Sara, John Parachini, and William Rosenau. 2005. *Aum Shinrikyo, Al Qaeda, and the Kinshasa Reactor: Implications of Three Case Studies for Combating Nuclear Terrorism*. Santa Monica, CA: RAND Corp.

Danieli, Yael, Brian Engdahl, and William E. Schlenger. 2004. The psychosocial aftermath of terrorism. In *Understanding Terrorism: Psychosocial Roots, Consequences, and Interventions*, ed. Fathali M. Moghaddam and Anthony J. Marsella, 233–46. Washington, DC: American Psychological Association.

Davies, Barry. 2003. *Terrorism: Inside a World Phenomenon*. London: Virgin Books.

Davis, Paul K., and Brian Michael Jenkins. 2002. *Deterrence and Influence in Counterterrorism: A Component in the War on Al Qaeda*. Santa Monica, CA: RAND Corp.

Della Porta, Donatella.1992. Introduction: On individual motivations in underground political organizations. In *Social Movements and Violence: Participation in Underground Organizations*, ed. Donatella Della Porta, 3–28. Greenwich, CT: JAI Press.

Der Derian, James. 2002. In terrorem: Before and after 9/11. In *Worlds in Collision: Terror and the Future of the Global Order*, ed. Ken Booth and Tim Dunne, 101–17. New York: Macmillan Palgrave.

DeVoe, R. F, Jr. 1997. The natural disaster boom theory: Or window-breaking our way to prosperity. In *Economic Consequences of Earthquakes: Preparing for the Unexpected*, ed. B. G. Jones, 181–88. Report No. NCEER-SP-0001. Buffalo: State University of New York at Buffalo, Multidisciplinary Center for Earthquake Engineering Research.

Domke, David. 2004. *God Willing? Political Fundamentalism in the White House, the "War on Terror," and the Echoing Press*. Ann Arbor, MI: Pluto Press.

Dow, K., and S. L. Cutter. 1998. "Crying wolf": Repeat responses to hurricane evacuation orders. *Coastal Management* 26:237–52.

————. 2000. Public orders and personal opinions: Household strategies for hurricane risk assessment. *Environment* 2:143–155.

Downton, James V., Jr. 1979. *Sacred Journeys: The Conversion of Young Americans to Divine Light Mission*. New York: Columbia University Press.

Doyle, Michael. 1983. Kant: Liberal legacies and foreign policy. *Philosophy and Public Affairs* 12(1, 2):205–35, 323–53.

Drabek, Thomas E. 1994. Disaster in aisle 13 revisited. In *Disasters, Collective Behavior, and Social Organization*, ed. Russell R. Dynes and Kathleeen J. Tierney, 26–44. Newark, NJ: University of Delaware Press.

Drabek, T. E., and D. A. McEntire. 2002. Emergent phenomena and multiorganizational coordination in disasters: Lessons from the research literature. *International Journal of Mass Emergencies and Disasters* 20(2):197–224.

Drake, C. J. M. 1998. *Terrorists' Target Selection*. New York: St. Martin's Press.

Du Bois, Cora. 1939. *The 1870 Ghost Dance*. Berkeley: University of California Press.

Durkheim, Émile.1951 [1895]. *Suicide*, trans. John A. Spaulding and George Simpson, ed. with an introduction by George Simpson. Glencoe, IL: Free Press.

———. 1958 [1839]. *The Rules of Sociological Method*, trans. Sarah A. Solovay and John H. Mueller, ed. George E. G. Catlin. Glencoe, IL: Free Press.

Dynes, Russell. 1970. *Organized Behavior in Disaster*. Lexington, MA: D. C. Heath.

———. 1994. Community emergency planning: False assumptions and inappropriate analogies. *International Journal of Mass Emergencies and Disasters* 12:141–58.

Dynes, Russell, and Kathleen J. Tierney, eds. 1994. *Disasters, Collective Behavior, and Social Organization*. Newark: University of Delaware Press.

Eisendrath, Craig R., and Melvin A. Goodman. 2005. *Bush League Diplomacy: How the Neoconservatives Are Putting the World at Risk*. Amherst, NY: Prometheus Press.

Eltzbacher, Paul. 1960. *Anarchism: Exponents of the Anarchist Philosophy*, trans. Steven Byngton. New York: Libertarian Book Club.

Enders, W., T. Sandler, and J. Cauley. 1988. UN conventions, technology and retaliation in the fight against terrorism: An econometric evaluation. *Terrorism and Political Violence* 21(2):83–105.

Engels, Friedrich. 1959 [1880]. Socialism: Utopian and scientific. In *Marx and Engels: Basic Writings on Politics and Philosophy*, ed. Lewis S. Feuer, 68–111. Garden City, NY: Doubleday.

———. 1993 [1845]. *The Condition of the Working Class in England in 1844*. Oxford: Oxford University Press.

Erikson, Kai. 1976. *Everything in Its Path: Destruction of Community in the Buffalo Creek Flood*. New York: Simon and Schuster.

Evans, Robert H. 1994. Italy and international terrorism. In *The Deadly Sin of Terrorism: Its Effect on Democracy and Civil Liberty in Six Countries*, ed. David A. Charters, 73–102. Westport, CT: Greenwood Press.

Eyerman, Ron. 2004. Cultural trauma: Slavery and the formation of African American identity. In *Cultural Trauma and Collective Identity*, by Jeffrey C. Alexander, Ron Eyerman, Bernhard Giesen, Neil J. Smelser, and Piotr Sztompka, 60–111. Berkeley and Los Angeles: University of California Press.

Ezekiel, Raphael S., and Jerrold M. Post. 1991. Worlds in collision, worlds in collusion: The uneasy relationship between the policy community and the academic community. In *Terrorism Research and Public Policy*, ed. Clark McCauley, 117–25. London: Frank Cass.

Falk, Richard. 2003. *The Great Terror War*. New York: Olive Branch Press.

Falkenrath, Richard A., Robert D. Newman, and Bradley A. Thayer. 1998. *America's Achilles' Heel: Nuclear, Biological Terrorism and Covert Attack*. Cambridge, MA: MIT Press.

Farah, Douglas. 2005. *Blood from Stones: The Secret Financial Network of Terror.* New York: Broadway Books.

Farnam, Julie. 2005. *US Immigration Laws under the Threat of Terrorism.* New York: Algora Publishing.

Federal Research Division, Library of Congress. 2002. *A Global Overview of Narcotics-funded Terrorist and Other Other Extremist Groups.* http://purl.access.gpo.gov/GPO/LPS49436.

Fitzpatrick, Colleen, and Dennis S. Mileti. 1994. Public risk communication. In *Disasters, Collective Behavior, and Social Organization,* ed. Russell R. Dynes and Kathleen J. Tierney, 71–84. Newark: University of Delaware Press.

Fleming, Marie. 1982. Propaganda by the deed: Terrorism and anarchist theory in late nineteenth century Europe. In *Terrorism in Europe,* ed. Yonah Alexander and Kenneth A. Myers, 8–26. New York: St. Martin's Press.

Flint, Colin. 2003. Geographies of inclusion/exclusion. In *The Geographical Dimensions of Terrorism,* ed. Susan L. Cutter, Douglas B. Richardson, and Thomas J. Wilbanks, 53–58. New York: Routledge.

Fong, Mak Lau. 1981. *The Sociology of Secret Societies: A Study of Chinese Secret Societies in Singapore and Peninsular Malaysia.* Kuala Lumpur: Oxford University Press.

Fothergill, A. 2003. The stigma of charity: Gender, class, and disaster assistance. *Sociological Quarterly* 44(4):659–80.

Fothergill, A., E. Maestas, and J. D. Darlington. 1999. Race, ethnicity and disasters in the U.S.: A review of the literature. *Disasters* 23(2):156–73.

Foulkes, S. H. 1964. *Therapeutic Group Analysis.* New York: International Universities Press.

Friedland, Nehemia. 1992. Becoming a terrorist: Social and individual antecedents. In *Terrorism: Roots, Impact, Responses,* ed. Lawrence Howard, 81–93. New York: Praeger.

Friedman, Lawrence. 2004. *Deterrence.* Cambridge: Polity Press.

Fritz, Charles, and J. H. Mathewson. 1957. *Convergence Behavior in Disasters: A Problem in Social Control.* Washington, DC: National Academy of Sciences-National Research Council.

Fukuyama, Francis. 1992. *The End of History and The Last Man.* New York: Free Press.

———. 2002. History and September 11. In *Worlds in Collision: Terror and the Future of Global Order,* ed. Ken Booth and Tim Dunne, 27–47. New York: Palgrave Macmillan.

Gal-Or, Noemi. 1994. Countering terrorism in Israel. In *The Deadly Sin of Terrorism: Its Effect on Democracy and Civil Liberty in Six Countries,* ed. David A. Charters, 136–72. Westport, CT: Greenwood Press.

Galanter, Marc. 1999. *Cults: Faith, Healing, and Coercion,* 2nd ed. New York: Oxford University Press.

Gallie, W. B. 1956. Essentially contested concepts. *Proceedings of the Philosophical Society* 52:157–98.

Gareau, Frederick. 2005. *State Terrorism and the United States: From Counterinsurgency to the War on Terrorism.* Atlanta, GA: Clarity Press.

Gearty, Conor. 1991. *Terror.* London: Faber and Faber.

Geertz, Clifford. 1973. The integrative revolution: Primordial sentiments and civil politics in the new states. In C. Geertz, *The Interpretation of Cultures: Selected Essays,* 255–310. New York: Basic Books.

Gellner, Ernest. 1983. *Nations and Nationalism*. Ithaca, NY: Cornell University Press.

Gerbner, George. 1990. Symbolic functions of violence and terror. In *Terrorism and the Media: Dilemmas for Government, Journalists and the Public*, ed. Yonah Alexander and Richard Latter, 93–98. Washington, D.: Brassey's (US).

Gerrity, E. T., and B. W. Flynn. 1997. Mental health consequences of disasters. In *The Public Health Consequences of Disasters*, ed. E. K. Noji, 101–21. New York: Oxford University Press.

Gilbert, Paul. 1990. Community and civil strife. In *Terrorism, Protest and Power*, ed. Martin Warner and Roger Crisp, 17–32. Aldershot, UK: Edward Elgar.

———. 1994. *Terrorism, Security, and Nationality: An Introductory Study in Applied Political Philosophy*. London: Routledge.

Gill, K.P.S. 2002. Introduction. In *The Global Threat of Terror: Ideological, Material, and Political Linkages*, ed. K.P.S. Gill and Ajai Sahni, 1–5. New Delhi: Bulwark Books.

Gillespie, Richard. 1970. Political violence in Argentina: Guerrillas, terrorists and Carapintadas. In *Terrorism in Context*, ed. Martha Crenshaw, 211–48. University Park: Pennsylvania State University Press.

Gilpin, Robert. 2001. *Global Political Economy: Understanding the International Order*. Princeton, NJ: Princeton University Press.

Giroux, Henry. 2004. *Proto-Fascism in America: Neoliberalism and the Demise of Democracy*. Bloomington, IN: Phi Delta Kappa Educational Foundation.

Gitlin, Todd. 1980. *The Whole World Is Watching: Mass Media in the Making and Unmaking of the New Left*. Berkeley and Los Angeles: University of California Press.

Gladwin, C. H., H. Gladwin, and W. G. Peacock. 2001. Modeling hurricane evacuation decisions with ethnographic methods. *International Journal of Mass Emergencies and Disasters* 19(2):117–43.

Glass, T., and M. Schoch-Spana. 2002. Bioterrorism and the people: How to vaccinate a city against panic. *Confronting Biological Weapons, CID* 34:217–23.

Goldstick, Danny. 2002. Defining terrorism. In *Essential Readings on Political Terrorism: Analyses of Problems and Prospects of the 21st Century*, ed. Harvey W. Kushner, 17–21. Lincoln, NB: Gordian Knot Books.

Goss, John Peter. 1986. Response to "Is nuclear terrorism possible?" by Brian M. Jenkins. In *Nuclear Terrorism: Defining the Threat*, ed. Paul Leventhal and Yonah Alexander, 39–43. Washington, DC: Pergamon-Brassey's.

Green, Jerrold D. 1995. Terrorism and politics in Iran. In *Terrorism in Context*, ed. Martha Crenshaw, 553–94. University Park: Pennsylvania State University Press.

Greenberg, Maurice R., William F. Wechsler, and Lee S. Wolosky. 2002. *Terrorist Financing: Report of an Independent Task Force, Sponsored by the Council of Foreign Relations*. New York: Council on Foreign Relations.

Gross, Feliks. 1969. Political violence and terror in 19th and 20th century Russia and Eastern Europe .In *Assassination and Political Violence: A Report to the National Commission on the Causes and Prevention of Violence*, ed. J. F. Kirckham, Sheldon G. Levy, and William J. Crotty, 419–76. Washington, DC: U. S. Government Printing Office.

Gunaratna, Rohan. 2002. *Inside Al Qaeda: Global Network of Terror*. New York: Columbia University Press.

Gurr, Ted Robert. 2000. *People versus States: Minorities at Risk in the New Century*. Washington, DC: United States Institute of Peace.

Gurr, Ted Robert, and Barbara Harff. 1994. *Ethnic Conflict in World Politics.* Boulder, CO: Westview Press, 1994.

Habakkuk, H. J. 1967. *American and British Technology in the Nineteenth Century: The Search for Labour-saving Inventions.* Cambridge: Cambridge University Press.

Hannerz, Ulf. 1990. Cosmopolitans and locals in world culture. In *Global Culture: Nationalism, Globalization, and Modernity: A Theory. Culture and Society Special Issue,* ed. Mike Featherstone. London: Sage.

Hanson, Jim. 1996. *The Next Cold War? American Alternatives for the Twenty-First Century.* Westport, CT: Praeger.

Harrison, Michael M. 1994. France and international terrorism: Problem and response. In *The Deadly Sin of Terrorism: Its Effect on Democracy and Civil Liberty in Six Countries,* ed. David A. Charters, 103–36. Westport, CT: Greenwood Press.

Hastings, Tom H. 2004. *Nonviolent Response to Terrorism.* Jefferson, NC: McFarland.

Hess, Stephen, and Marvin Kalb, eds. 2003. *The Media and the War on Terrorism.* Washington, DC: Brookings Institution.

Hetherington, Marc J. 2001. Resurgent mass partisanship: The role of elite polarization. *American Political Science Review* 95(3):619–31.

Hewings, Geoffrey J. D., and Yasuhide Okuyama. 2003. Economic assessments of unexpected events. In *The Geographical Dimensions of Terrorism,* ed. Susan L. Cutter, Douglas B. Richardson, and Thomas J. Wilbanks, 153–60. New York: Routledge.

Hewitt, Christopher .1970. *Understanding Terrorism in America: From the Klan to al Qaeda.* London: Routledge.

Hills, A. 2002. Responding to catastrophic terrorism. *Studies in Conflict and Terrorism* 25:245–61.

Hocking, Jennifer Jane. 1970. Governments' perspectives. In *Terrorism and the Media,* ed. D. L. Paletz and A. P. Schmid, 86–104. Newbury Park, CA: Sage.

Hodgkinson, Peter E., and Michael Stewart. 1998. *Coping with Catastrophe: A Handbook of Post-Disaster Psychosocial Aftercare,* 2nd ed. London: Routledge.

Hoffman, Bruce. 1986. *Right-wing Terrorism in the United States.* Santa Monica, CA: RAND Corp.

———. 1990. Recent trends and future prospects of Iranian sponsored international terrorism. *Rand Report.* Reprinted in *Middle East Terrorism: Current Threats and Future Prospects,* ed. Yonah Alexander, 41–82. New York: G. K. Hall.

———. 1998. *Inside Terrorism. New York:* Columbia University Press.

———. 2002. The mind of the terrorist: Perspectives from social psychology. In *Essential Readings on Political Terrorism: Analyses of Problems and Prospects of the 21st Century,* ed. Harvey W. Kushner, 62–69. Lincoln, NB: Gordian Knot Books.

Horowitz, Irving L. 1983. The routinization of terrorism and its unanticipated consequences. In *Terrorism, Legitimacy and Power: The Consequences of Political Violence,* ed. Martha Crenshaw, 38–51. Middletown, CT: Wesleyan University Press.

Huntington, Samuel P. 1991. *The Third Wave: Democratization in the Late Twentieth Century.* Norman: University of Oklahoma Press.

———. 1996. *The Clash of Civilizations and the Remaking of World Order.* New York: Simon & Schuster.

———. 2004. *Who Are We? The Challenges to America's National Identity.* New York: Simon and Schuster.

Hyman, Anthony. 1994. Muslim fundamentalism. In *Middle East Terrorism: Current Threats and Future Prospects*, ed. Yonah Alexander, 254–57. New York: G. K. Hall.

Irwin, Cynthia. 1989. Terrorists' perspectives: Interviews. In *Terrorism and the Media*, ed. David L. Paletz and Alex P. Schmid, 63–85. Newbury Park, CA: Sage.

Jacobsen, C. G. 1996. *The New World Order's Defining Crises: The Clash of Promise and Essence.* Aldershot: Dartmouth Publishing Co.

Jamieson, Alison. 1989. *The Heart Attacked: Terrorism and Conflict in the Italian State.* London: Marion Boyers.

Janis, Irving. 1951. *Air War and Emotional Stress.* New York: McGraw-Hill.

Jenkins, Bruce N. 1980. *The Study of Terrorism: Definitional Problems.* Santa Monica, CA: RAND Corp.

Jenkins, Philip. 2003. *Images of Terror: What we Can and Can't Know About Terrorism.* New York: Aldine de Gruyter.

Johnson, Norris R., William E. Feinberg, and Drue M. Johnston. 1994. Microstructure and panic: The impact of social bonds on individual action in collective flight from the Beverly Hills Supper Club fire. In *Disasters, Collective Behavior, and Social Disorganization*, ed. Russell R. Dynes and Kathleen J. Tierney, 168–89. Newark: University of Delaware Press.

Jones, David Martin, and Mike Smith. 2004. Contemporary political violence: New terror and the global village. In *Globalization and the New Terror: The Asian Pacific Dimension*, ed. David Martin Jones, 1–23. Cheltenham, UK: Edward Elgar.

Judt, Tony. 1970. America and the war. In *Striking Terror: America's New War*, ed. Robert B. Silvers and Barbara Epstein, 15–30. New York: New York Review of Books.

Juergensmeyer, Mark. 1983. *Terror in the Mind of God: The Global Rise of Religious Violence.* Berkeley and Los Angeles: University of California Press.

Kagan, Robert. 2003. *Of Paradise and Power.* New York: Alfred A. Knopf.

Kamrava, Mehran. 2005. Repression, fundamentalism, and terrorism in the Middle East. In *Democratic Development and Political Terrorism: The Global Perspective*, ed. William Crotty, 167–91. Boston: Northeastern University Press.

Kaplan, Robert. 2000. T*he Coming Anarchy: Shattering the Dreams of the Post Cold War.* New York: Random House.

Kaufmann, Arnold F., Martin L. Meltzer, and George P. Schmid. 2004. The economic impact of a bioterrorist attack: Are prevention and postattack intervention programs justifiable? In *The War Next Time: Countering Rogue States and Terrorists Armed with Chemical and Biological Weapons*, ed. Barry R. Schneider and Jim A. Davis, 195–218. Maxwell Air Force Base, AB: U.S. Counterproliferation Center.

Kellen, Konrad. 1990. Ideology and rebellion: Terrorism in West Germany. In *Origins of Terrorism: Psychologies, Ideologies, Theologies, States of Mind*, ed. Walter Reich, 43–58. Cambridge: Cambridge University Press.

Kellner, Douglas. 2003. *From 9/11 to Terror War: The Dangers of the Bush Legacy.* London: Rowman and Littlefield.

Kelly, J. D. 2001. Postcoloniality. In *International Encyclopedia of the Social and Behavioral Sciences*, ed. Neil J. Smelser and Paul B. Baltes, 17:11844–48. Oxford: Elsevier Science.

Kennedy, Paul. 1987. *The Rise and Fall of Great Powers: Economic Change and Military Conflict from 1500 to 2000.* New York: Random House.

Keohane, Robert O. 2002. The public deligitimation of terrorism and coalitional politics. In *Worlds in Collision: Terror and the Future of the Global Order*, ed. Ken Booth and Tim Dunne, 141–51. New York: Macmillan Palgrave.

Kettl, Donald F. 2004. *System Under Stress: Homeland Security and American Politics*. Washington, DC: CQ Press.

Kriesi, Hanspeter. 2004. Political context and opportunity. In *The Blackwell Companion to Social Movements*, ed. David A. Snow, Sarah A. Soule, and Hanspeter Kriesi, 67–90. Oxford: Blackwell.

Krueger, Alan B., and Jitka Maleckovà. 2002. *Education, Poverty, Political Violence, and Terrorism: Is There a Causal Connection?* Cambridge, MA: National Bureau of Economic Research.

Kupperman, Robert H. 1986. Vulnerable America. In *Contemporary Research on Terrorism*, ed. Paul Wilkinson and Alasdair M. Stewart, 570–80. Aberdeen: Aberdeen University Press.

La Barre, Weston. 1970. *The Ghost Dance: Origins of Religion*. Garden City, NY: Doubleday.

Laqueur, Walter. 1977. *Terrorism*. London: Weidenfeld and Nicolson.

———. 1978. *The Terrorism Reader: A Historical Anthology*. Philadelphia: Temple University Press.

———. 1999. *The New Terrorism: Fanaticism and the Arms of Mass Destruction*. New York: Oxford University Press.

Lasswell, Harold D. 1960. *Psychopathology and Politics*. New York: Viking.

Leemon, Thomas A. 1972. *The Rites of Passage in a Student Culture: A Study of the Dynamics of Transition*. New York: Teachers College Press.

Lenain, Patrick. 2004. The economic consequences of terrorism. In *Business and Security: Public-Private Sector Relations in a New Security Environment*, ed. Alyson J. K. Bailes and Isabel Frommelt, 219–31. Oxford: Oxford University Press.

Lester, David. 1987. *Suicide as a Learned Behavior*. Springfield, IL: Charles C. Thomas.

Levitt, Geoffrey M. 1988. *Democracies Against Terror: The Western Response to State-Supported Terrorism*, with a foreword by Walter Laqueur. New York: Praeger.

Lieven, Anatol. 2004. *America Right or Wrong: An Anatomy of American Nationalism*. Oxford: Oxford University Press.

Lifton, Robert Jay. 1969. *Thought Reform and the Psychology of Totalism: The Study of "Brainwashing" in Communist China*. New York: Norton.

Lindell, M. K., and R. W. Perry. 2004. *Communicating Environmental Risk in Multiethnic Communities*. Thousand Oaks, CA: Sage.

Livingstone, Neil C. 1982. *The War Against Terrorism*. Toronto: Lexington Press.

Lodge, Juliet, ed. 1981. *Terrrorism: A Challenge to the State*. New York: St. Martin's Press.

Lofland, John. 1981. *Doomsday Cult: A Study of Conversion, Proselytization, and Maintenance of Faith*, enlarged ed. New York: Irvington.

Lofland, John, and Rodney Stark. 1965. Becoming a world-saver: A theory of conversion to a deviant perspective. *American Sociological Review* 30(6):862–75.

Long, David E. 1990. *The Anatomy of Terrorism*. New York: Free Press.

Maley, William. 2002. Messianism and political action: Some contextual characteristics. In *The Global Threat of Terror: Ideological, Material and Political Linkages*, ed. K.P. S. Gill and Ajai Sahni, 71–83. New Delhi: Bulwark Books.

Maniscalco, Paul M., and Hank T. Christen. 2001. *Understanding Terrorism and Managing the Consequences*. Upper Saddle River, NJ: Prentice-Hall.

Manning, Frederick J., and Lewis Goldfrank, eds. 2002. *Preparing for Terrorism: Tools for Evaluating the Metropolitan Medical Response System Program*. Washington, DC: National Academy Press.

Martin, Robert C. 1987. Religious violence in Islam: Towards an understanding of discourse on Jihad in modern Egypt. In *Contemporary Research on Terrorism*, ed. Paul Wilkinson and Alasdair M. Stewart, 55–71. Aberdeen: Aberdeen University Press.

Marx, Gary T. 1970. Issueless riots. *Annals of the American Academy of Political and Social Science* 391(3): 21–33.

Marx, Karl, and Friedrich Engels. 1954 [1848]. *Communist Manifesto*. Chicago: Henry Regnery.

Mathewson, Kent, and Michael Steinberg. 2003. Drug production, commerce, and terrorism. In *The Geographical Dimensions of Terrorism*, ed. Susan L. Cutter, Douglas B. Richardson, and Thomas J. Wilbanks, 39–66. London: Routledge.

McAdam, Doug, Sidney Tarrow, and Charles Tilly. 2001. *Dynamics of Contention*. New York: Cambridge University Press.

McCauley, Clark. 2004. Psychological issues in understanding terrorism and the response to terrorism. In *Psychology of Terrorism, Condensed Edition: Coping with the Continuing Threat*, ed. Chris E. Stout, 33–63. Westport, CT: Praeger.

McGlown, K. Joanne, ed. 2004. *Terrorism and Disaster Management: Preparing Healthcare Leaders for the New Reality*. Chicago: Health Administration Press.

Mead, Margaret. 1965 [1942]. *And Keep Your Powder Dry: An Anthropologist Looks at America*. New York: William Morrow.

Merari, Ariel. 1991. Academic research and government policy on terrorism. In *Terrorism Research and Public Policy*, ed. Clark McCauley, 88–102. London: Frank Cass.

Merkl, Peter H. 1986. Rollerball or Neo-Nazi violence. In *Political Violence and Terror: Motifs and Motivations*, ed. Peter Merkl, 229–55. Berkeley and Los Angeles: University of California Press.

———. 1991. German left-wing terrorism. In *Terrorism in Context*, ed. Martha Crenshaw, 160–210. University Park: Pennsylvania State University Press.

Midlarsky, Manus I., Martha Crenshaw, and Fumihiko Yoshida. 1980. Why violence spreads: The contagion of international terrorism. *International Studies Quarterly* 24(2):262–98.

Miller, Lawrence. 2002. Psychological interventions for terroristic trauma: Symptoms, syndromes, and treatment strategies. *Psychotherapy: Theory/Research/Practice/Training* 39(4):283–96.

Miller, Richard B. 1991. *Interpretations of Conflict: Ethics, Pacification and the Just War*. Chicago: University of Chicago Press.

Minnite, Lorraine. 2005. Outside the circle: The impact of post-9/11 responses on the immigrant communities of New York. In *Contentious City: The Politics of Recovery in New York City*, ed. John Mollenkopf, 165–204. New York: Russell Sage Foundation.

Mooney, James. 1896. The Ghost Dance religion and the Sioux outbreak of 1890. *United States Bureau of American Ethnology, Annual Report*, Vol. 14, No. 2.

Murphy, John F. 1989. *State Support of International Terrorism: Legal, Political and Economic Dimensions.* Boulder, CO: Westview Press.

Nacos, Brigitte L. 2003. *Mass-mediated Terrorism: The Central Role of the Media in Terrorism and Counter-terrorism.* Lanham, MD: Roman and Littlefield.

Naimark, Norman M. 2001. *Fires of Hatred: Ethnic Cleansing in Twentieth-Century Europe.* Cambridge, MA: Harvard University Press.

Narang, A. S. 2001. Introduction. In *Terrorism: The Global Perspective*, ed. A. S. Narang and Pramila Srivastava, 1–6. New Delhi: Kanishka Publishers.

National Commission on Terrorist Attacks Upon the United States. 2004. *The 9/11 Report.* New York: St. Martin's Press.

National Strategy Forum. 2004. Prudent preparation. www.nationalwstrategy.com. Reprinted in *Psychology of Terrorism: Coping with the Continuing Threat*, ed. Chris E. Stout, 131–34. Westport, CT: Praeger.

New York Times. 2005a. Our unnecessary insecurity. Editorial. February 20.

New York Times. 2005b. Our terrorist-friendly borders. Editorial. March 21

New York Times. 2005c. Chairman exerts pressure on PBS, alleging biases. May 2.

New York Times. 2005d. Flooding recedes in New Orleans; U.S. inquiry is set. September 8.

Newhouse, John. 2003. *Imperial America: The Bush Assault on the World Order.* New York: Alfred A. Knopf.

Noji, Eric K. 2004. Public health aspects of weapons of mass destruction. In *Terrorism and Disaster Management: Preparing Healthcare Leaders for the New Reality*, ed. K. Joanne McGlown, 177–96. Chicago: Health Administration Press.

Nye, Joseph S. 2003. *The Paradox of American Power: Why the World's Only Superpower Can't Go It Alone.* Oxford: Oxford University Press.

Nye, Joseph S., Jr. 2004. *Power in the Global Information Age.* London: Routledge.

Ochberg, Frank M. 1979. Preparing for terrorist victimization. In *Political Terrorism and Business: The Threat and Response*, ed. Yonah Alexander and Robert A. Kilmarx, 113–22. New York: Praeger.

Oliver, Anne Marie, and Paul Steinberg. 2005. *The Road to Martyrs' Square: A Journey into the World of the Suicide Bomber.* New York: Oxford University Press.

Organisation for Economic Cooperation and Development. 2004. *The Security Economy.* Paris: OECD.

Otubanjo, Femi. 1994. African guerrillas and indigenous governments. In *Terrorism in Africa*, ed. Martha Crenshaw, 115–24. New York: G. K. Hall.

Paletz, David L., and John Boiney. 1992. Researchers' perspectives. In *Terrorism and the Media*, ed. David L. Paletz and Alex P. Schmid, 6–28. Newbury Park, CA: Sage.

Paletz, David L, and Alex P. Schmid, eds. 1992. *Terrorism and the Media.* Newbury Park, CA: Sage.

Palmer, David Scott. 1995. Revolutionary terrorism of Peru's Shining Path. In *Terrorism in Context*, ed. Martha Crenshaw, 249–308. University Park: Pennsylvania State University Press.

Parrott, James A., and Oliver D. Cooke, 2005. The economic impact of 9/11 on New York City's low-wage workers and households. In *Resilient City: The Economic Impact of 9/11*, ed. Howard Chernick, 193–231. New York: Russell Sage Foundation.

Parsons, Talcott. 1970. *The Social System.* Glencoe, IL: Free Press.

Pearlstein, Richard M. 1991. The Mind of the Political Terrorist. Wilmington, DE: SR Books.

Peña, Charles V. 2005. The homeland security advisory system does not work. In *Homeland Security*, ed. Andrea C. Nakaya, 99–100. Farmington Hills, MI: Greenhaven Press.

Perrow, Charles. 1984. *Normal Accidents: Living with High-Risk Technologies*. New York: Basic Books.

Perry, Ronald W. 1993. A model of evacuation as compliance behavior. In *Disasters, Collective Behavior, and Social Organization*, ed. Russell R. Dynes and Kathleen J. Tierney, 85–98. Newark: University of Delaware Press.

Perry, Ronald W., and M. K. Lindell. 1991. The effects of ethnicity on evacuation decision making. *International Journal of Mass Emergencies and Disasters* 9:47–68.

Picard, Robert G. 1993. *Media Portrayals of Terrorism: Functions and Meaning of News Coverage*. Ames: Iowa State University Press.

Piszkiewicz, Dennis. 2004. *Terrorism's War with America: A History*. Westport, CT: Praeger.

Poole, Keith T., and Howard Rosenthal. 1997. *Congress: A Political-Economic History of Roll Call Voting*. Oxford: Oxford University Press.

Post, Jerrold M. 1984. Narcissism and the charismatic leader-follower relationship. *Political Psychology* 7(4):675–88.

———. 1987. Prospects for nuclear terrorism: psychological motivations and constraints. In *Preventing Nuclear Terrorism: The Report and Papers of the International Task force on the Prevention of Nuclear Terrorism*, ed. Paul Leventhal and Yohan Alexander, 91–103. Lexington, MA: Lexington Books.

———. 1988. Terrorist psycho-logic: Terrorist behavior as a product of psychological forces. In *Origins of Terrorism: Psychologies, Ideologies, Theologies, States of Mind*, ed. Walter Reich. 26–42. Washington, DC: Woodrow Wilson Center Press.

———. 1990. Notes on a psychodynamic theory of terrorist behaviour. *Terrorism: An International Journal* 7:241–86.

———. 2003. Killing in the name of God: Osama Bin Laden and Al Qaeda. In *Know Thy Enemy: Profiles of Adversary Leaders and Their Strategic Cultures*, ed. Barry Schneider and Jerrold M. Post, 17–40. Maxwell Air Force Base, AB: USAF Counterproliferation Center.

———. 2004. Prospects for chemical/biological terrorism: Psychological incentives and constraints. In *Bioterrorism: Psychological and Public Health Interventions*, ed. Robert J. Ursano, Ann E. Norwood, and Carol S. Fullerton, 71–87. Cambridge: Cambridge University Press.

Prados, John. 2002. Bin Laden statement, October 7, 2001: "The Sword Fell." In America *Confronts Terrorism: Understanding the Danger and How to Think About It*, ed. John Prados, 23–24. Chicago: Ivan R. Dee.

Pridham, Geoffrey. 1981. Terrorism and the state in West Germany during the 1970s: A threat to stability or a case of political over-reaction?" In *Terrorism: A Challenge to the State*, ed. Juliet Lodge, 11–56. New York: St. Martin's Press.

Quinton, Anthony. 1990. Reflections on terrorism and violence. In *Terrorism, Protest and Power*, ed. Martin Warner and Roger Crisp, 35–43. Aldershot, UK: Edward Elgar.

Raphael, Beverly. 1886. *When Disaster Strikes: How Individuals and Communities Cope with Catastrophe*. New York: Basic Books.

Rapoport, David C. 1987. Why does religious messianism produce terror? In *Contemporary Research on Terrorism*, ed. Paul Wilkinson and Alasdair M. Stewart, 72–88. Aberdeen: Aberdeen University Press.

Ridge, Tom. 2005. The homeland security advisory system is effective. In *Homeland Security*, ed. Andrea C. Nakaya, 86–89. Farmington Hills, MI: Greenhaven Press.

Right Honorable Lord Chalfont. 1990. Terrorism and international security. In *Terrorism and the Media: Dilemmas for Government, Journalists and the Public*, ed. Richard Latter, 12–22. Washington, DC: Brassey's (US).

Ringstrom, Philip A. 2002. Thoughts on September 11, 2001. In *Terrorism and Unconscious Dynamics of Political Violence*, ed. Coline Covington, Paul Williams, Jean Arundel, and Jean Knox, 35–49. London: Karmak.

Robertson, R. 2001. Globality. In *International Encyclopedia of the Social and Behavioral Sciences*, ed. Neil J. Smelser and Paul B. Baltes, 9:6354–458. Oxford: Elsevier.

Robins, Robert S., and Jerrold M. Post. 1997. *Political Paranoia: The Psychopolitics of Hatred*. New Haven, CT: Yale University Press.

Ross, Jeffrey Ian, and Ted Robert Gurr. 1989. Why terrorism subsides: A comparative study of Canada and the United States. *Comparative Politics* 212 (4):405–26.

Roudi, Farzaneh. 2002. *Population Trends and Challenges in the Middle East and North Africa*. Washington, DC: Population Reference Bureau.

Rubin, Barry, ed. 1990. T*he Politics of Counter-Terrorism: The Ordeal of Democratic States*. Washington, DC: Foreign Policy Institute.

Rubin, Barry, and Judith Colp Rubin, eds. 2002. *Anti-American Terrorism and the Middle East: A Documentary Reader*. New York: Oxford University Press.

Rutherford, Danilyn. 2005. Nationalism and millenarianism in West Papua: Institutional power, interpretive practice, and the pursuit of Christian truth. In *Social Movements: An Anthropological Reader*, ed. June Nash, 146–67. Oxford: Blackwell.

Ryn, Claes G. 2003. *America the Virtuous: The Crisis of Democracy and the Quest for Empire*. New Brunswick, NJ: Transaction Publishers.

Sageman, Marc. 2004. *Understanding Terror Networks*. Philadelphia: University of Pennsylvania Press.

San Francisco Chronicle. 2005. In Hurricane Katrina's wake, some question whether battle against terrorism is the right fight. September 11.

Sanchez-Cuenca, Ignacio. 2004. *Terrorism as War of Attrition: ETA and the IRA*. Madrid: Istituto Juan March de Estudios e Investigaciones.

Schaffert, Richard W. 1992. *Media Coverage and Political Terrorists: A Quantitative Analysis*. New York: Praeger.

Schein, Edgar H., with Inge Schneier and Curtis H. Barker. 1961. *Coercive Persuasion: A Socio-psychological Analysis of the "Brainwashing" of American Civilian Prisoners by the Chinese Communists*. New York: W. W. Norton.

Schenger, William E. 2005. Psychological impact of the September 11, 2001 terrorist attacks: Summary of empirical findings. In *The Trauma of Terrorism: Sharing Knowledge and Shared Costs*, ed. Yael Daniels, Danny Brom, and Joe Sills, 97–108. New York: Maltreatment and Trauma Press.

Schiller, David T. 2001. A battlegroup divided: The Palesinian Fedayeen. In *Inside Terrorist Organizations*, 2nd ed. ed. David C. Rapoport, 90–108. London: Frank Cass.

Schmid, Alex P. 1993a. The response problem as a definition problem. In *Western Responses to Terrorism*, ed. Alex P. Schmid and Ronald D. Crelinson, 7–30. London: Frank Cass.

———. 1993b. Countering terrorism in the Netherlands. In *Western Responses to Terrorism*, ed. Alex P. Schmid and Ronald D. Crelinson, 79–109. London: Frank Cass.

———. 1998. Goals and objectives of international terrorism. In *Current Perspectives on International Terrorism*, ed. Robert O. Slater and Michael Stohl, 47–87. New York: St. Martin's Press.

Schmid, Alex P., and Jenny de Graaf. 1982. *Violence as Communication: Insurgent Terrorism and the News Media*. London: Sage.

Schmid, Alex P., Albert J. Jongman, et al. 1988. *Political Terrorism: A Research Guide to Concepts, Theories, Data Bases and Literature*. Amsterdam: North Holland.

Schoch-Spana, Monica. 2003. Educating informing, and mobilizing the public. In *Terrorism and Public Health: A Balanced Approach to Strengthening Systems and Protecting People*, ed. Barry S. Levy and Victor W. Sidel, 118–35. New York: Oxford University Press.

Schoenberg, Harris O. 2003. *Combatting Terrorism: The Role of the UN*. Wayne, NJ: Center for UN Reform Education.

Schraub, Kimber M. 1990. The rise and fall of the Red Brigades. In *The Politics of Counterterrorism: The Ordeal of Democratic States*, ed. Barry Rubin, 137–62. Washington, DC: Foreign Policy Institute.

Shabad, Goldie, and Francisco Jos Llera Ramo. 1995. Political violence in a democratic state: Basque terrorism in Spain. In *Terrorism in Context*, ed. Martha Crenshaw, 410–69. University Park: Pennsylvania State University Press.

Sharkansky, Ira. 2003. *Coping with Terror: An Israeli Perspective*. Lanham, MD: Lexington Books.

Shai, Shaul. 2004. *The Shaids: Islam and Suicide Attacks*, trans. Rachel Lieberman. New Brunswick, NJ: Transaction Publishers.

Sidel, Mark. 2003. *More Secure, Less Free: Antiterrorism Policy and Civil Liberties After September 11*. Ann Arbor: University of Michigan Press.

Siegel, J. M., K. J. Shoaf, and L. B. Bourque. 2000. The C-Mississippi Scale for PTSD in postearthquake communities. *International Journal of Mass Emergencies and Disasters* 18:339–46.

Silke, Andrew. 2003. The psychology of suicide terrorism. In *Terrorists, Victims and Society: Psychological Perspectives on Terrorism and Its Consequences*, ed. Andrew Silke, 93–108. Hoboken, NJ: Wiley.

Silberstein, Sandra. 2002. *War of Words: Language, Politics and 9/11*. London: Routledge.

Silvers, Robert B., and Barbara Epstein, eds. 2002. Appendix: The British summary. In *Striking Terror: America's New War*, ed. Robert B. Silvers and Barbara Epstein, 353–72. New York: New York Review of Books.

Simmons, Anna, and David Tucker. 2003. United States special operations forces and the war on terrorism In *Grand Strategy in the War Against Terrorism*, ed. Thomas Mockaitis and Paul B. Rich, 77–91. London: Frank Cass.

Simon, Jeffrey D. 1987. Misunderstanding terrorism. *Foreign Policy* 67:104–20.

———. 1990. *US Countermeasures against International Terrorism*. Santa Monica, CA: RAND Corp.

Simpson, O. P. 2001. Community emergency response training (CERTs): A recent history and review. *Natural Hazards Review* 2:54–63.

Smelser, Neil J. 1959. *Social Change in the Industrial Revolution: An Application of Theory to the British Cotton Industry.* London: Routledge and Kegan Paul, and Chicago: University of Chicago Press, 1959.

———. 1962. *Theory of Collective Behavior.* New York: Free Press.

———. 1976. *Comparative Methods in the Social Sciences.* Englewood Cliffs, NJ: Prentice-Hall.

———. 1990. The rational and the ambivalent in the social sciences. *American Sociological Review* 63(1):1–15.

———. 2004a. Psychological trauma and cultural trauma. In Jeffrey C. Alexander, Ron Eyerman, Bernhard Giesen, Neil J. Smelser, and Piotr Sztompka, *Cultural Trauma and Collective Identity,* 31–59. Berkeley and Los Angeles: University of California Press.

———. 2004b. September 11, 2001 as cultural trauma. In Jeffrey C. Alexander, Ron Eyerman, Bernhard Giesen, Neil J. Smelser and Piotr Sztompka, *Cultural Trauma and Collective Identity,* 264–82. Berkeley and Los Angeles: University of California Press.

Smelser, Neil J., and Faith Mitchell, eds. 2002a. *Terrorism: Perspectives from the Behavioral and Social Sciences.* Washington, DC: National Academies Press.

———. 2002b. *Discouraging Terrorism: Some Implications of 9/11.* Washington, DC: National Academies Press.

Smith, Steve. 2002. Unanswered questions. In *Worlds in Collision: Terror and the Future of the Global Order,* ed. Ken Booth and Tim Dunne, 48–59. New York: Macmillan Palgrave.

Sobiek, Stephen M. 1994. Democratic responses to international terrorism in Germany. In *The Deadly Sin of Terrorism: Its Effect on Democracy and Civil Liberty in Six Countries,* ed. David A. Charters, 43–72.. Westport, CT: Greenwood Press.

Sprinzak, Ehud. 1988. From messianic pioneering to vigilante terrorism: the case of Gush Eunim underground. In *Inside Terrorist Organizations,* ed. David C. Rapoport, 194–216. New York: Columbia University Press.

———. 1991. The great superterrorism scare. *Foreign Policy* 112:110–24.

———. 2001. The lone gunmen: The global war on terrorism faces a new brand of enemy. *Foreign Policy* 127:72–73.

———. 2002. Rational fanatics. *Foreign Policy* 120:66–73.

Stark, Rodney, and William Sims Bainbridge. 1980. Works of faith: Interpersonal bonds and recruitment to cults and sects. *American Journal of Sociology* 85(4):1376–95.

Swabish, Jonathan A., and Joshua Chang. 2005. Insurance coverage for New York City in an age of terrorist risk. In *Resilient City: The Economic Impact of 9/11,* ed. Howard Chernick, 158–90. New York: Russell Sage Foundation.

Tarrow, Sidney. 1996. States and opportunities: The political structuring of social movements. In *Perspectives on Social Movements: Political Opportunities, Mobilizing Structures, and Cultural Framings,* ed. Doug McAdam, John D. McCarthy, and Mayer N. Zald, 41–61. Cambridge: Cambridge University Press.

Taylor, Maxwell. 1988. *The Terrorist.* London: Brassey's Defence Publishers.

Taylor, Robert W. 1987. Liberation theology, politics, and violence in Latin America. In *Contemporary Research on Terrorism*, ed. Paul Wilkinson and Alasdair M. Stewart, 45–54. Aberdeen: Aberdeen University Press.

Terrell, Robert, and Kristina Ross. 1992. The voluntary guidelines' threat to U.S. Press Freedom. In *In the Camera's Eye: News Coverage of Terrorist Events*, ed. Yonah Alexander and Robert G. Picard, 75–102. Washington, DC: Brassey's (US).

Tetrais, Bruno. 2004. *War Without End: The View from Abroad*, trans. Franklin Philip. New York: New Press.

Thackrah, John Richard. 1987a. Terrorism: A definitional problem. In *Contemporary Research on Terrorism*, ed. Paul Wilkinson and Alasdair M. Stewart, 24–41. Aberdeen: Aberdeen University Press.

Thackrah, John Richard. 1987b. *Encyclopedia of Terrorism and Political Violence*. London: Routledge.

Thornton, Thomas Perry. 1964. Terror as a weapon of political agitation. In *Internal War: Problems and Approaches*, ed. Harry Eckstein, 71–99. New York: Free Press.

Tocqueville, Alexis de. 1955 [1856]. *The Old Regime and the French Revolution*, trans. Stuart Gilbert. Garden City, NY: Doubleday.

Todd, Emmanuel. 2003. *After the Empire: The Breaking of the American Order*, trans. C. Jon Degolu. New York: Columbia University Press.

Toth, James. 2005. Local Islam gone global: The roots of religious militancy in Egypt and its transnational transformation. In *Social Movements: An Anthropological Reader*, ed. June Nash, 117–45. Oxford: Blackwell.

Turner, Ralph H. 1994. Rumor as intensified information seeking: Earthquake rumors in China and the United States. In *Disasters, Collective Behavior, and Social Organization*, ed. Russell R. Dynes and Kathleen J. Tierney, 244–66. Newark: University of Delaware Press.

Turner, Victor. 1979. *Process, Performance, and Pilgrimage: A Study in Comparative Symbology*. New Delhi: Concept Publishing Co.

Tuveson, E. L. 1949. *Millenarianism and Utopia: A Study of the Background of Idea of Progress*. Berkeley and Los Angeles: University of California Press.

Twenlow, Stuart W., and Frank C. Sacco. 2002. Reflections on the making of a terrorist. In *Terrorism and Unconscious Dynamics of Political Violence*, ed. Coline Covington, Paul Williams, Jean Arundel, and Jean Knox, 97–123. London: Karnac.

Ullman, Harlan. 2004. *Finishing Business: Ten Steps to Defeat Global Terror*. Annapolis, MD: Naval Institute Press.

United States Department of Homeland Security. 2004. *National Response Plan*. Washington, DC: Department of Homeland Security. http://purl.access.gpo.gov/GPO/LPS56895.

United States Department of State. 1988. *Patterns of Global Terrorism*. Washington, DC: U.S. Department of State.

United States General Accounting Office. 2004. *Homeland Security Advisory Systems: Preliminary Observations Involving Threat Level Increases*. Washington: DC: General Accounting Office. http://purl.access.gop.gov/GPO/LPS52063.

United States House of Representatives. 2004. Hearing before the Select Committee on Homeland Security July 17, 2003. Washington, DC: U.S. Government Printing Office. http://purl.access.gpo.gov/GPO/LPS57566.

United States Strategic Bombing Survey. 1947. *The Effects of Strategic Bombing on German Morale.* Vol. I. Washington, DC: U.S. Government Printing Office.

Victor, Barbara. 2003. *Army of Roses: Inside the World of Palestinian Women Suicide Bombers.* Emmaus, PA: Rodale.

Volkan, Vamik. 2004. *Blind Trust: Large Groups and Their Leaders in Times of Crisis and Terror.* Charlottesville, VA: Pitchstone Publishing.

Wallace, Anthony F. C. 1956. Revitalization movements. *American Anthropologist* 58:264–81.

Wallace, Paul. 1995. Political violence and terrorism in India: The crisis of identity. In *Terrorism in Context*, ed. Martha Crenshaw, 352–409. University Park: Pennsylvania State University Press.

Wallerstein, Immanuel. 2003. *The Decline of American Power: The US in a Chaotic World.* New York: Metropolitan Books.

Wardlaw, Grant. 1988. State responses to international terrorism: Some cautionary comments. In *Current Perspectives on International Terrorism*, ed. Robert O. Slater and Michael Stohl, 206–45. New York: St. Martin's Press.

——— 1989. *Political Terrorism: Theory, Tactics, and Counter-measures*, 2nd rev., extended. Cambridge: Cambridge University Press.

Warner, Bruce W. 1993. Great Britain and the response to international terrorism. In *The Deadly Sin of Terrorism: Its Effect on Civil Liberty in Six Countries*, ed. David A. Charters, 13–42. Westport, CT: Greenwood Press.

Wasmund, Klaus. 1986. The political socialization of West German terrorists. In *Political Violence and Terror Motifs and Motivations*, ed. Peter Merkl, 229–55. Berkeley and Los Angeles: University of California Press.

Webel, Charles P. 2004. *Terror, Terrorism, and the Human Condition.* New York: Palgrave Macmillan.

Weber, Max. 1949. *The Methodology of the Social Sciences*, trans.-ed. Edward A. Shils and Henry Finch. New York: Free Press.

———. 1950. *General Economic History*, trans. Frank Knight. Glencoe, IL: Free Press.

———. 1968. *Economy and Society: An Outline of Interpretive Sociology*, ed. Guenther Roth and Claus Wittich. 3 vols. New York: Bedminster Press.

Weinberg, Leonard, and William Lee Eubank. 1988. Neo-Fascist and far left terrorists in Italy: Some biographical observations. *British Journal of Political Science* 18(4):531–49.

Weinberg, Leonard, and Ami Pedahzur. 2003. *Political Parties and Terrorist Groups.* London: Routledge.

Welsh, David. 1995. Right-wing terrorism in South Africa. In *Terror from the Extreme Right*, ed. Tore Bjørgo, 239–64. London: Frank Cass.

Whitehead, Harriet. 1987. *Renunciation and Reformulation: A Study of Conversion in an American Sect.* Ithaca, NY: Cornell University Press.

Whittaker, David J. 2002. *Terrorism: Understanding the Global Threat.* London: Longman-Pearson Education.

———. 2003. *The Terrorism Reader*, 2nd ed. London: Routledge.

Wieviorka, Michel. 1995. Terrorism in the context of academic research. In *Terrorism in Context*, ed. Martha Crenshaw, 597–606. University Park: Pennsylvania State University Press.

Wilkinson, Paul. 1983. The Orange and the Green: Extremism in Northern Ireland. In *Terrorism, Legitimacy and Power: The Consequences of Political Violence*, ed. Martha Crenshaw, 105–23. Middletown, CT: Wesleyan University Press.

———. 1987. Terrorism: An international research agenda? In *Contemporary Research on Terrorism*, ed. Paul Wilkinson and Alasdair M. Stewart, xi–xx. Aberdeen: Aberdeen University Press.

———. 1988. Support mechanisms in international terrorism. In *Current Perspectives on International Terrorism*, ed. Robert O. Slater and Michael Stohl, 88–1154. New York: St. Martin's Press.

———. 1990. Terrorism and propaganda. In *Terrorism and the Media: Dilemmas for Government, Journalists and the Public*, ed. Yonah Alexander and Richard Latter, 26–33. Washington, DC: Brassey's (US).

———. 2001. *Terrorism Versus Democracy: The Liberal State Response*. London: Frank Cass.

Williams, Clive. 2004. Islamic extremism and Wahhabism. In *Globalisation and the New Terror: The Asian Pacific Dimension*, ed. David Martin Jones, 70–75. Cheltenham, UK: Edward Elgar.

Williams, Paul L. 2002. *Al Qaeda: Brotherhood of Terror*. Parsippany, NJ: Alpha Books.

Wilson, Bryan. 1973. *Magic and the Millennium: A Sociological Study of Religious Movements among Tribal and Third-World Peoples*. New York: Harper and Row.

Wilson, J. Brent. 1994. The United States' response to international terrorism. In *The Deadly Sin of Terrorism: Its Effect on Democracy and Civil Liberty in Six Countries*, ed. David A. Charters. 173–210. Westport, CT: Greenwood Press.

Wilson, William Julius. 1987. *The Truly Disadvantaged: The Inner City, the Underclass, and Public Policy*. Chicago: University of Chicago Press.

Winchester, Simon. 2003. *Krakatoa: The Day the World Exploded: August 27, 1883*. New York: HarperCollins.

Winder, Jonathan M. 2002. Globalization, terrorist finance and global conflict: Time for a white list? In *Financing Terrorism*, ed. Mark Pieth, 5–40. Boston: Kluwer Academic.

Wirth, Hans. 2005. *9/11 as a Collective Trauma and Other Essays on Psychoanalysis and Society*. Giessen: Psychosozial-Verlag.

Wolfenstein, E. Victor. 1967. *The Revolutionary Personality: Lenin, Trotsky, Gandhi*. Princeton, NJ: Princeton University Press.

Wolfenstein, Martha. 1957. *Disaster: A Psychological Essay*. Glencoe IL: Free Press and Falcon's Wing Press.

Woodward, Bob. 2004. *Plan of Attack*. New York: Simon and Schuster.

Wuthnow, Robert, ed. 1995. *Rethinking Materialism: Perspectives on the Spiritual Dimension of Economic Behavior*. Grand Rapids, MI: William B. Eerdmans.

Young, James E. 2005. The memorial process: A juror report from ground zero. In *Contentious City: The Politics of Recovery in New York City*, ed. John Mollenkopf, 140–64. New York: Russell Sage Foundation.

Zartman, I. William. 1995. *Collapsed States: The Disintegration and Restoration of Legitimate Authority*. Boulder, CO: Lynne Rienner.

Index